Ray Graves' Guide to Modern Football Defense

Ray Graves' Guide to Modern Football Defense

Ray Graves

West Nyack
New York

Parker
Publishing
Company, Inc.

LIBRARY OF CONGRESS
CATALOG CARD NUMBER: 66-14072

PRINTED IN THE UNITED STATES OF AMERICA

75322—BC

To my wife, Opal—

Who can always find a smile in defeat—and has helped me to make friends with the inevitable—

And to all football coaches' wives, the unsung heroes of the game.

the author acknowledges . . .

The recording of my thoughts on defensive football was a very exciting proposition to me when plans for this book first began to materialize.

However, as I started getting into the material, it became evident that a major portion of what I was writing was actually a collection of the ideas and theories of the men who taught me the game. This has only made me more aware of the debt owed these men in contributing to any success I have enjoyed.

First of all, I was fortunate to have had the opportunity to play under the late General R. R. Neyland at the University of Tennessee. Neyland, who was years ahead of most of his teaching contemporaries in defensive coaching techniques, had no peers in defensive organization.

Neyland stressed all phases of defensive football with a philosophy that a team is never on defense, always on offense, because there are more ways to score on defense than there are on offense. Of this we were reminded every day.

One other lasting memory of the General was the way he instilled confidence in his players. Without his players being aware of it, he put in them the pride you must have to be a champion.

The success of any team can only be made possible by the pride, ability, and dedication of the individual players who must carry out their responsibilities on the field of battle. It has been my pleasure to coach some outstanding athletes, which is one of the great rewards in sports.

With this collegiate background, it then became my good fortune to play professional football for the Philadelphia Eagles under Earl "Greasy" Neal, one of the greatest and most colorful coaches of all time. He had more football imagination than anyone I have ever known. His "Eagle Defense" is still one of the most popular defenses in modern football.

I am grateful for the confidence Coach Bobby Dodd had in me during my coaching career at Georgia Tech. He gave me responsibilities and with them a chance to prove some of my personal defensive theories. Under his leadership I had an opportunity to spend many hours with some of the top coaches in the game.

I would be remiss in failing to mention Arkansas head coach Frank Broyles and the value of having been a coaching associate of his at Georgia Tech. During my seven years as head defensive coach at Tech, Frank spent much time as head offensive coach.

Trying to defense Frank's offensive ideas really kept me and the defensive staff up late at night. However, out of this period, came the famous "Belly Series" from his offensive staff and the "Monster Defense" from the defensive staff.

Last, but not least, is deserved recognition and thanks to my defensive staff at the University of Florida—Gene Ellenson, Billy Kinard, and Don Brown. Ellenson is my assistant head coach as well as head defensive coach. He is recognized as one of the top defensive coaches in the game and has made many personal innovations in modern defensive football. His "Rover Defense" is now one of our major defenses. Gene rendered valuable assistance in making this book a reality.

In closing, I hope this detailed discussion of our defensive ideas, as well as philosophy, will benefit coaches and perhaps challenge their thinking. It is further hoped that the material, while partially technical in nature, will be interesting to the football fan who desires to expand his knowledge of the game of football.

RAY GRAVES

foreword . . .

Down through the years football in the Deep South has been dominated traditionally by teams which were primarily oriented in the defensive aspects of the game.

Out of this has come some of the finest defensive players and also many coaches who have made valuable contributions in their specialty.

Among these coaches is Ray Graves, a man whose background in defensive football includes lessons learned first-hand as a player under the late General R. R. Neyland, the acknowledged master of this phase of the game.

Ray learned his lessons well, first as a player and later as a coach under some of the game's greatest teachers. Out of his exposure to the ideas of these men came a sound and basic understanding of defense.

Being of imaginative mind, Graves was not content to simply pass on the teachings and theories of other coaches. He experimented with many revisions of standard defensive tactics and now many of his defensive variations have become trends of the game.

Among these is the "monster defense," which Graves and his defensive staff came up with at Georgia Tech. This defense, with the "monster" being a sort of roving linebacker who lines up to either side in a position predetermined by the defensive signals, is now standard.

Graves' accomplishment as head football coach at the University of Florida, where he has compiled the best record in Gator grid history, is evidence enough that he is well-qualified to chronicle his thoughts for fellow coaches and fans. His record has been built primarily around the techniques described in this book.

FRED RUSSELL
Sports Editor
Nashville Banner

Contents

Part I

Introduction

1

History and Personal Defensive Philosophy

I am going to take some liberties, as the author, to ramble and reminisce with you in this opening chapter. It might give you a little insight into what will come later. Thinking about the history of football, and my experience in the game, has made me aware of the responsibility we coaches have in maintaining the heritage which has been handed down by some dedicated coaches and players of the past.

Some of these great coaches left their mark on the offensive strategy of the game. Often they stand out more than defense-minded coaches who were selling their players the idea that it's easier to win a close game by keeping the opposition from scoring than by scoring yourself.

I had the opportunity to play under the late General R. R. Neyland, whose view of defense as offense had a profound influence on modern football. He stressed all the defensive areas of football, with the philosophy that you are not on defense, you are on offense. A sign over the dressing room door at Tennessee is implanted in my memory, "There are more ways to score on defense than there are on offense." If you count them, you will find this is true. How many close games are won on a pass interception, punt return, blocked kick or safety.

General Neyland also used the kicking game as an offensive weapon. He proved that, by kicking the ball when in dangerous territory and playing sound defense, you could move the ball closer to your opponent's goal line than if you kept it on offense. Let your opponents handle the ball more at their end of the field, knowing that more critical mistakes such as fumbles and penalties occur on offense than on defense.

General Neyland used much of his army training and tactics in coaching football. To break your opponent's morale and win, he believed, you whip a team at its strength. Two of his main ingredients for winning, "relentless pursuit by eleven men" and "gang tackling," were developed from General Sheridan's famous Civil War statement that to win, you have to "Get there first with the most."

Some of General Neyland's game axioms, still the winning edge in football, are:

1. Relentless pursuit by eleven men.
2. Gang Tackling, the most demoralizing thing in football.
3. If at first the game or a break goes against you, don't slow down—put on more steam!
4. Rush their kicker and passer. Here is where the breaks are made.
5. Intercept their forward pass. A well known chant to all who knew Neyland was his famous OSKI - WOW - WOW, meaning—take advantage of moving to the ball while the forward pass is in the air; be in position to block if we intercept, or tackle if the pass is completed.
6. Play your position first—then react.
7. Your value to the team varies inversely with your distance from the ball.
8. Know the down and distance at all times.

The last thing he always wrote up on the board before every game was "Carry the fight to Alabama and keep it there all day." (Alabama was the Big Game for every Tennessee boy.)

Most of these axioms still apply to the game of football.

After World War II football changed greatly. During the war many coaches were thinking football and experimenting with service teams on offensive and defensive maneuvers which they had not had a chance to experiment with in college. Out of this period came the Don Faurot Split-T offense. Many coaches began using a multiple type of offense. The "pro set" (a wide flanker and split end) became more common, with motion, extended motion and the quick fly of backs giving the defense many headaches.

Every year the offense created more problems for the defense. From week to week a defense might face the Single Wing, coach Matty Bell's spread formations, the Split T, or any combinations of these offenses.

My coaching career began at Tennessee as line coach under John

Barnhill, and we were doing all right with our 60 Defense until we ran into the Split-T Ray Morrison devised for Temple University. We were a stronger team physically, but they split our defensive 6-man-line so badly that all the quarterback had to do was decide which hole he wanted to sneak through for five yards. With this game chalked up to experience, I called my good friend, coach Herman Hickman, who had already started some variations of the 60 Defense at Army, and asked for his advice on how to stop the Split-T.

Since that day, I have always believed defense must be approached with a multiple theory. You need multiple defenses, and the defense should surprise the offense sometimes—the element of surprise should not be reserved for the offense only. Never let the offense come out and put all the pressure on the defense. So, by Shifting, Stunting and Concealing defenses, the offense is never given a reason to call an offensive play.

Personal Defensive Theory

First, you must have complete knowledge of what you are trying to coach. You also must believe in what you are teaching. Believe it is the best defensive plan in the business, and sell your team that it is the best. Knowledge and teaching are related, but some of the smartest coaches are not always the most successful coaches. One of my teachers in college left me with a lasting theory about teaching. He said, "It's not what you know, it's what you teach." The more you think about this statement the truer it seems. Always try to improve your teaching technique as well as your knowledge of defensive football.

In coaching defensive football, teach the weakness as well as the strength of every defensive maneuver. If the players know both, it will give them confidence. For example, if in a defense you are giving the offense a flat passing zone for a rush and the offense completes a pass in this flat zone, the team will not get rattled or tend to criticize anyone for not carrying out their responsibilities. They are aware that the opponent hit the weakness of the defense. When an opponent attacks you at a weakness you know of, you are better prepared to adjust your defenses. Both offense and defense are guessing games, but the defense has the advantage of being able to change defenses and not be stereotyped.

This brings me to something I have always believed in—a multiple defensive theory. You cannot line up with, and play, any one defense all afternoon and get the maximum results. The offense gains a tremendous advantage when they know what you are going to do on defense. My experience has been that boys will learn what you give them. Expect them to know they can win and be the best and they will. This is why, in my defensive coaching, I have always tried to bring new defensive theories and innovations into this phase of the game. Football is a game–make it a game by giving the boys something new. Make them think you are always a step ahead of the offense.

A sound multiple defense requires two or three basic defenses with stunts, and a sound goal line defense. Beside the basic defenses, you must have at least one stunt that gives everyone some variation of his initial basic responsibility. This can also be supported by shifting defenses. This is a big defensive advantage. The rules permit this defensive movement as long as it does not interfere with the offensive snap count. The offense knows the snap count and can vary plays. Defensive men can move around and cause changes in offensive assignments which confuse and demoralize the offense. Every time some defensive maneuver makes the offense think, it has accomplished something. If the offensive man is wondering *who* to block, he is less effective than if he is thinking about *how* to block.

Team Objectives

A good defense requires team objectives—something for eleven men to work for in complete harmony.

1. *Prevent a Score.* You can't lose a football game if the opposition can't score. This is the ultimate in defensive football. Never worry about a first down, worry about touchdowns. A touchdown prevented is a touchdown scored.
2. *Gang Tackle the Ball Carrier.* If there is anyone a defense player hates, it is an offensive football player. Take it out on the ball carrier. Gang tackling is a demonstration of desire to win. It is still the most demoralizing thing in the game.
3. *Switch from Defense to Offense Instantly.* Remember you are always on offense. There are five ways to score on defense.

- Recover a fumble over the goal line.
- Block a kick.
- Intercept a forward pass.

- Force a safety.
- Return a punt.

4. *Be Mentally Alert for Fumbles.* Recovering fumbles is not accidental. The team getting the ball is the team which is always after the ball. Sometimes it is luck when you recover a fumble, but luck is when opportunity meets with preparation.
5. *Know the Situation at All Times.* This will always play an important part in the final score. The player must be aware of down and distance, time remaining, score, weather, wind, personnel in the game, and a dozen other factors that can change the way he will play his defensive responsibility. Be smarter than your opponents.
6. *Take Pride in Your Job.* To be the best, it is imperative that everyone take pride in winning and believe in each other. This one ingredient can make the difference between winning or losing.

Remember!!

We Want Fumbles.
We Want Punt Returns.
We Want to Block That Kick.
We Want Pass Interceptions.
We Want to Win!!

In conclusion, I would like to summarize and underline some "Defensive Coaching Reminders" that have helped us in carrying out our defensive responsibilities.

1. Position—Play your responsibility first, then react. Always be in the right position.
2. *Rush* passer hand high. Force a high pass.
3. *Don't* let faking backs through free of charge.
4. *Punish* pass blockers. They might usher you in the next time.
5. Pass defenders must play the ball at its height.
6. Make the opponent throw. They have only five receivers; we have eleven.
7. When they catch the ball in front of us, give them a headache.
8. The only place on the field the defense has the advantage is on the *Goal Line.*

9. Relentless pursuit by eleven men is a *must*. You can't win with *Ten Men*.
10. *One* interception is worth five completions.
11. Don't make mistakes—the team that makes the fewest mistakes usually wins.
12. Remember, there is no *score* given for a *first down*.
13. Never give up the easy touchdown—make them work for it.
14. Always think, THEY SHALL NOT SCORE.

Part II

Alignments and Responsibilities

2

Basic Monster Defense

The Monster had a rather unusual origin. In 1950 at Georgia Tech we were having our troubles stopping the Split T offense. Coach Bobby Dodd called Coach Bud Wilkinson and asked him how you stopped this monster he and Don Faurot had created. After several phone calls Coach Wilkinson tried to give us the Oklahoma 5-4-2 defense by long distance. However, Coach Dodd decided I had better go out and see it in action. I received all the University of Oklahoma hospitality of Coach Bud Wilkinson and Coach Gomer Jones, and returned with a briefcase full of notes and diagrams. I was sold on the 7 front, but not sold entirely on going to the four deep. I was a little scared to take that three deep safety out of our defense. I couldn't go back on my Tennessee rearing. I was also wondering how quickly we could brainwash our halfbacks and safety men, who were schooled and sold on the three deep defense.

Our problem was also magnified because we had already completed spring practice and would have to put in the Oklahoma 5-4-2 in the fall pre-season practice. I knew we would have to do it with as little change as possible. With this background the Monster was born. I sold Coach Dodd on going to the Oklahoma 7 front, keeping our same three deep with our fullback as a swinging monster. To make our opponents think we were four deep, we (to use an East Tennessee expression) "squirmed" our three deep away from Monster.

It was not a true three deep lineup, but after the snap we went to three zone responsibilities. In doing this we eliminated teaching our halfback to play corner. One position (Monster) had all the coaching attention to play the corner position. A lot has happened to the Monster since 1950, but it is still the basic defense of many of the top teams in the country.

Before going into the actual assignments of each player, some basic tenets should be discussed.

Selection of Personnel

First, of course, is the selection of personnel from your particular squad. The most important choice is the Monster himself. He certainly should be one of your best athletes. He must be big and rugged enough to play end against a power sweep. This means he has to be well grounded in the techniques of warding off blockers and he must be a good shoulder tackler. He also must be fast enough to rotate to safety, and therefore play center field, and/or be able to cover a tight end man-to-man.

This type of athlete is not always easy to find. One attribute may outweigh the other. One simple way to select Monster is to pick out the four or five secondary men who can defend against the pass and pick the biggest one. In this way, you follow the safety pattern. If your Monster is a big, tough, rugged line backer or end, but not much of a pass defender, opponents will isolate him all day and pit a faster, more clever receiver against him and beat you with this one strategy. Conversely, if your Monster is a slim, race horse sort of kid that can cover well, your opponents will have to try to beat him with their running game. You can do something in this area to help him out. Cross charges, line slants, firing line backers, etc., should relieve pressure on a lightweight Monster.

Once in a while you will get a youngster that has everything. The University of Miami had such a player some years ago. His name was Don Bossler; he has since played fullback for the Washington Redskins. He has played all-offense for the Pros, but he was a great defensive corner in college. Don was about six feet one inches in height and weighed 215, with good speed. But such players are unusual.

The selection of personnel for the rest of a defensive team using the Monster defense should be picked using the following yardsticks:

Left End (LE)— Your strongest end. Could be a fast tackle.

Left Tackle (LT)— Your second best interior lineman.

Left Linebacker (LLB)— Your best, fastest linebacker.

Middle Guard (MG)— Your best interior lineman, must have speed, but size is not too important.

Right Linebacker (RLB)— Your second best linebacker, but should be big enough to play a 60 guard.

Right Tackle (RT)— Here, a tackle that has quickness. Sometimes an ex-end can play this spot.

Right End (RE)— Your fanciest end. Should be able to double cover.

Left Halfback (LHB)— Your lightest player, good pass defender, can get by being just a fair tackler.

Right Halfback (RHB)— Bigger, stronger Halfback—good tackler.

Safety (SAF)— Always play your best secondary man in this position.

Monster Rules

The next step is the rules for declaring Monster—the rules governing the Monster's position. Since Monster is a swinging corner, he must have some simple guides to follow in order to line up properly. His declaration will set the pattern for the whole defense. His declaring rules are:

1. *Field*—Generally Monster should declare away from the hash mark, or to the field.
2. *Formation*—This can change the above rule. A strong set into the side line should supersede his "field" rule. Also a tight slot could change the "field" rule.
3. *Game Plan*—This can change either of the above rules and is based on what your opponent does well.
4. *Split End*—Monster should never declare to a split end.
5. *Defense Called*—Certain defenses will call for Monster to align in four deep immediately.
6. *Rule of Thumb*—Declare to the offensive strength anywhere. If there is a dead T, then declare to wide side.

The third step is the actual mechanics of Monster declaration. The defensive huddle is formed as shown in Figure 1.

Notice that the Monster and safety man are facing the signal caller and the offensive team. Calling the defense then proceeds as follows:

1. Inside right linebacker calls original defense, for example: "Slant."

   1-a. Safety man calls basic secondary coverage; "Blue."
2. Defensive team lines up in a basic 54 alignment with Monster in the middle. The three interior linemen line up down on one knee so Monster and signal caller (right inside linebacker) can see the offensive huddle "break."
3. Offensive team "breaks" from their huddle and declares their formation.
4. Monster now knows on which side he must declare or line up. As he runs to his proper position (based on rules for declaring) he shouts "Monster right" (or left).
5. Signal caller now knows where Monster is going to be. Based on his game plan, he now shouts direction of slant. It will be either to or away from Monster—usually away. His code word is "Roger" for right or "Lucy" for left.
6. Perimeter Captain (safety man) calls out secondary coverage. The coverage is usually "Blue" for this defense; however, a wide formation may change this to "Black."
7. One other change may be made after all this adjusting and alignment. This is caused by long motion by the offense. Such an offensive maneuver causes the line slant to change if the motion is towards Monster. Signal caller shouts "Check Lucy" which changes line slant from right to left. If, on the other hand, the long motion is away from Monster, the secondary must rotate from left to right and the line slant remains the same.

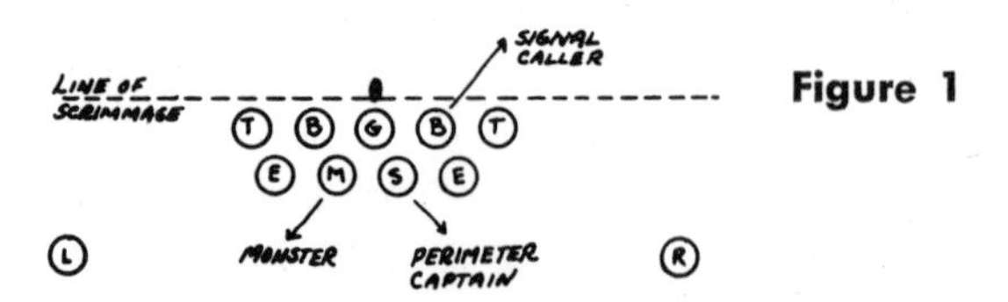

Figure 1

Two Monster Categories

Before the basic Monster is covered, it should be mentioned that there are two general categories within the Monster structure. One is the *Reading* category and the other is the *Pressing* category. A reading defense is one where the up front defenders react upon offensive moves or actions. Naturally, this becomes a containing defense that will bend but shouldn't break. It is a maximum pursuit defense. When playing this style defense up front, the secondary should, as much as possible, play zone pass defense.

Pressing is a penetrating style which features ends and linebackers coming hard. This is where the defense makes the first move. You are more apt to make a big play or deny offensive gain, but you do it at the risk of having a long gainer against you. This is true because you cut down on pursuit. The secondary now plays a man-to-man pass defense. Your pass defenders can jump on a receiver quickly and cover him close for a short distance. The theory follows that the pressing defense will give you a hard rush; therefore offensive receivers should not be able to get deep. If you cover close, the passer can't throw early, and if your rush is good, he can't throw late. Since this is gamble defense, you should call about two "reads" for every press.

54 Regular

The first defense of the Basic Monster is a "read" and is called 54 Regular (Figure 2). It will feature a backside eagle. That is an eagle away from Monster. Here are the rules of play for this defense.

Situation: Offense comes out with a tight flanker to our left. Our Monster shouts "Monster left." Out right linebacker shouts "Right eagle," and moves to that alignment.

Individual rules (numbers refer to defensive men in Figure 2):

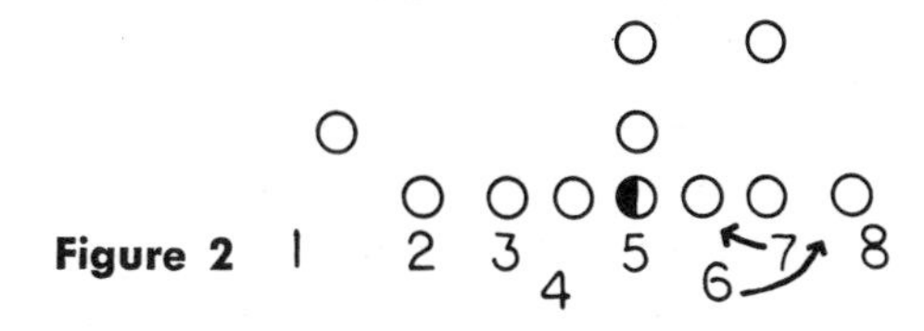

Figure 2

1. *Monster*—Use declaring rules for the day.
   Ball action toward you—force.
   Ball action straight back—take respective flat.
   Ball action away—rotate to deep left halfback.
2. *Anchor*—Align on the nose of the offensive end and read his release. Do not let him off the line. Meet him tough. Don't let him in on our linebacker or let him release deep as a receiver. Don't let him block you out on the off-tackle play. Pursue laterally.
   Ball action toward you—defend your area.
   Ball action straight back—contain rush.
   Ball action away—spy. (play slow.) Stay back and look for delayed plays or comebacks.
   Roll out or play pass to you—back up Monster by covering short flat.
3. *Regular*—Align on offensive tackle's nose. Head read him. Do not get hooked in or turned out by him. If he tries to make an inside release, flatten out his angle and brace for trapper.
   Ball action toward you—keep relative distance to Anchor.
   Ball action straight back—rush to inside.
   Ball action away—pursue on 45 degree angle looking for cutbacks.
4. *Regular*—Align even with middle guard's feet but slightly outside of the offensive guard. Use parallel stance and read the quarterback. Keep outside leverage on the guard. Keep pace with the quarterback. If he is faking or spinning in his original position, hold your ground.
   Ball action toward your side—fill off tackle hole first, then pursue.
   Ball action straight back—take your hook spot.
   Ball action away—think throwback, retreat first, then cross the center when sure it is not a counter.
   Pass play away—deep middle.
5. *Regular*—Align 1½ to three feet deep on center's nose. Head read the center. Pursue the ball side-line to side-line. Keep rush lanes with your tackles. Keep double-team triangle in your vision—center's block will tell you if it's a double. Find power and get under it.

Ball action straight back—don't commit around center until draw possibility has passed.

6. *Eagle Regular*—Align on outside shoulder of offensive guard. Read the guard. Follow the same rules as #3 Regular. The only difference is that you are one man in *and* slightly outside.
7. *Eagle Regular*—Align on inside shoulder of offensive end. Use two-point stance with outside foot forward. On the snap, jab-step with up foot into the inside shoulder of offensive end. You and our end should eliminate the offensive end. If tackle turns out on you, use a reverse pivot back to the inside.
   Play pass your way—take respective hook area.
   Straight drop—take flat.
8. *Eagle Regular*—Align on offensive end's outside shoulder with your inside foot forward. Jab end on the snap. Key near halfback.
   Ball action toward you—read blockers: end first, near half-back second, fullback or guards third. Keep inside or outside leverage on keys.
   Roll out or straight drop—contain.
   Ball action away—chase.
9. *Squirm*—Align five yards deep, three yards outside offensive end. Key nearest eligible receiver.
   If he blocks—come up and force in same plane as Monster. Keep relative distance to your end, never get deeper than the ball.
   If he releases outside—cover him until safety can support you. Then flatten out into your flat.
   Ball action away—rotate back to deep halfback your side, keeping outside leverage on all eligibles.
10. *Safety*—Align over offensive guard, away from Monster, about ten yards deep.
    Ball action to your side—
    If no eligibles release—support inside Squirm man (#9).
    If eligibles release—take deep outside.
    Ball action straight back or away—rotate back to middle.
    If eligibles release—play center field.
    If no eligibles release—back up Strong Halfback (#11).

11. *Strong Halfback*—Align back of Monster vs. tight formation ten yards deep.

    Ball action to your side—

    If no eligibles out—support straight at off tackle hole, then take pursuit angle.

    If eligibles out—take deep 1/3 your side.

    Ball action straight back—take deep 1/3 your side.

    Ball action away from your side—rotate to safety.

These are general rules for each position. They do not take into account adjustments in the secondary. (Chapter 9 on Secondary Play covers adjustments in detail).

3

Monster Stunts

This chapter deals entirely with what should be done with a Monster set-up in order to make it hold up against any possible offensive strategy.

Secondary coverages are explained in chapter 9; however, to show the coordination a quick run-down will precede this chapter.

Coverage	*Type*
Blue	Swinging corner, squirmed 3 deep zone
Orange	Fully rotated three deep zone
Black	Four deep man-to-man

CATEGORY

READ		PRESS	
Up Front	*Secondary*	*Up Front*	*Secondary*
54 Regular	Blue	54 Fire	Black
Slant Regular	Blue	Slant Fire	Black
(a) Combo	Blue		
(b) Switch	Blue		
(c) Bullets	Orange		
Roger X Regular	Blue	Roger X Fire	Orange
DI Regular	Blue	DI Fire	Orange
Split DI Regular	Blue	Split DI Fire	Orange

The most basic stunt is SLANT REGULAR. Any term can be used to designate the direction of the slant. "Roger" and "Lucy" have been a very compatible pair, but any code words which mean right or left will do.

It should be stressed that game plan has a lot to do with whether the slant should be called to or away from Monster. Your opponent should not be able to predict your slant; however, the defense is sound enough even when they know which way you are slanting. This is made possible because you mix enough straight up defenses along with Rovers and Eagles to make prediction impossible.

Your basic problem with slanting away from Monster is covering a roll-out, or sprint-out type pass, in the flat, to the side they have forced your Monster to contain the passer. Therefore, Monster knows any time the slant is towards him, he has flat responsibility and is relieved of containment. It should be pointed out that such a pass can be covered, even if Monster is containing. If the anchor end does a good job, the eligibles release on about the same plane and your half-back can cover both of them, provided Monster puts on a quick contain and makes the passer pull up early.

Here is a basic rule to follow in declaring direction of line slant.

1. Against a tight formation—slant away from Monster.
2. Against a wide flanker—slant to the Monster.

Reading Category

Slant Regular—Roger (Figure 3)

1. *Monster*—Align outside widest eligible, up to five yards, no deeper than two yards off the line of scrimmage. Use current rules for declaring.
   Ball action toward you, force.
   Ball action straight back, flat.
   Ball action away, rotate.
2. Anchor—Same rules as written under Basic Monster (preceding chapter).
3. *Slant*—Align head on offensive tackle. Take all the ball you can without being offsides. On the snap, charge the offensive guard's outside shoulder. You must close to your middle guard.

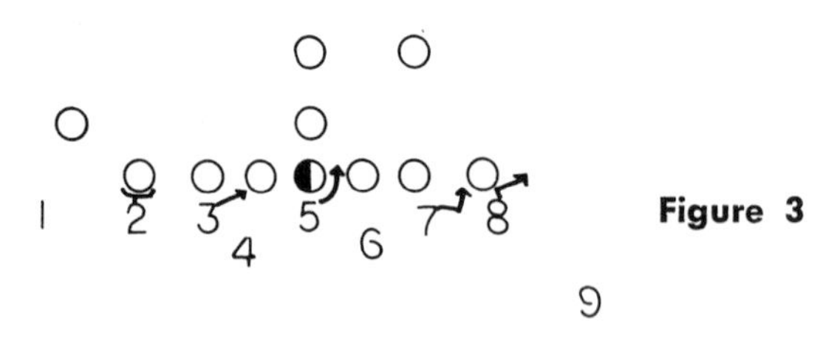

Figure 3

Never get turned up-field on flow away. If the tackle blocks down on you, optional pursuit back; either run around his block or pivot outside. Use cross over lead step (see Figure 3a).

4. *Scrape Off*—Align on the outside shoulder of the offensive guard with your feet parallel. Key ball flow.

    Ball flow toward you, "scrape off" behind your slanting tackle.

    Play pass toward you, scrape off on through and rush or fall back to hook area.

    Ball flow straight back, respective hook.

    Ball flow away, counter step then pursue.

5. *Quick Around*—Align on center's nose close to line of scrimmage. On the snap use quick lead step into center-guard gap in direction of the call. If center lead blocks the way you are going, keep leverage and flatten out. If he leads the other way, run around his block. If either guard blocks down on you, keep low enough to create a pile on their side of the line of scrimmage. Don't go for deep penetration; if shut off at the gap, slide parallel to the line of scrimmage (Figure 3b).
6. *Filler*—Align the same as Scrape Off. Key near halfback first, then ball flow. If near halfback dives straight ahead, fill the hole tough. If near halfback goes anywhere else (or if there is no near halfback) key ball flow. Use same rules described under Regular in last chapter.
7. *Loop*—Align on outside ear of offensive tackle slightly off the ball. On the snap, loop to the tight end's inside shoulder. Think of breaking up double team first. If end releases, you and your end should slow him up and make releasing difficult. Square up and look for trapper. Don't cross the line of scrimmage. Contain back up pass and roll out if their end is split (Figure 3c).
8. *Blood*—Align on outside shoulder of tight end. Double cover on split end. On snap jab, end into your looping tackle. Then step laterally to outside and play wide responsibility.

    Ball flow towards you, play static. Keep outside leverage on blockers.

    Ball deep, get up field.

    Ball flow straight back, drop off in flat.

    Ball flow away, rotate.

3 INTERIOR LINEMEN – "ROGER" CALLED

Figure 3 a – *LEFT TACKLE*

Figure 3 b – *MIDDLE GUARD*

Figure 3 c – *RIGHT TACKLE*

In double cover position, play inside shoulder of split man, taking away the "look in" pattern. Delay split end dropping off as you do; you have the wide flat. If your tackle fails to contain, come back up and force.

9, 10, 11. *Blue Coverage* as explained in the chapter under secondary coverage.

Slant Regular—Lucy (Figure 4)

The same rules apply to each corresponding position. Just reverse responsibilities. There are a couple of coaching points in regard to end play. If your slant is toward the Monster, the Anchor End disguises an anchor technique but must loosen enough to make an out charge that will keep leverage on a close flanker. Also the other end now would normally become the anchor end, but inasmuch as you have no Monster support he must not anchor as thoroughly. This is a weakness in slanting toward Monster. The Scrape-Off linebacker must look for the end getting off on him and be ready for it. There is one other way to strengthen yourself while slanting to Monster and that is to *execute* the slant on the back side. This takes away the crack down by the end. It is simply an eagle adjustment. Example:

Adjustments when slanting are fairly simple. The secondary uses the same adjustments as described in Chapter 9. Since a line slant can be changed quickly from one direction to another, it is just a matter of recognition. Following is a quick run-down on line adjustments when a slant has been called.

1. Tight flanker—call slant away from Monster.
2. Wide flanker—call slant to Monster.

Figure 4 **Figure 5**

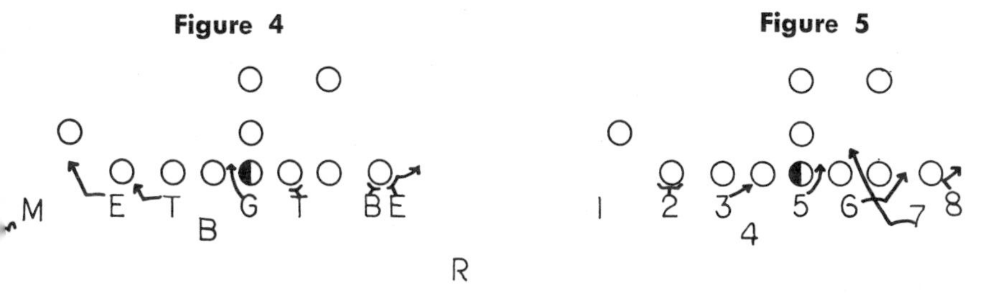

3. Extended motion—call slant to motion executed.
4. Split end—if possible, slant to split end.
5. Two wide out—call slant to Monster.
6. 3 receivers on side—call slant to receivers' side.
7. Unbalanced line—call slant to long side of line.
8. I formations—let flankers and split ends dictate slant.
9. Shifts—check to a slant executed.
10. Spreads—check to a spread defense.

Slant Regular Combo—Roger called (Figure 5)

1. *Monster*—same as Slant Regular.
2. *Anchor*—same as Slant Regular.
3. *Slant*—same as Slant Regular.
4. *Scrape Off*—same as Slant Regular.
5. *Quick Around*—same as Slant Regular.
6. *Combo*—align in the eagle position, receive gap charge instructions from your linebacker. Take either gap hard and penetrate.
7. *Combo*—align in the eagle position, give gap charge direction to your tackle. You take the other gap using a "fire" technique.
8. *Blood*—same as Slant Regular.

9, 10, 11—Blue Coverage and adjustments.

Combo vs. Split End (Figure 6)

(This is the only set that would affect this stunt.)

When using Combo disregard split end. Your end to Combo side plays very slow. It is possible, of course, to continue double cover.

Another stunt to use against a split end if your game plan does not call for double coverage, or if you are getting hurt by the running

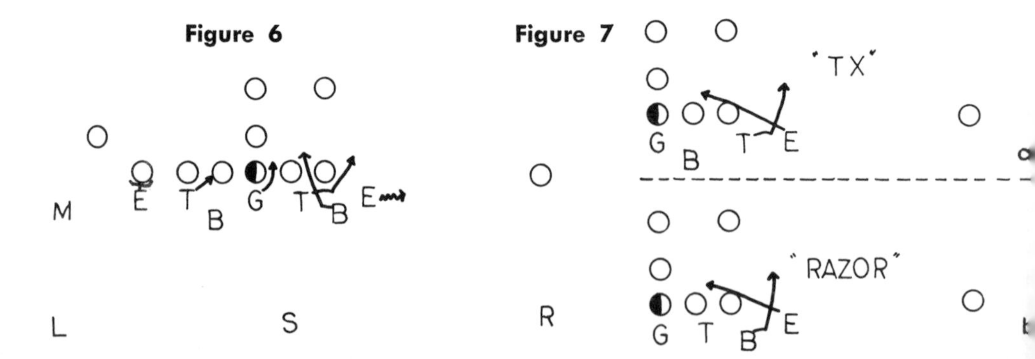

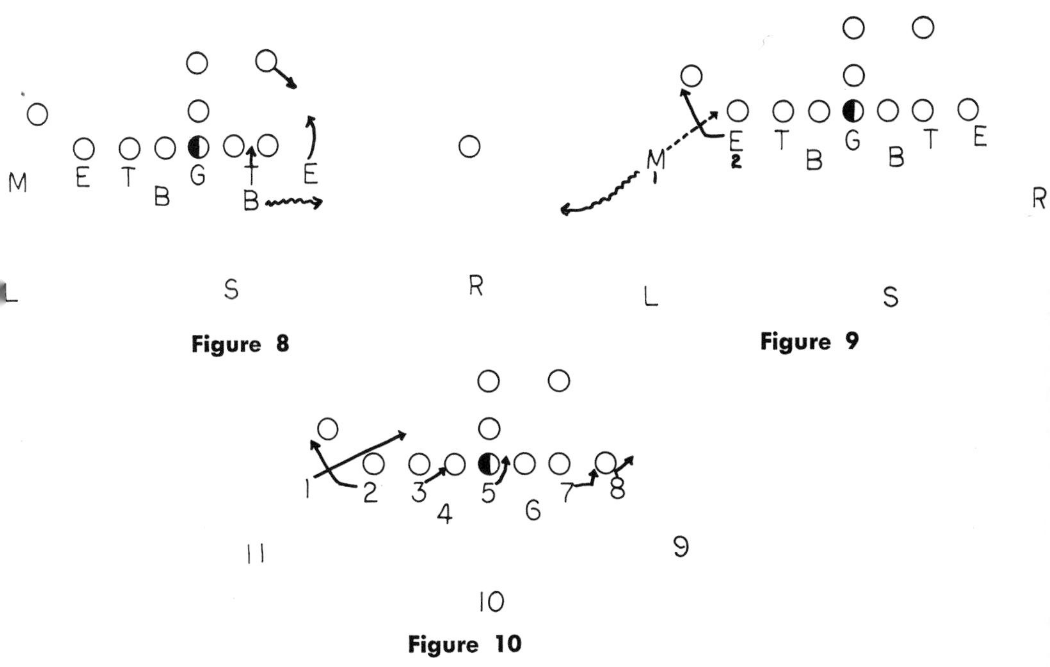

Figure 8

Figure 9

Figure 10

game to that side, is a cross charge by the end. If he has a tackle next to him it is called a TX (Figure 7a). If he has a linebacker next to him, he calls Razor (Figure 7b).

Examples:

These two stunts are very effective against the option play. They both provide penetration and containment.

By not committing the line backer on a rush, you can get help on flat coverage to the split end side (Figure 8).

Slant Regular Switch (Figure 9)

(Use on long yardage only.)

1. *Monster*—lay back off the line a little and key the offensive end first. (You still have ball flow keys.) If end blocks, support inside. If end releases, take flat. If ball flows away, rotate.
2. *Anchor*—execute a "Lucy" on the snap.

Everyone else play Slant Regular.

Adjustments to Switch stunt—Any kind of motion or wide flanker to that side will take Switch off and call for Slant Regular.

Slant Regular Bullets (Figure 10)

1. *Monster*—align on line and execute a reckless inside charge aiming for the offensive fullback.

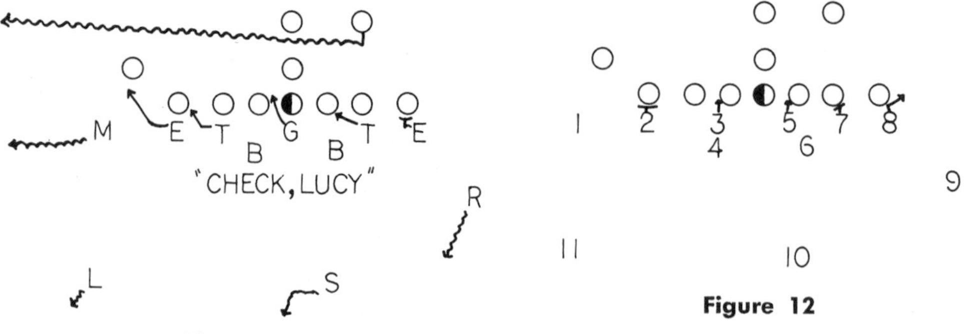

Figure 11

Figure 12

2. *Anchor*—cross behind Monster and force.
3, 4, 5, 6, 7 and 8—execute Slant Regular.
9, 10, 11—automatic orange.

Adjustments—The only thing that takes Bullets off is extended motion to Monster. Line slants toward motion and Monster goes with motion man (Figure 11). The Signal Caller shouts "Check Lucy" as soon as he spots the motion.

The line slant frees the Anchor to contain, which allows Monster to cover the motion man. There is only one receiver left on the backside, and only one running back left in the backfield, so the right end can play a good snug anchor. The right halfback can come off the squirm position and get square on the remaining eligible. The safety can come over and favor the heavy side. The left halfback can deepen as the running threat has all but been eliminated.

Roger X Regular (Figure 12)

1. *Monster*—Same as Slant Regular.
2. *Anchor*—Same as Slant Regular.
3. *Eagle*—Align on guard's outside shoulder. Charge hard on snap. Don't get hooked in by the guard. Same rules as 54 Regular tackle, you are simply one man removed to the inside.
4. *Spy*—Hide behind your tackle. Apply 54 Regular rules.
5. *Bang*—Align on guard's inside shoulder and "bang" his shoulder hard on the snap. Keep him from getting an easy release on your linebacker. Don't let center overblock you.
6. *Regular*—apply 54 Regular rules.
7. *Regular*—apply 54 Regular rules.
8. *Blood*—apply Slant Regular rules.

9, 10, 11—Blue coverage.

Adjustments on Roger X Regular are the same for Monster and

the secondary as covered in the chapter on Secondary Play. *One basic thing to remember: when extended motion comes toward Monster,* SLANT. *When extended motion comes away from Monster,* ROTATE.

If your opponent shifts his strength so that your "squirmed" side is threatened by a flanker, move that side out to a wide tackle six position and go Orange in the secondary (Figure 13).

1. *Monster*—Same as Roger X Regular.
2. *Anchor*—Same as Roger X Regular.
3. *Eagle*—Same as Roger X Regular.
4. *Spy*—Same as Roger X Regular.
5. *Nose*—Move out to guard's nose on command "Check 60." Apply 54 Regular rules to guard as if he were the center. Do not penetrate.
6. 60—Align on the tackle's nose, two yards off the line. Read the tackle. If he blocks down or out, fill quickly and look for the lead back. You never have any other pass defense responsibility but the hook area.
7. *Anchor*—Apply anchor rules. (When threatened by close flanker play outside ear of the tight end.)
8. *Blood X*—Apply Blood technique executed. Ball flow straight back, take flat. Ball flow towards, contain and force. Ball flow away, rotate to 3 deep halfback.

9, 10, 11—Orange coverage. Use quick rotation vs. tight formations in order to cover either flat with corresponding halfback. This is only when offensive quarterback is sprinting out either way. On straight back action the flats are covered by Monster and Blood end.

D. I. Regular (Figure 14)

D. I. stands for double i. This is a running defense primarily, but the same secondary rules apply. Since a direction must be given to the

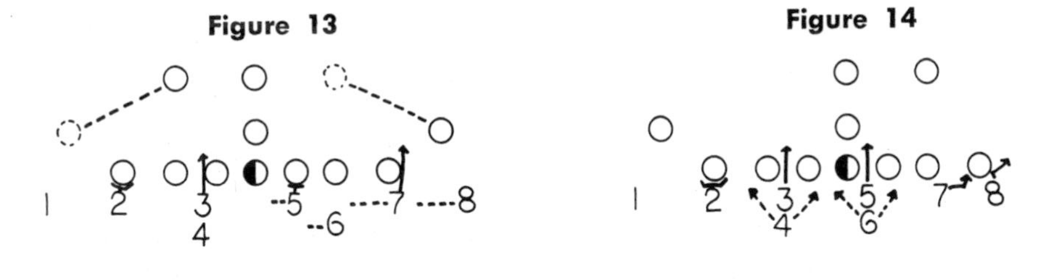

Figure 13 **Figure 14**

line, it is similar to the slant. Whatever rule you establish to determine which way to slant, apply to the shift. Use the term "Over Right"—"Over Left." Again a simple rule: shift over *away* from Monster against tight formations and shift over *towards* Monster against a wide flanker.

1. *Monster*—apply Slant Regular rules.
2. *Anchor*—apply Slant Regular rules.
3. *Gapper*—align on the offensive guard-tackle gap and drive hard on the snap straight ahead. Keep low enough to "turn" any overblock from either side. When in this position always give with pressure, because everyone will "over" block you. This means to pursue in the immediate direction of the block.
4. *Stack*—align behind tackle, if in over right; the middle guard if in over left. Read the fullback. If he takes one step to your side of the center, fire the next gap *outside* the gapper you are lined up behind. If the fullback takes one step the other side of the center, fire the next gap *inside* your gapper.
5. *Gapper*—align in center—guard gap to your right (same gap to your left, if the call is over left) and apply the same rules as outlined in #3 Gapper.
6. *Stack*—Same as #4 Stack.
7. *Lucy*—apply Lucy rules.
8. *Blood*—apply Blood rules.

9, 10, 11—Blue coverage and adjustments.

Line Adjustments: When in over left, reverse rule appropriately.

Apply the same rule concerning motion—Motion to Monster; slant, from this stacked formation. Motion away, rotate. Linebackers read on motion and do not fire (Figures 15 and 16).

Since this is basically a read defense, your end goes out with an offensive split end (Figure 17).

There is one exception regarding split end double coverage on Slants and DI's. When faced by a wide flanker one way and a split end the other side, you will slant and double stack towards the Monster side. This means your backside end should not go out on double coverage (Figures 18—Slant, and 19—DI). This keeps you from having to contain the back side with your linebacker. This is because Monster has gone back to the four deep position and can no longer force. If you aren't too worried about your opponent's throwing game, you could keep Monster up, slant or DI the other way, and free your backside end.

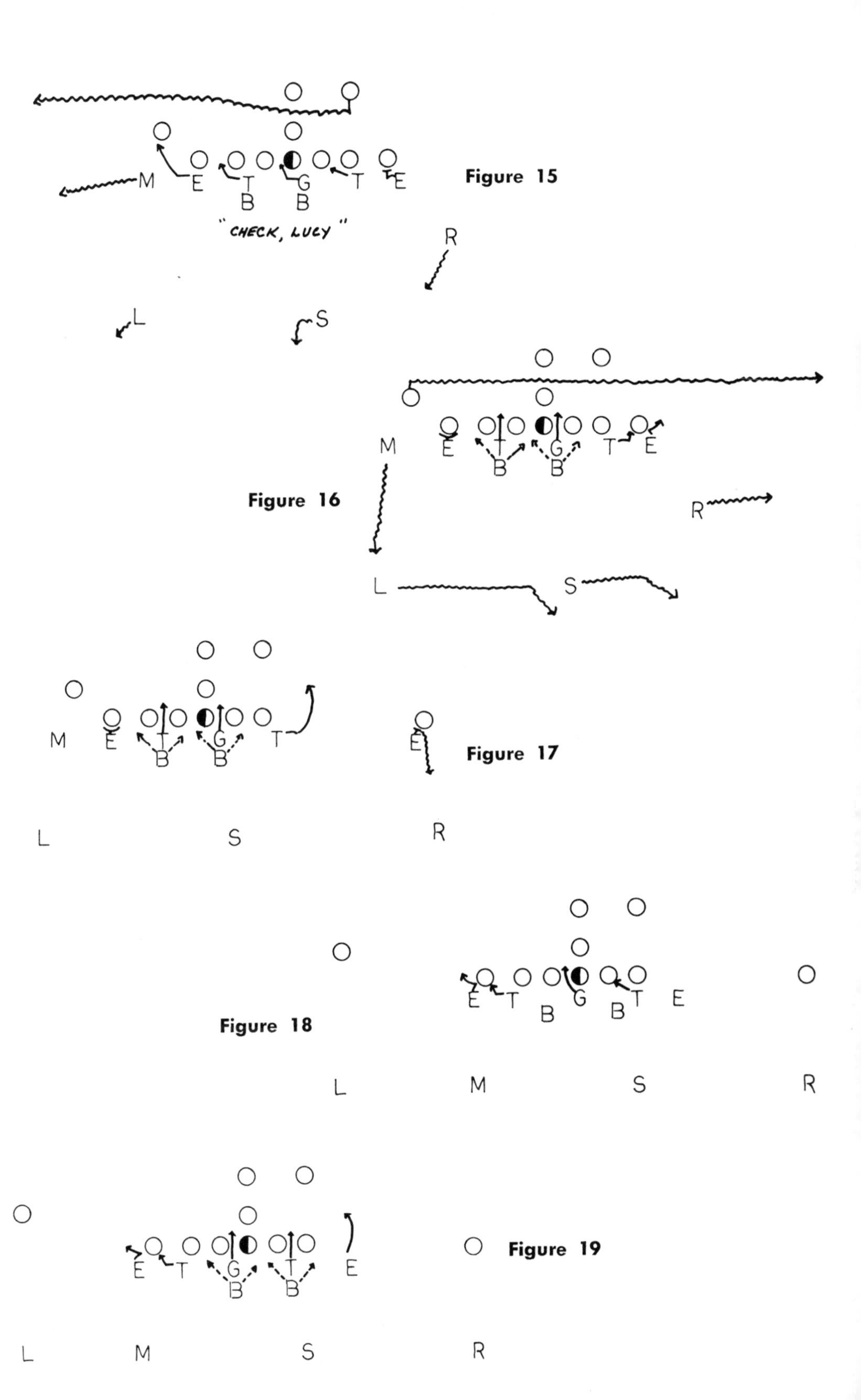

Figure 15

Figure 16

Figure 17

Figure 18

Figure 19

Split DI Regular (Figure 20)

Use the same rules for shifting over right or left as you used in Slant Regular and DI Regular.

1. *Monster*—Apply same rules for declaring and alignment. You are now relieved of forcing and containing.
   Ball flow your way, you have the flat until run has clearly been established.
   Ball flow straight back, take flat.
   Ball flow away, rotate.
2. *Lucy*—Apply Lucy rules.
3. *Loop*—Apply Loop technique. Clear the offensive tackle. You may have to align a shade deeper to do this. End up square to the line after your loop.
4. *Fire*—Go on the snap. Aim directly over the offensive guard. Break laterally as soon as pursuit angle is established.
5. *Loop*—Loop across offensive guard get to his outside shoulder use lead step.
6. *Fire*—Same as #4 Fire. Your aiming point is offensive center.
7. *Roger*—Apply Roger rules.
8. *Blood*—Apply Blood technique.

9, 10, 11—Blue coverage and adjustments.

No adjustments are necessary as Monster is free to go anywhere.

Pressing Category

54 Fire—Black Coverage

"Ray" or "Lin" designates middle guards action (Figure 21).

1. *Fire*—If threatened by a close flanker, line up in Regular position, in 3 point stance, and lay your ears back and split the

Figure 20

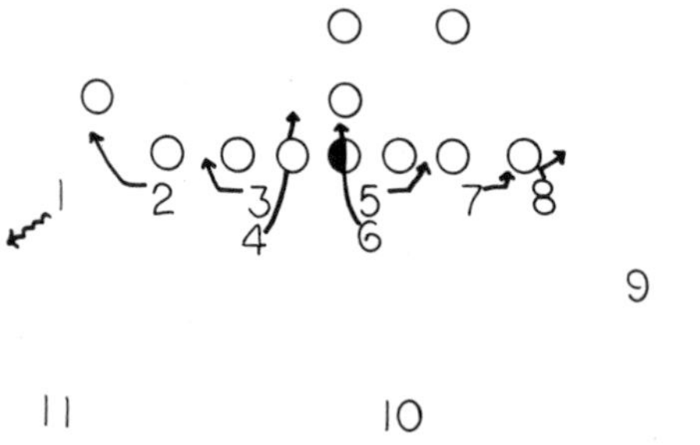

Figure 21

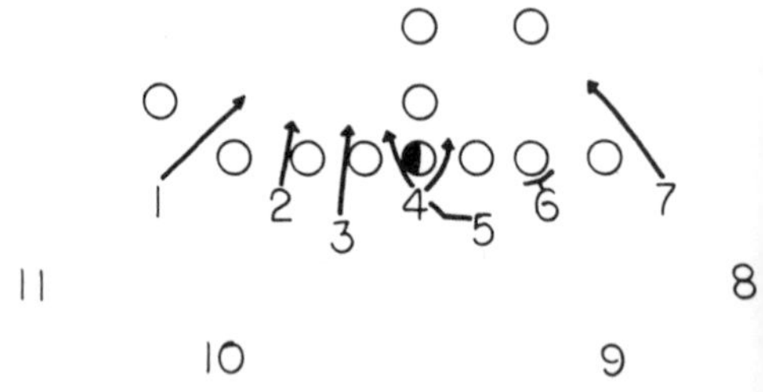

seam. If not threatened by a close flanker, line up wider and come hard keeping outside leverage on near half, but squeeze the off-tackle hole.

2. *Press*—Align in 54 position but come hard on the snap. Try to keep pace with your end. Don't worry about draws or traps.
3. *Fire*—"Ray" called, you fire through guards outside shoulder. If "Lin" were called, and you know you're the left linebacker, you would stagger step and cross behind your middle guard.
4. *Slant*—"Ray" called apply Roger rules.
5. *Fire*—"Ray" called and you are right linebacker cross behind middle guard. "Lin" called, fire over offensive guards outside shoulder.
6. *Anchor*—"Ray" called, you are right tackle, anchor and play carefully as your linebacker has gone. "Lin" called, use Press technique (#2).
7. *Fire*—Same as written above in #1.

8, 9, 10, 11—Black.

The off-tackle hole in "Ray" is vulnerable. The safety is keying the offensive end and should support quickly, if his man blocks. If they run anywhere else you should be in good shape. Since you are in Black Coverage, no line adjustments are necessary.

Slant Fire, Lucy called (Figure 22)

Notice the changing of Monster and Left Half Back. This can be done against tight sets. It will probably fit your personnel better. Since this is Black Coverage, the slant should be called towards the strength (Monster side). Right Line Backer calls for a slant already executed by the opposite side. This will prevent the offensive end from cracking down on the scrape-off line backer. A good feature of this defense is the pressure you put on the offensive center. He is used to getting guard help on his pass protection blocks. Now he has to block that slanting middle guard by himself or else the firing linebacker is clean.

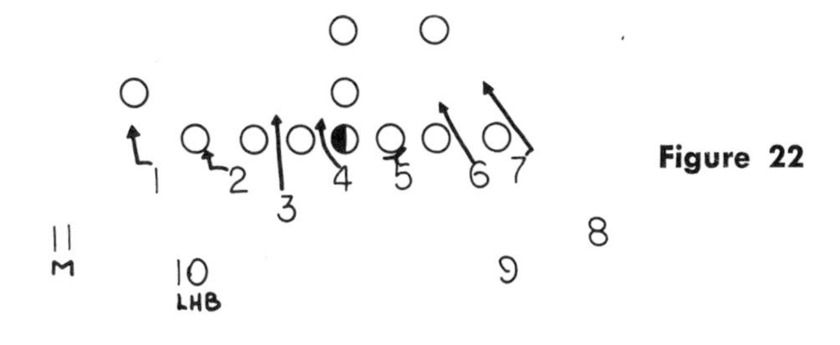

Figure 22

1. *Lucy*—apply Lucy rules.
2. *Lucy*—apply Lucy rules.
3. *Fire*—Fire through offensive guards outside shoulder. Do not get hooked in by the guard since you can always expand to the outside.
4. *Quick Around*—apply Roger or Lucy rules.
5. *Eagle*—align on outside shoulder of offensive guard and apply Eagle rules. You are the anchor for stunting men on either side of you.
6. *Eagle Fire*—align in the Eagle position. Disguise a regular, but fire hard on the snap.
7. *Eagle Fire*—align in the Eagle position but widen just before the ball snap. Come hard aiming at near backs outside shoulder. Squeeze the off-tackle hole. The near back should tell you if he is making a kick out block or a hook in block. Anytime the triangle (QB, FB, near HB) comes at you without a trailer (pitch man) you can put your head inside the near half back's block.

8 and 11—Against tight formations you are a true corner back. Align no more than three yards deep. Key your eligible and do not look into the offensive backfield. You have time to make a run-pass decision, do not hurry it.

9 and 10—Align five to six yards deep over your eligible. If he releases, cover him, if he blocks support.

By adding the word "Bullets" to this defense, you can get an eight-man rush (Figure 23). This could call for Orange coverage automatically.

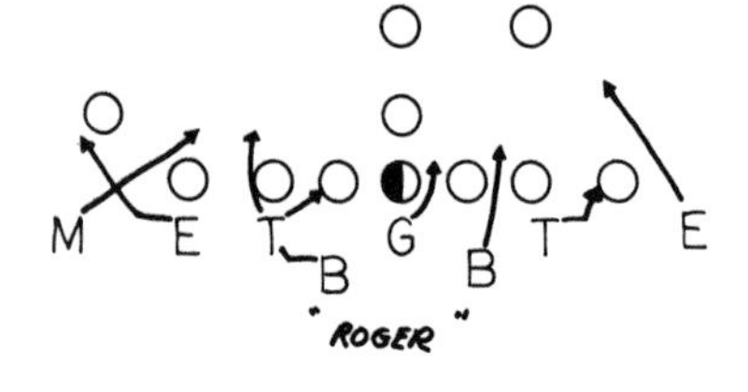

Figure 23

Figure 24

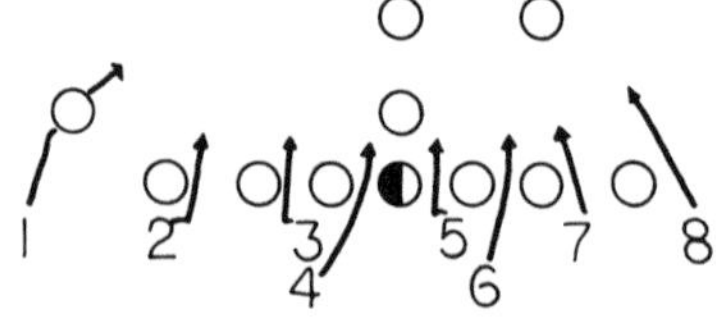

Roger X Fire (Figure 24)

1. *Monster*—Come hard on the snap. Keep leverage on close flanker, you are still outside container.
2. *Inside Fire*—Align in anchor position. On the snap, stagger step to inside and drive the end-tackle gap.
3. *Outside Fire*—Align in Roger X position. On the snap, stagger step to your outside and drive the tackle guard gap.
4. *Fire*—Align in tandem with your tackle. On the snap drive the guard-center gap.
5. *Inside Fire*—Align in Roger X position. On snap, stagger step to inside and drive the center-guard gap.
6. *Fire*—Align in Roger X position. On the snap, drive the guard-tackle gap.
7. *Press*—Same technique as 54 Fire.
8. *Fire*—Same technique as 54 Fire.
9. 10, 11—Orange coverage. Here again you can teach a fast rotation against tight sets to cover the flat, or you can give up the flats depending on game situation, etc.

Adjustments to different sets require a lot of teaching. If you want to go with this eight man rush, cross your fingers and don't try to adjust to everything. Only one thing should make you change, and that is extended motion. Apply your regular motion rules. Slant if motion is to Monster and rotate if away from Monster.

One adjustment that should be made is against the shift (Figure 25). This is about the same, except that your right side fires from a wider position. The same motion rules should apply.

DI Fire (Figure 26)

This is similar to DI Regular with a few changes. First, the line

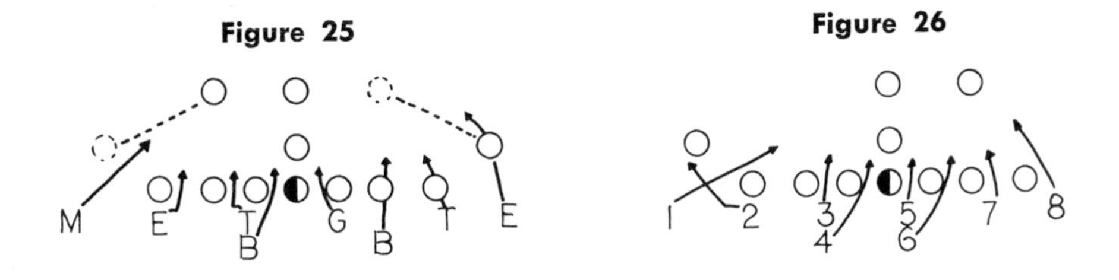

Figure 25

Figure 26

backers fire away from Monster. Monster and Anchor may fire straight or cross charge. The secondary plays a straight Orange.

1. *Monster*—Commit on the snap. Either call "Fire" or "Bullets" with the anchor.
2. *Anchor*—Stunt with Monster.
3. *Gapper*—Apply DI Regular rules.
4. *Fire*—Fire gap away from Monster side.
5. *Gapper*—Apply DI Regular rules.
6. *Fire*—Fire gap away from Monster side.
7. *Press*—Apply 54 *FIRE rules.*
8. *Fire*—Apply 54 *FIRE* rules.
9. 10, 11—*ORANGE* coverage. Line again apply motion rules.

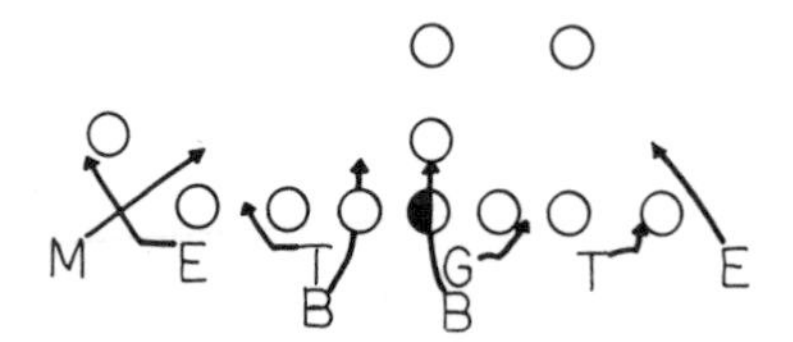

Figure 27

Split DI Fire (Figure 27)

This defense is pretty much the same as Split DI. We've added Bullets and used a fire technique on the side away from Monster. Of course, the secondary plays Orange.

We have now completed a Monster category of defenses. Not all of them have to be used. There also is a place for a 6—1 set-up, and an eagle style. They will be covered in subsequent chapters.

4

61 Rover

Rover has been good to us. Originally, it was called a 6—3 defense, but changes in the secondary (from corners and two deep) to four deep and the novel commitment of the middle linebacker, have brought about the name of 6—1 Rover. We keep records on the results of each of our defenses, and Rover is usually the leader in least yards gained per try. This is because of the way it is used. Certainly the results would be worse if we tried to make this a basic defense. A proper ratio is about eight to ten times a game. It becomes a surprise defense and prevents your opponent from setting a game plan to defeat Rover.

For a brief history of the evolution of Rover, we must go back to the middle 'fifties. Gene Ellenson, who is presently my defensive coach, was coaching at the University of Miami at that time. He helped to create Rover, and has always carried it in our defensive repertory. We keep its' use at a minimum, but have always had great results with it. The original Rover was a moving middle line backer who always seemed to be jumping into the line where the offense was running. At that time Miami had both corners up and this maneuver created almost a ten-man line, if the attack and Rover were on the same side. Needless to say, it was effective.

With the advent of extended motion and wide flankers, along with split ends, the old Rover required changing. By pulling the corners back into four deep and changing the end play, and by restricting Rover's use, we have shown it to be effective against the pro style attack.

We consider this a pressing defense, so our secondary plays a man-to-man defense. This handles the adjustments problem. Rover is still free to rove. The secret is having the middle line backer (Rover) jump into the guard-tackle gap just before the offensive snap. If he is there too early, the offense can utilize a blocking pattern that will provide a blocker for every defender. This is predicated on at least three offensive men all shifting blocking plans. By moving Rover in and out and in again, you can cause a lot of offensive mental gearshifting. Therefore, if Rover comes in just before the snap, somebody is going to block the wrong plan and the defense has a man clean.

Another interesting point is how Rover picks his side. Every offensive quarterback will subconsciously cast his eyes to the side of the play called when he observes Rover about to move. This is natural. So Rover gets his tip in this manner. Should you find a quarterback who won't look to either side, Rover uses his knowledge of his opponent (through scouting, pictures, etc.,) to dictate the most probable side in this situation. This raises the odds of his being right. If he is wrong, your defense may be a little weaker, but it should not cave in. If Rover is right, the defense should get a big play. If the offensive quarterback gives an audible change-off or takes an abnormally long count, Rover should switch sides.

If 61—Rover is called and Rover doesn't rove, the defense is a straight 6-1-4 defense. The following position rules are given without Rover in the line.

61 Rover (Figure 28)

1. *Fire*—apply 54 Fire rules.
2. *Press*—apply 54 Fire rules.
3. *Nose*—play on offensive guard's nose. Head read and play it as if you were on the center's nose. Lateral pursuit is necessary from this position.
4. *Rover*—If playing straight away, key flow and back up the line from end to end. It is better to meet the center with good defensive leverage, and then locate the attack, than to run out of the middle fast, which leaves you open to being blocked *by* the hole. Pass responsibility is either hook. Normally, it would be the hook area to the strength or roll-out direction. However, the receiver may have to go away from quarterback direction and look for the throw back hook.
5. *Nose*—Same as #3 Nose.
6. *Press*—Apply 54 Fire rules.
7. *Fire*—Apply 54 Fire rules.

8, 9, 10, 11—Black coverage (man to man).

Adjustments are all handled by the secondary, except when an un-

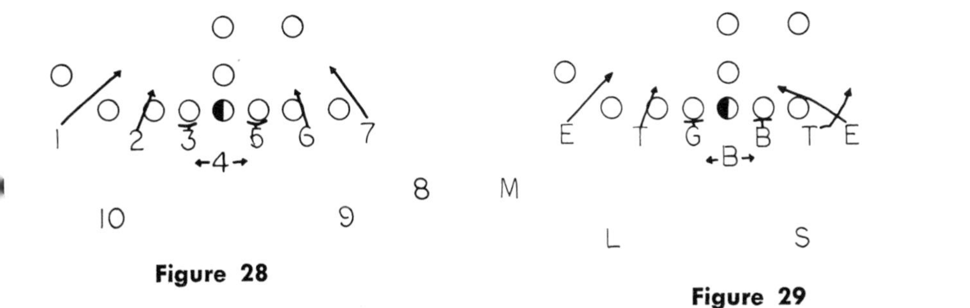

Figure 28

Figure 29

balanced line calls for the whole line to move over one man to the unbalanced side. Since this is a press defense your end will stay in and press against a split end (Figure 29). Note the TX between right end and right tackle.

Rover and one of the guards can work out a "game," without committing Rover. The guard simply takes either gap, with Rover being mentally aware of the open side.

Rover Over (Figure 30)

When Rover Over is called the following rules apply: Rover picks his side and hollers "in." He jumps into the guard-tackle gap with his outside foot up in an upright stance (Figure 30a). He also taps the guard

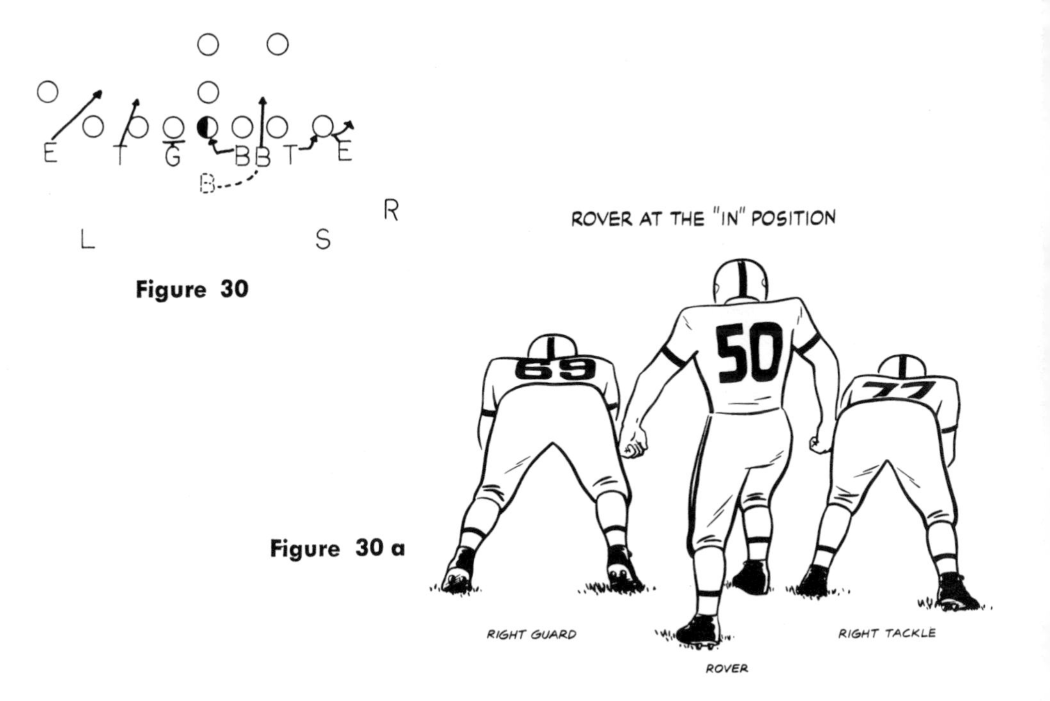

Figure 30

Figure 30 a

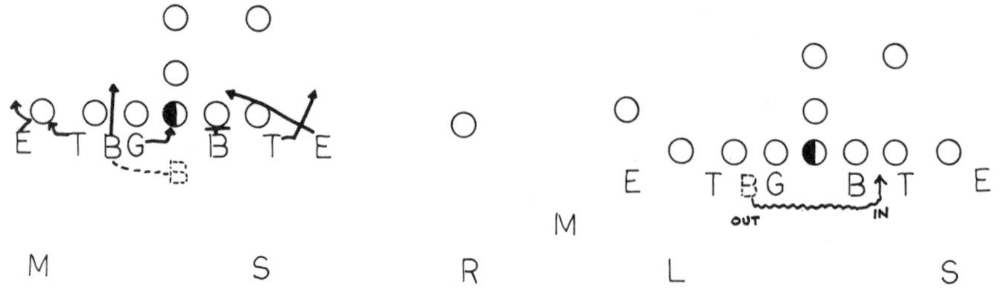

Figure 31

Figure 32

and tackle on their inside hips as he arrives. The ball snaps while in this alignment the guard loops back to a nose position on the center. (Sometimes you can let him take the gap.) The tackle does a Roger (or Lucy if it is on the left side). The end does a Blood technique. The tackle and end should "lock" the offensive end, which takes away the quickie pass. This is particularly good when one end is split (Figure 31).

Of course, Rover dives the gap on the snap. If Rover hollers in, taps, and arrives, and then nothing happens for two seconds, he hollers "out" and leaves. He may go to the other side or go right back in where he came from (Figure 32 shows him going to the other side).

A common mistake by a Rover is that after he breaks clean, he runs by all the action. He must be ready, and have enough football sense to break off into a pursuit angle.

It doesn't make too much difference if his guard, tackle, and end miss his "ins" or "outs." It would be more sound, but very often they are helped by not making the predicted move.

61—Running Rover (Figure 33)

The same rules apply. Rover gives a verbal signal from his middle position, such as "Rip" for right or "Liz" for left. He now runs through the hole after the snap. It is very risky to call and not run through. There is a strong temptation to call the stunt, then have Rover key. There are two things wrong with this. One, he gets there a step or two late. Two, he can get hit by a counter play.

This stunt can be combined with Bullets for a sound short yardage defense (Figure 34).

Figure 33

Figure 34

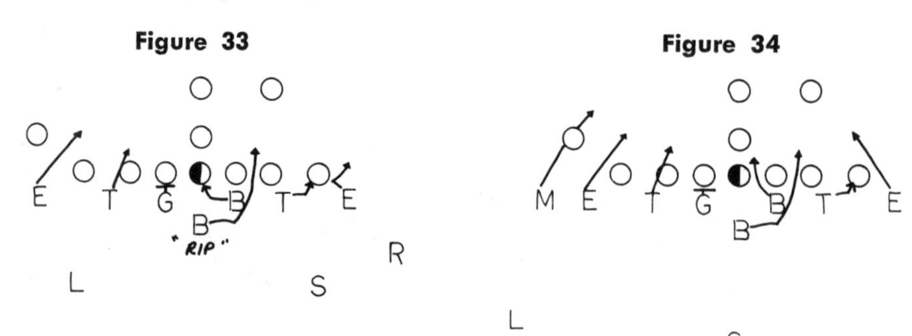

Rover calls away from Monster and the secondary, as always on Bullets, is Orange.

61 Rover 5

To combat people from sneaking out five receivers against a man-to-man four deep, Rover 5 is called. This places the middle linebacker on the fifth receiver. Rover's instructions are to locate the middle man of the back three offensive backs and line up over him and take him man-to-man if he releases (Figure 35).

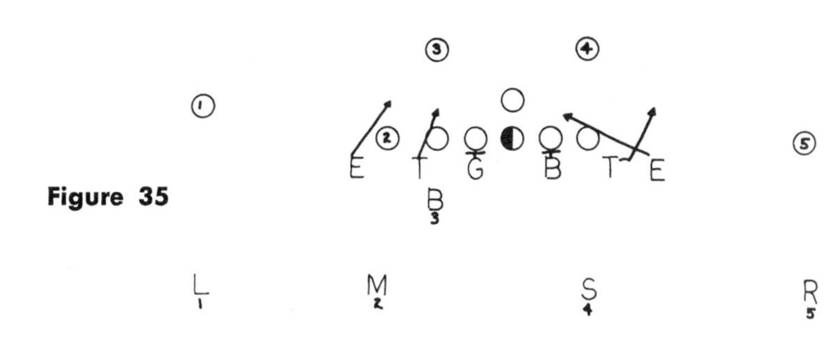

Figure 35

This gives you a pretty good six man rush, with five receivers covered.

A few more tips on using Rover. Very often it is advisable to shift into a 6-1 set up from a 54 alignment. This discourages automatics. Another important point is selection of personnel for Rover. It takes a reckless type that likes to shoot gaps. Some linebackers are "smellers." They have a knack of getting in front of almost any play, and do not take well to a "give up" type of charge. These kids usually make poor Rovers. So find a kind of show-off type kid and let him Rove. Of course, another decision can take precedence. Of your two inside linebackers, one will be better suited to play guard in the line. That will just leave the other one to be Rover. Down through the years, the defense seemed to work better when Rover had a personality that fitted the position.

5

The Eagle

We have touched on some Eagle play as parts of other defenses. It will be necessary to cover the full Eagle separately, however. The Eagle has a definite place in any defensive repertory. Like 61 Rover, it is hard to make it hold up as a base defense. The 61 Rover is basically a rush defense, while the Eagle is primarily a pass defense. Each has possibilities to hold up its weak area, but your opponents can pick away at it. If you played the 61 all the time, you'd invite the passing game, particularly hook and curl passes. If you played the Eagle all the time, you'd get a steady dose of off-tackle and inside attack. Also you'd find exaggerated line splits which spread your middle mighty thin.

The advantage the Eagle has for run defense is that it confuses most normal blocking rules; its advantage as a pass defense is the position of the linebackers. They are wide enough to cover flats, or provide a good hold up on tight ends. We have also found that the Eagle can provide a really fine pass rush. The rush comes more from the outside, and outside rushes are always harder to block than inside rushes. The Eagle also fits a Monster secondary well. Monster can declare either side, or stay in the middle, or declare a four deep and never affect the play of the rest of the line.

While any combination of secondary coverages will fit the Eagle, we usually go Orange and give the back side flat to the linebacker away from Monster. This is because it gives us one defense that will allow double coverage by Monster with a maximum prevent by the three deep. In certain situations we can get double coverage on both sides, with three deep.

Following are the position rules for the basic Eagle defense.

Eagle Regular (Figure 36)

1. *Monster*—Use rules for declaring. Contain and force are relieved so you have flat on everything but motion and flow away.

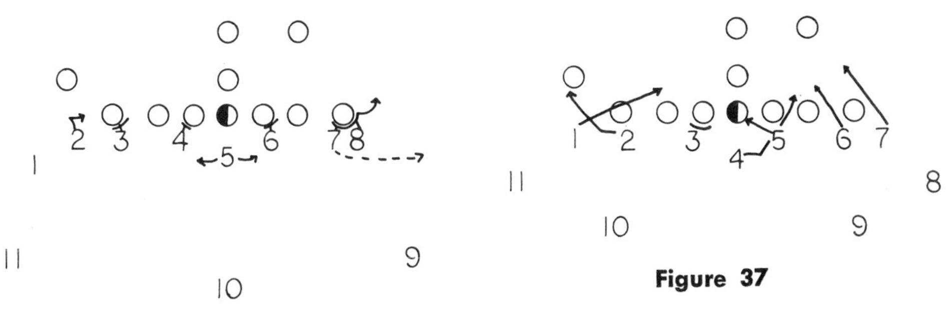

Figure 36

Figure 37

Against a wide flanker you have three options. Double, walk off, or regular.

2. *Regular*—Apply 54 Regular rules.
3. *Eagle Regular*—Align on inside shoulder of off-side end with outside foot forward, upright stance. Jab end on snap. React to blocking pressure. If you are on Monster side, you take the hook area. If you are on side away from Monster, you take flat, your side, on pass show. There is one exception to the flat coverage—if your end is double covering a split end, you go back to 54 Regular position, key near halfback and take him wherever he goes.
4. *Eagle Regular*—Align on outside shoulder of offensive guard. Use 54 Regular rules applied to the guard instead of the tackle.
5. *Middle Guard*—Align on center's nose in an upright stance, your feet even with the feet of the two tackles. Key center, Quarterback, fullback tandem. Flow either way, fill outside tackle to corresponding side first. Any pass show, check draw first, then take hook area away from Monster.
6. *Eagle Regular*—Apply rules in #4 above.
7. *Eagle Regular*—Apply rules in #3 above.
8. *Regular*—Apply rules in #1 above.

9, 10, 11—Orange coverage.

Line adjustments are simple. No adjustments are made except to a split end. That side goes back to a 54 Regular if your end double covers. If your end stays in, you can cross charge with him (Razor) or take "flat" from Eagle position. Middle guard always comes back up tight, if he has a half Eagle only.

The companion defense with Eagle Regular is Eagle Fire. We regard this as one of our best pass rushes.

Eagle Fire (Figure 37)

1. *Fire*—Align in Eagle position. Call a straight fire or Razor with

your linebacker. If a straight fire, you have contain rush responsibility. If a Razor, you close down to anchor tackle.

2. *Fire*—Align in Eagle position. Get call from your end. If Fire, dummy a hold-up, but fire on snap inside end-tackle gap. If Razor, stagger step to outside and take contain rush responsibility.
3. *Eagle Fire*—Align in Eagle position, get call from your middle guard. If he calls the other tackle, you become anchor. Apply Spy rules. If he calls you, do a Roger into the offensive center.
4. *Eagle Fire*—Align in Eagle position. Call to either tackle for a cross charge. Simply holler his name. After call and on snap, stagger step in that direction and charge through area in which that tackle lined up. Do not run a "circle" route. Stagger and straight. Game plan will determine which tackle is best to cross (the Eagle fire cross is shown in Figure 37a).
5. *Eagle Fire*—Apply #3 rules above.
6. *Fire*—Apply #2 rules above.
7. *Fire*—Apply #1 rules above.

8, 9, 10, 11—Black coverage.

3 INTERIOR MEN EXECUTING EAGLE FIRE CROSS

Figure 37 a

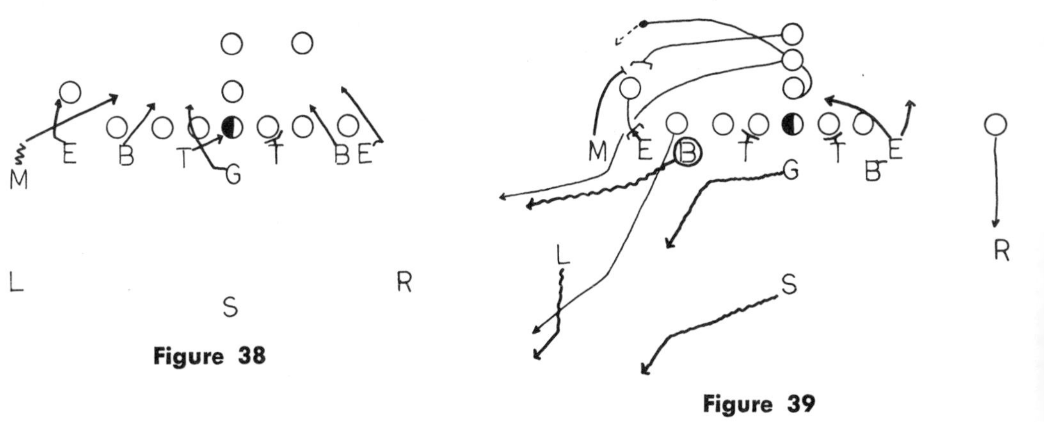

Figure 38

Figure 39

No line adjustments. Your end always stays in and Razors with his linebacker against a split end.

You can make this into an eight-man rush by calling Eagle Fire Bullets (Figure 38). This will call for an automatic Orange in the secondary.

Note the linebacker to Monster side must use "fire" technique only. Remember that motion always calls for Bullets to come off. Use same motion coverage as explained before.

Here is a special defense combining Eagle and Eagle Fire to meet a special offense (Figure 39).

This play creates a tough problem for the containing end and flat-and-hook coverage. By containing with a wider man (Monster) you can force a pull up by the Quarterback. By being in the Eagle your linebacker can cover the flat. Also your middle guard can cover the hook and you have a strong back side rush. If they roll the other way, your linebacker should be in the passer's face. If they "reach" block with their tackle on your crashing end, put the Eagle cross into the flow and your middle guard should get to the passer (Figure 40). An alternate plan would call for not committing the linebacker, and covering the flat with him (Figure 41).

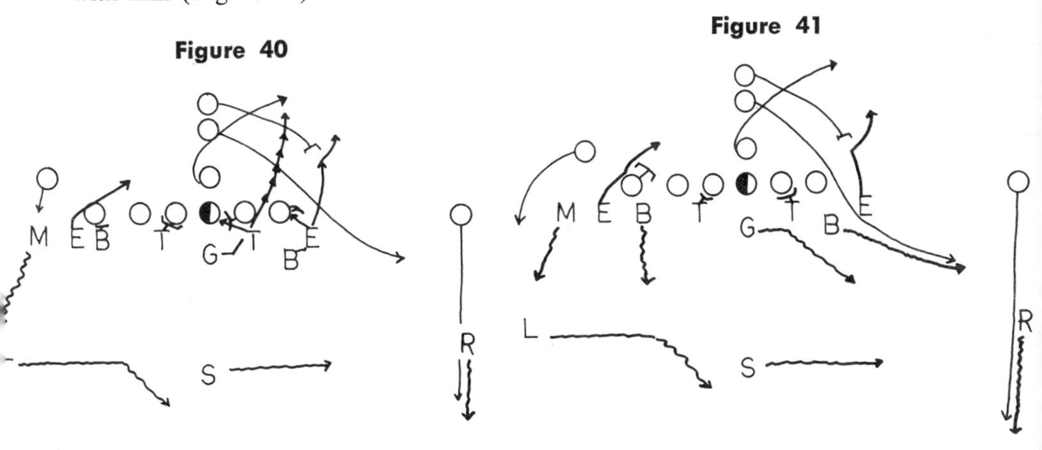

Figure 40

Figure 41

6

60 Defense

The 60 Defense is probably the oldest of all the basic defenses in modern football. From this alignment has evolved overshift defenses and variations of the five and seven man lines. All of these 8 front defenses are supported by a three deep zone secondary. However, there has been a gradual evolution in the past ten years with many more offensive variations and the necessary adjustments that have to be made to meet these spread formations. The cycle of offense has changed, and with the "I" formation, double wing and all types of motion, it is still necessary to keep the even defense in any defensive plan that is sound in meeting offensive strength with defensive strength. The teams that maintain an odd basic defense with the Monster or four deep secondary are forced to slant or shift into an even defense often. So it follows that there will always be a place for this basic defense.

The basic defense we will call "60 Heads." This is a reading defense and is the toughest part of the defense to play. It requires much more time in teaching because the major portion of the responsibility is based on the defense's recognition of the offensive play. It is important that everyone play his responsibility first, and then react in this defense. It also follows that pursuit is one of the advantages in this type of defense, but the angle of pursuit varies greatly depending on the type of play. The pursuit angle of the team is a major coaching responsibility. Keeping a perimeter around the ball is a must at all times.

Figure 42 gives an example of the correct angle of pursuit on a sweep. Notice that the ball carrier is always in the middle of the wheel.

Guard's Play in 60 Heads Defense

Position. In 60 Heads guards are lined nose-up on the offensive guards about two feet off the ball. It is important to emphasize two feet

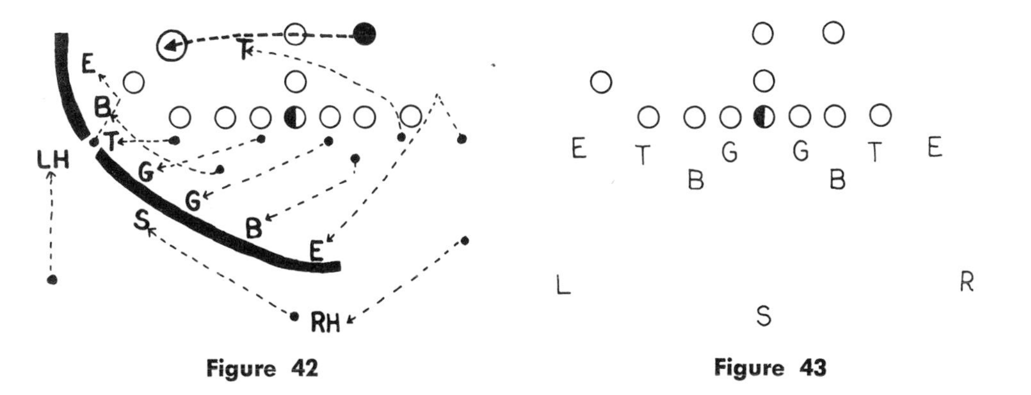

Figure 42 **Figure 43**

off the ball, because invariably they want to line up two feet off the offensive man, and consequently, they will be too close.

Stance. Guards should use a four point stance with the feet on line and about shoulder width apart. A four point stance is desirable (but not necessary) because it will tend to keep the guards low. It is important that they maintain a neutral stance with legs in a coiled position to provide explosive power. In playing a reaction style defense in 60 Heads, the neutral stance and a "low center of gravity" gives good lateral movement to either side.

Keys. Guards key the offensive tackle, guard, and center.

Play. Guards play a reaction style defense. When either the offensive center or tackle blocks toward them, the defensive guards will take a short lateral step toward the potential blocker. When blocked by the offensive guard, the defensive guard defeats him with a shiver, or a forearm shoulder lift, fighting against the pressure of the offensive blocker. Insist that they keep their shoulders parallel at all times, to give them greater lateral movement to the backside in case the ball carrier attempts to cut back on them. The defensive guard slides or spins across the head of his offensive opponent; he never takes the easy way around the blockers. When he senses a trap, he holds his position, sits low and meets the trapper by exploding into him, driving him down the line. Since the guard is lined up two feet off the ball, he cannot afford to give any more ground. As soon as your keys commit, DECLARE WAR!

Splits. The split rule for guards is 12 inches. As long as the offensive guard takes a 12″ or less split, he should play nose up. If he takes a greater split than 12″, he should stay at a relative distance from the center, and play the guard in the same manner defensive tackles play the end, with inside-out leverage. That is, on the snap take a short lateral jab step with outside foot toward the guard, using a hand shiver or forearm shoulder lift, playing pressure from him while keying the quarterback for the sneak. Guards are primarily responsible for the area between them. If they are getting hurt in this area, they should move in tighter. Any time the offensive guard's split is great enough, the defensive guards have the option to fire the gap.

"Me and You." The defensive guards can play "me and you" any time. Establish one as the captain to call "me" or "you." One of them plays slower and more cautiously than the other. The slow guard has a greater responsibility for the draw play, a screen pass, and a trap. The other guard plays more aggressively and can afford to commit quicker. This is a good stunt to use to break one guard clean to rush the passer.

Rushing the Passer. Guards are so close to the ball that they should be able to put more pressure on the passer quicker than any other lineman most of the time. Much work should be done on this because of its value to the pass defense. Stress the importance of the guards' staying in their rushing lanes and keeping their hands up as they rush the passer. If they should be forced out of their rushing lane, they should work quickly to get back into their lane, never giving the passer an opening to run between them. By staying in their rushing lanes, they discourage the passer from tucking the ball under his arm and running through the big hole that would be created if they ran around blockers.

Pursuit. Guards should figure in all pursuit. They are closer to the ball, and are able to determine the flow quicker than any other lineman. The angle they take in their pursuit will be determined by the point of attack of the offensive and how soon they are able to read the play.

Tackle Play In 60 Heads

Stance. The tackles are in either a three or four point stance, and like the guards, they keep a low "center of gravity" with their weight balanced. The outside foot of the tackle should be slightly in front of the inside foot and the legs should be coiled. The width of his base is slightly wider than his shoulders.

Position. The defensive tackle lines up approximately 18″ off the ball with his inside eye on the outside eye of the offensive end.

Key. The defensive tackle keys the offensive tackle.

Play. On the snap of the ball the defensive tackle takes a short lateral jab step with his outside foot toward the end and simultaneously strikes the end with a hand shiver or forearm shoulder left. As he moves to control the end, he watches the offensive tackle.

If the offensive end is blocking him, the defensive tackle feels him

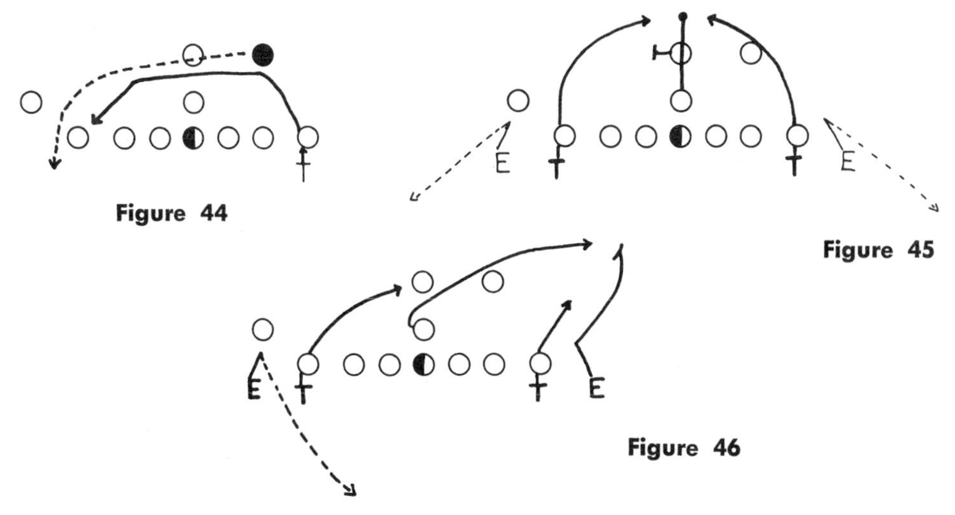

Figure 44

Figure 45

Figure 46

and fights pressure laterally in or out against the block of the end. If the end has released, the defensive tackle reacts to the key given him by the offensive tackle's block. He must defeat the turn-out block or the hook block by the tackle and rush hard when the offensive tackle pass-blocks. If neither the offensive end nor tackle blocks on him, he must set for a trap block by a back or a pulling interior lineman. His technique for meeting the trap block should be the same as for a guard.

Splits. The defensive tackle maintains a constant split of about 2½ yards from his defensive guard as long as the offensive halfback on his side is in his normal position, regardless of the split of the offensive lineman. When the offensive halfback is not in his normal position, the defensive tackle moves to a nose-up position on the offensive end. His play in the basic 60 defense is initially on the line of scrimmage until he locates the ball.

Plays away from tackle. On plays away from the defensive tackle, he becomes the "chase" man and crosses the scrimmage line and chases the play, staying as deep as the ball until it crosses the line of scrimmage (Figure 44). The chase man is responsible for deep reverses, bootlegs and slow cut back plays.

Rushing the Passer. On straight drop back passes, the tackles have the added responsibility of containing the passer. Therefore they should keep outside leverage on the passer and rush with their arms up if the passer is facing in their direction (Figure 45). If he is facing away from them they can come in lower, always trying to keep the pocket the passer is throwing from as narrow as possible.

On roll passes to his side, the tackle should rush through his lane to prevent an opening through which the passer might be able to run back (Figure 46). The tackle does not have the responsibility of con-

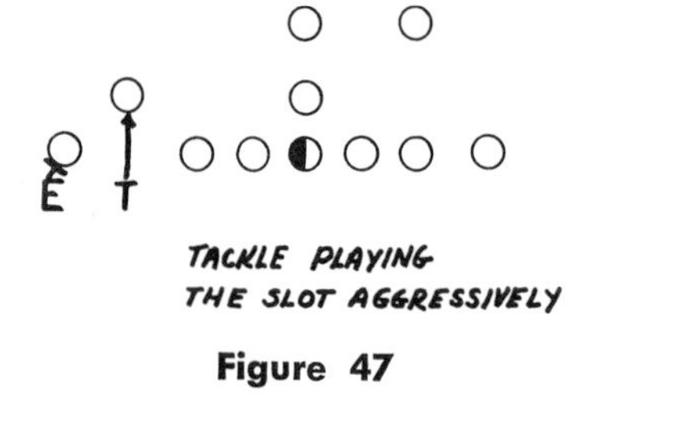

Figure 47

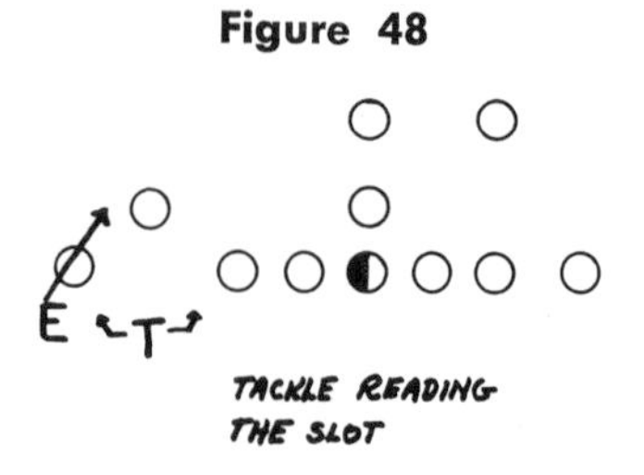

Figure 48

taining a fan or roll-out pass to his side on 60 Heads. The tackle making the backside rush must contain the passer and prevent him from running back to the off-side, rushing the backside shoulder of the passer.

Playing slot or wingback sets. If a normal slot is to his side, the tackle plays slot back as he would the offensive end. He has two options in playing this:

(1) play aggressively into slot back trying to get maximum penetration (Figure 47). The tackle should expect to be doubled by the end and should be mentally strong to his outside.

(2) play a good 18" off ball and read the end, slot back, and tackle, and react to their movement (Figure 48). Play the wingback situation in the same manner.

End Play in 60 Heads

In this defense the play of the ends is vital. They have more responsibility. They are half linemen and half halfbacks. They have more pursuit area and more adjustments to make with flankers and offensive motion.

Stance. The defensive end lines up in a crouched position with outside foot back, shoulders parallel to the line of scrimmage, and weight forward on the balls of his feet. He should take as much of the ball as he can get, so that on the snap he can get across the line of scrimmage as quickly as possible. Stress that the ends should stay low and keep their shoulders parallel. It is important that they do not box upfield. This makes them easy targets to be blocked out and opens up the off tackle hole.

Position. The defensive end lines up on the line of scrimmage about two or two and one-half yards from his defensive tackle.

Key. The defensive end keys the onside halfback. If the halfback is not in his normal position, the end keys the offensive fullback, then any pulling lineman.

Play. On the snap of the ball, the defensive end takes a two step charge across the line at an angle of 60 degrees to the line of scrimmage. In taking his charge, the end steps with his outside foot first and then advances his inside foot—he takes a regular step with the outside back foot and a short hop with the inside foot. Just as he plants his inside foot, he slides his outside foot slightly to the rear, which helps him to settle in a stationary position. This two step charge puts the defensive end about one yard, or four feet, across the line of scrimmage, with his shoulders still parallel to the line and his outside foot back and slightly to the outside to give him a solid base to operate from. (The moves of the left end are shown in Figure 4).

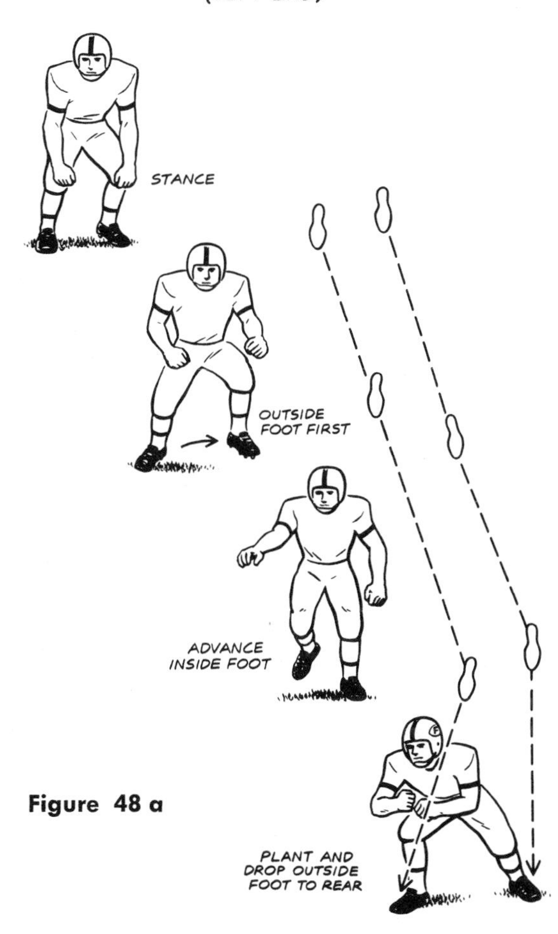

Figure 48 a

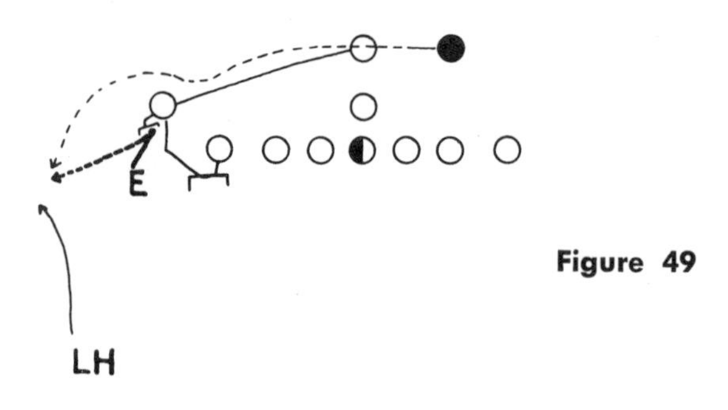

Figure 49

The end should be stationary momentarily, until he diagnoses the play. To do this he watches the offensive halfback, who frequently will block him in or out on sweeps or off-tackle plays. If the halfback dives or goes away, the defensive ends look immediately to the inside for blockers. When meeting inside plays, the end sets tough and fights the blocker with a shoulder and forearm left, thus limiting the off-tackle hole. The end should remember to keep his shoulders parallel so he will be able to fall back into the hole if the play cuts inside, or fall back to the outside if the play goes outside. The end should never get caught in a box position (shoulders at 90 degree angle to line) where he is an easy target to be driven out. If the end's key indicates a sweep, then he should try to get up field more, slide laterally, and ward off blockers with his hands. He gives ground grudgingly, always trying to force the sweep deep and wide and stringing it out. If an end gets caught, he should fall back to his outside and take an angle toward his goal which will cross the path of the ball carrier (Figure 49).

Flankers. The end will recognize any flanker who has outside position on him up to a width of five yards. When the flanker is more than five yards from the original position of the end, the defensive end will ignore him and assume his regular responsibilities.

When there are two men flanked out on his side and a pass play is indicated, the end will play in the flat zone. When this occurs, the tackle must contain the passer.

The end must coordinate his play opposite a slot with his tackle. If the tackle is playing tough and attempting to penetrate the end, who has lined up on the outside shoulder, the defensive end must play the offensive end strong and attempt to keep him from doubling down on the tackle. If the tackle is playing off and reading, then the defensive end will be more aggressive and get depth quicker.

Plays away from end. On plays away from the defensive end, he retreats back through his original position and then takes a deep pursuit angle through the safety man's zone, thus becoming the second safety.

Pass Defense Responsibilities. On any straight drop-back pass, both ends drop off and cover the flats. They do this in the same manner as described when the running play goes away from them.

On any roll out, fan, or play pattern pass to his side, the end is responsible for containing the passer. The offside end will fall back over his otuside shoulder to help cover the flat or throw-back pass to his side.

On long yardage downs or in short yardage situations where they come across at a 60 degree angle, the ends should charge up field more than normally.

General Rules for Defensive Ends

1. You must be alert, agile, and nifty in your movements.
2. Remember you have two holes to protect: first, the sweep and second, the off-tackle hole.
3. Your outside support is a long way off, so if you are circled and the ball carrier gets turned down field, a long run may result.
4. You do not get the internal support given to other linemen, and the blocks you must defeat are made by running backs or linemen who have generated considerable power and force when they hit you. You must break their initial charge; meet force with force, and finesse.
5. Never be knocked down or tied up by *one man.*
6. You are playing the *best position on the football team*—you are a combination back and lineman. Take pride in your position and work hard to excel at it.

Linebacker Play in 60 Heads

Never has there been a great defense without great linebackers. They, like the ends, have a lot of adjustments to make.

Stance. The linebacker should be comfortable in his stance, physically relaxed and mentally alert. Feet should be spread the width of the shoulders, with the otuside foot slightly back and the weight evenly distributed. Knees should be slightly bent, head up, and eyes looking ahead with split vision. He must be in a position from which he can move quickly, forward, backward and laterally. The arms and hands will be in a position to strike a blow (flipper or shiver) and protect the legs and body from blockers.

Position. Linebackers line up directly on the nose of the offensive tackle and about three yards from the line of scrimmage. Their depth will vary with down and distance—a little closer on short yardage and deeper on long yardage or passing downs.

Keys. Linebackers key through the offensive tackles into the backfield. They should be aware of the tackles' block and the backfield action.

Play against the Run. If the offensive tackle releases directly at the linebacker, the linebacker steps up to meet him vigorously and squarely. If the offensive tackle takes either an inside angle or an outside angle on the linebacker, the backer will rapidly move laterally in order to avoid the tackle's block. When the offensive tackle uses a turn-out block on the defensive tackle, the backer steps into the hole in a crouched position to meet the blockers leading through the hole.

The linebackers are not expected on 60 Heads to make the tackle for no gain. Therefore they should not commit themselves until they know where the ball is. If they lose the ball, they should retreat back. They should always keep leverage on the ball carrier. On plays directed to their outside, they should hit from the inside out and on plays to their inside, they should hit from the outside. When the play is directed away from them, they should keep an inside-out position on the ball at all times and be a little slower in leaving their position to eliminate the cutback.

Play against the Pass. When the linebacker recognizes a straight-drop-back pass, he retreats over his outside shoulder to his hook zone and pulls up just as the quarterback starts his throw; he then breaks in the direction of the throw.

On a pass thrown from a play fake, or sprint out action, the backer is responsible for his hook zone first, and then the flat. You must work with your linebackers in deciding when they can release for the flat. If the quarterback continues past his offensive tackle, he automatically eliminates the onside hook, and linebackers should be coached to recognize this as early as possible. It is difficult to cover the flats from 60 Head, but with work you can do an adequate job.

General Rules for Linebackers

1. You must not be cut off from lateral pursuit by releasing lineman.

2. If you are the removed linebacker from the point of attack, you must not commit to the strong side quickly, but play it cautiously and look for the counter or cut-back play.
3. You must locate the ball—then hit hard and fast and drive the ball carrier back.
4. Be decisive—aggressive and hard nosed; you are the backbone of the internal defense.
5. You should get more tackles and be in more defensive plays than any other man on the team.
6. On wide plays you hit from the inside out on plays your way. If you are the removed linebacker, get slight depth and play for the cut-back.
7. Be tough, straight ahead and pursue from side line to side line. Great defensive teams are made by great linebackers—be the BEST!

Stunts from 60 Defense

Split 6—Figure 50

End. On the Split 6 stunt, the end play is the same as in 60 Heads Defense.

Tackle. Line up 18 inches off the ball. This should force the opposing end to take at least two steps to make contact. Take a short lateral step with the outside foot and a crossover step with the inside foot at the same time coming up with a forearm lift or shiver to be ready to defeat the end if he should be blocking down on you. The tackle must not be cut off by the end. Once the tackle gains outside position on the offensive end's outside shoulder, he maintains this position until he locates the ball. This will keep him in the proper position to support back on inside plays.

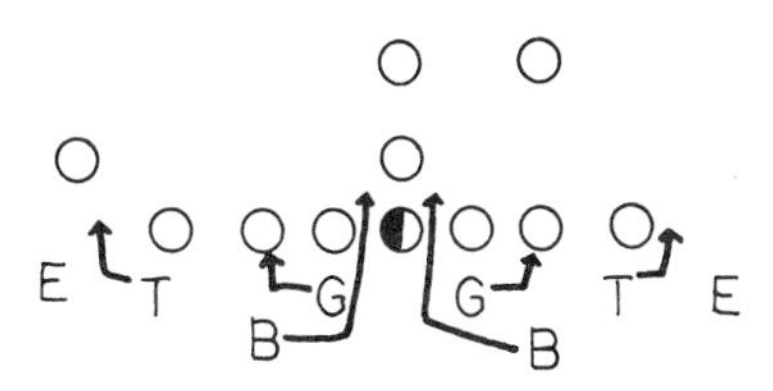

Figure 50

L S R

On a straight drop back, the tackle is responsible for containing the passer. On roll-out passes he recovers, and takes a hard inside rush as the end has contain responsibility.

If the play is away from his side, he becomes the chase man, and pursues behind the line as deep as the deepest man in the backfield. He is responsible for any reverses or delayed play to his side.

Guards. Line up 18 inches off the ball in a normal 60 Heads Stance. The first step should be a short step with the outside foot, at the same time protecting himself with a forearm shiver from the offensive guard. Then coming with a quick crossover lateral step, wind up parallel to the line of scrimmage in a low football position ready to fight pressure and diagnose the play. The guard cannot be cut off by the offensive tackle. If the tackle should get outside position on him, he must give ground to gain outside shoulder leverage on him. He must never release inside the offensive tackle unless the offensive tackle is split wide enough that he can beat him across the scrimmage line.

On pass plays, the guards should rush the passer through the offensive tackle's original position, and maintain this rushing lane.

Linebackers. Line up in a 60 Heads Stance. On the snap of the ball, both linebackers take a lateral step to their inside, keying the fullback. If the fullback comes their way outside of their original position, they should hold their position on the second step and should not cross the line of scrimmage. From this position, they should take the correct pursuit angle on any running play and play 60 Heads responsibility on passes (Figure 51). If the fullback goes away, the off linebacker fires over the backside shoulder of the off-center, and becomes a rushing lineman on a run or a pass. If the fullback fakes up the middle, both linebackers fire over the inside shoulder of the offensive guards.

The split 6 defense can be called on both sides or can be called as a stunt on either side with a 60 Heads play for the opposite side (Fig-

Figure 51 Figure 52

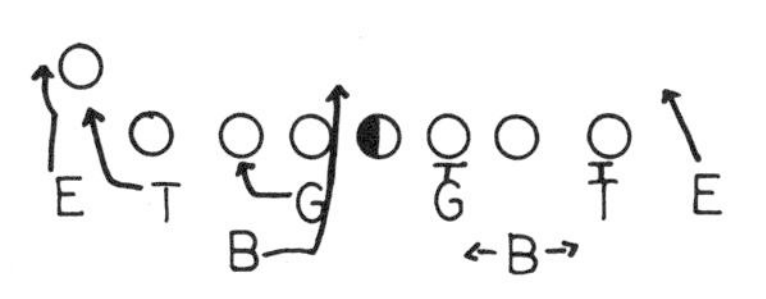

Figure 53

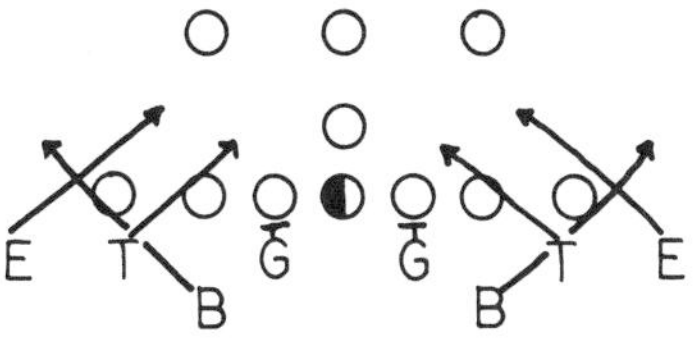

Figure 54

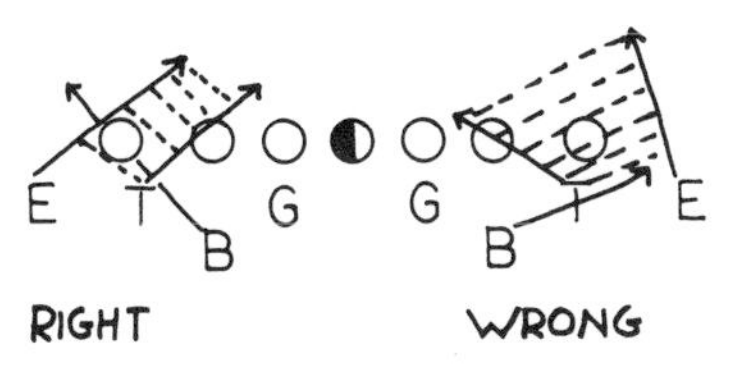

Figure 55

ure 52). This will enable you to adjust to offensive formations and put your linebackers in better position for pass defense and pursuit. For instance, one of the favorite times to have the Split 6 would be against a Wing set offensive formation, where the strong side defense loops at the wing and the short side keeps a 60 Heads position (Figure 53).

Ends, Tackle, Linebacker Stunt (Figure 54)

This stunt is one of the best for a tough off-tackle offense. It has a good hard pass rush with the linebacker in good position for the screen. This can also be combined with 60 Heads or any of the other stunts which can be called on either side.

Ends. The ends should come hard over the outside shoulder of the offensive end. The end must not be turned out by the offensive end. It is important that he maintain the same angle of rush as the tackle, and they must stay in the same plane (Figure 55).

If the play develops away from him, he becomes the chase man on this side. If a pass develops, the end is responsible for contain on straight drop back pass, but on roll-out passes, he rushes hard to the inside and tries to force the passer as deep as possible.

Tackles. Tackles line up in the same position as 60 Heads and come hard over the outside shoulder of the offensive tackle. They must not be turned out by the offensive tackle; they have all the running responsibility between them and the defensive guard, who is playing 60 Heads responsibility. If a pass develops, the tackle has no contain responsibility, but rushes hard from his inside position.

Linebacker. The linebacker should try to cheat a little from his 60 Heads position, and line up in the gap between the offensive tackle

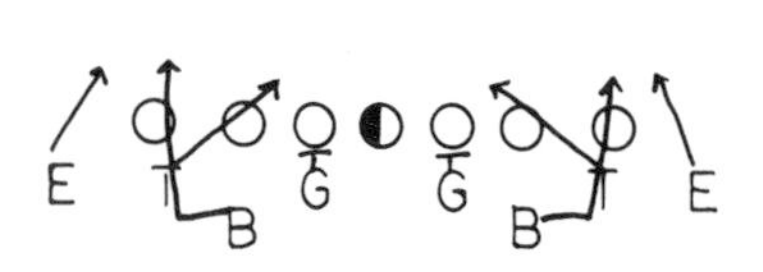

Figure 56

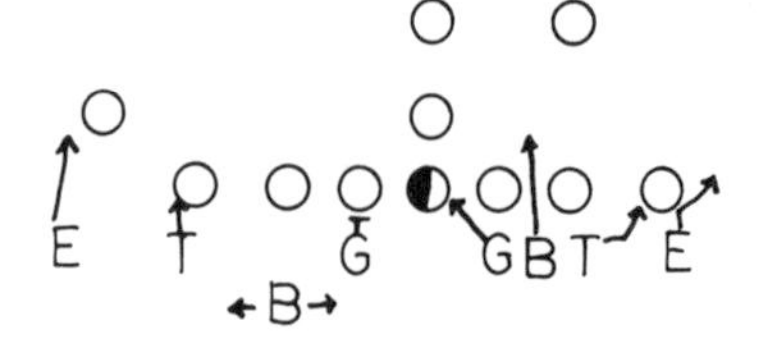

Figure 57

and the offensive end. On wide running plays, he is responsible for the outside, and must gain this position without flattening his angle of pursuit. He should come across quickly to gain this position on the snap of the ball; if the play develops away from him, he is slow to revolve back, looking first for any screen or throw-back pass.

Tackle Linebacker Stunt (Figure 56)

This stunt can be called on either side, and in this stunt the guard and end play is 60 Heads.

Tackle. The tackle lines up in a 60 Heads stance and comes hard over the outside shoulder of the offensive tackle. He is again responsible for all the running area between him and the defensive guard. He must not be out-blocked by the offensive tackle.

Linebacker. The linebacker lines up in a 60 Heads stance and position. On the snap of the ball, he first takes one lateral step, then with a quick crossover takes a position parallel to the line of scrimmage, square on the offensive end. From this position he comes across to diagnose the play, and becomes a hard inside rusher. On a straight drop back pass, he is responsible for containing the passer. On roll type action pass, he takes a hard inside rush and tries to force the passer as deep as possible as the defensive end will come up in a contain position. On play away, the linebacker has chase responsibilities.

The most common mistake made in this simple stunt is that the linebacker slants to his position over the offensive end, overruns running plays, and is in an awkward position to contain or rush the passer. This is a strong stunt for an offense that is double-teaming the tackle, and is definitely needed to protect the tackle in his 60 Heads play.

Eight Stunt (Figure 57)

This stunt is designed to give you the big defensive play. It cannot be used consistently, but may be used five or six times in a game. The element of surprise can make this a really tough defensive stunt for the offense to handle. This stunt can be called on only one side, preferably to the short side of the field. It is just as effective in passing as in running situations.

End. The end should conceal his position and line up at the last minute on the offensive end's outside shoulder. He must not get hooked by the offensive end; he should stay on the line, and on any wide play down the line of scrimmage. This defense must have quick support from the onside halfback if the offensive end blocks. It is also important that the end prevent the offensive end from making a clean release clean, by giving a good shiver on the snap of the ball. The end is responsible for containing on roll-out passes. On straight drop back passes he goes to the near flat.

Tackle. Lines up on the outside ear of the offensive tackle to try to draw an offensive block from him. On the snap of the ball, the tackle should charge out past the offensive end's inside shoulder, protecting himself with a good forearm as he is gaining this position. On a straight drop back pass, the tackle has contain responsibility. On a roll type pass he takes an inside rush.

Linebacker. From his normal 60 Heads position he conceals his position by moving in at the last moment as the quarterback moves under the center in position to take the ball. He should line up between the offensive guard and the offensive tackle, taking as much of the line of scrimmage as possible. On the snap he fires, and if he breaks clean, should square up on his second step and locate the ball. One of the most common weaknesses of the linebackers in this stunt is that they will penetrate too deeply and overrun plays. If executed correctly, the linebacker has the best chance to break clean.

Guard. The guard should line up in a 60 position, taking a sharp penetrating angle over the offensive center, and from this position, take the pursuit angle on the ball carrier or rush the passer.

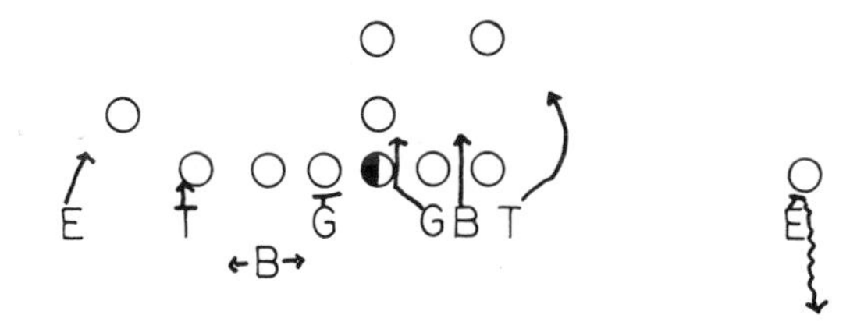

Figure 58

This stunt is a good one to use against a good passer and a good split end receiver (Figure 58).

In this adjustment the end will drop off in a flat position to double cover the split end with the tackle, linebacker and guard having the same responsibilities.

60 Red Dog (Figure 59)

This stunt is a must. It is a team stunt, and gives you a hard rush by the six front linemen from the 60 Defense.

Ends. On the snap, the ends come hard to the outside shoulder of the onside halfback. They still have outside responsibility, but there is no hesitation in moving on the snap to get penetration. They are responsible on passes to contain the passer on both straight drop back passes and roll out passes. If the play is away, they become the chase men.

Tackles. Lining up in the 60 Heads position, they come hard on the snap of the ball to the inside shoulder of the offensive end. They have no outside responsibility, and after diagnosing the play or pass, take their correct pursuit angle.

It is important that the tackle get quick penetration, and they should step with the outside foot and bring a forearm flipper at the same time to protect them from the offensive end.

Guards. Line up in the 60 heads position, but come hard on the snap of the ball to a meeting point behind the offensive center. If they break clean, they should be alert and ready to take their angle of pursuit without gaining more penetration. Every added step of penetration eliminates two steps of pursuit.

Linebackers. Line up in 60 Heads position and hang one count before moving to an outside position to protect the end.

Figure 59

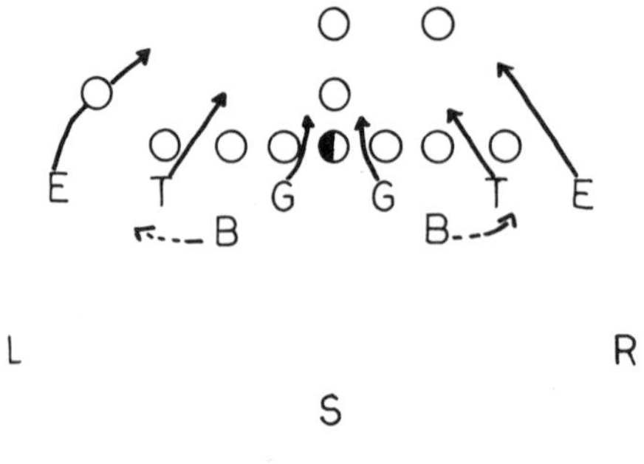

Figure 60

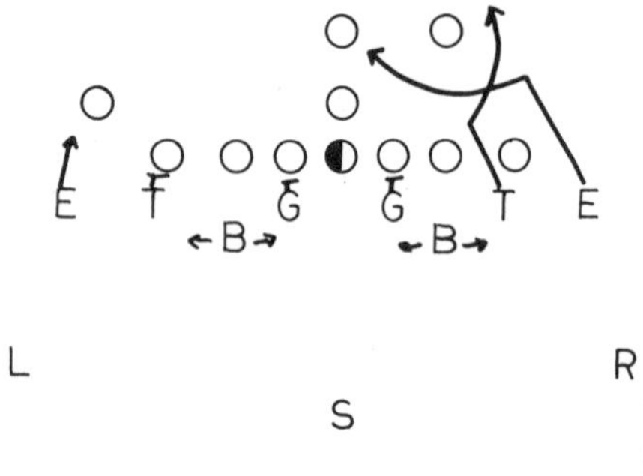

In coaching the linebackers in 60 Red, you can say play the same as in 60 Heads linebacker, but be more outside conscious, ready for a screen or inside-out support on sweeps.

End Tackle Variation—Delayed "X" (Figure 60)

This variation gives the end a chance to take the inside rush and gives the offense a blocking angle problem. The end and tackle swap responsibilities two yards across the line of scrimmage.

End. From his original 60 Heads position he starts across hard at the same angle as he would on 60 Red Dog. After he crosses two yards over the line, he takes a sharp inside rush, first looking for any inside pressure from pulling lineman or offensive backs. If a pass develops, he has no outside responsibility, and is a hard inside rusher. The end becomes the chase man. He goes first in the cross with the tackle.

Tackle. The tackle takes his Red Dog charge two yards across the line of scrimmage. He holds to give the end a chance to cross to his inside position, then he moves quickly to get his outside position. He has outside responsibility on runs and contains on all passes.

7

Defensing Spreads and Unusual Formations

Always be prepared to adjust your defense to unusual formations. Some can be met by variations of basic defenses. Your overall defensive plan should be to develop each basic defense against all the offensive formations you anticipate playing against. However, you must always be prepared to adjust to any unusual spread that might involve too many adjustments from your basic defenses. Therefore, it is advisable to have one automatic defense that will take care of these unusual formations. They are not sound formations for a balanced offense, so you only get hurt by them if you are not prepared, get confused, and don't make a sound defensive adjustment.

Spreads

A 5-3-2-1 defense is the easiest to make these adjustments from (Figure 61). This is also a good sound defense that is well concealed. It can be anything from an eight-man line to a three-man line. It is very flexible and is easily adjusted to flanker sets.

First, let's take up the basic defense and responsibilities.

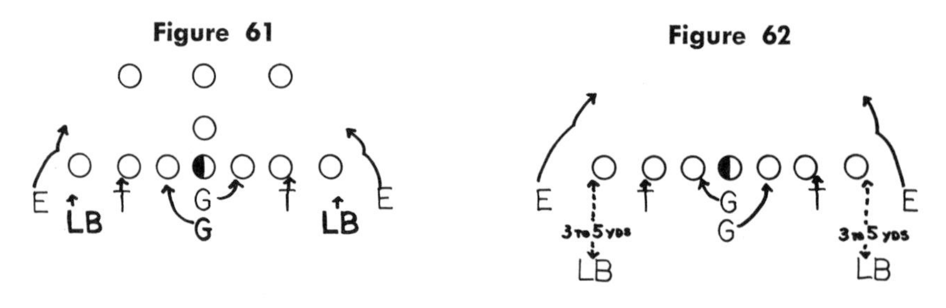

Figure 61

Figure 62

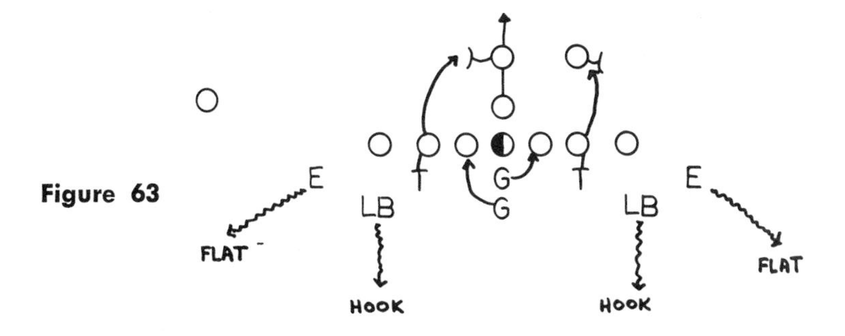

Figure 63

Ends. Does not commit on the snap. He stays on the line of scrimmage until the play develops. If a run develops his way, he is responsible for the outside, and should take the proper angle to flatten it out. On a straight drop-back pass, he has flat responsibility. On a roll-out pass, he is the container.

Linebackers. Lines up on outside shoulder of the offensive end. On the snap he forearm-shivers the end hard, forcing him to release inside on passes. This also helps throw him off balance if he is blocking down on the tackles, and protects himself on a single block. On straight drop-back passes, the linebacker should cover the outside spot. Usually, if an offensive end is forced to release inside the linebacker will hook back outside if this is his pattern, or if he is released outside, he will hook back inside. The linebackers are given the option of dropping out three to five yards, still lining up on the outside shoulder of the offensive end (Figure 62). This way they can play down and distance better.

Tackles. The tackles are the key to the defense. They line up on the outside shoulder of the offensive tackle. They must not be hooked by the offensive tackle. They step first with a hard forearm-shiver behind their inside foot, winding up in a strong outside position with his outside foot back. He must seal the inside if he gets pressure. We have three men outside that will permit this responsibility against the Split T and belly plays. If a straight drop-back pass shows, he must recover and take the proper angle to contain the passer. Work with the tackles to keep them coming back hard to the pass protection, and to keep the pocket of the passer as small as possible. We believe they have done their job well if they make the passer throw the pass on rhythm, and don't allow the extra seconds needed to pick out a second and third choice receiver. On roll-out passes the tackle takes his rush in the inside lane and the end is the container. Figure 63 shows pass defense responsibilities.

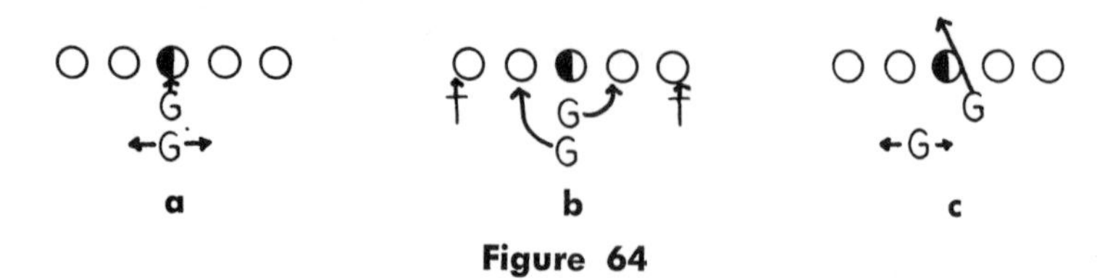

Figure 64

Guards. We let the guards operate as a separate unit. They have three options.

1. The middle guard lines up 18 inches off the ball and plays slow. He must draw two blockers on any trap. If a pass shows, he rushes through the center, and the out guard has middle pass responsibility (Figure 64a).

2. From the same position the middle guard charges hard over the offensive guard. The out guard indicates by a tap which way he is to charge. Then the out guard charges hard over the opposite offensive guard on the snap (Figure 64b).

3. They can line up with a staggered position in an even set. One goes hard and the other plays slow for a draw or trap. This stunt helps to keep the offensive guards from taking over exaggerated splits (Figure 64c).

Rules for Adjustments

One man out—the end takes him.

Two men out—the end takes the first one; the linebacker takes the second.

Three men out—the other end plays the outside shoulder of widest man (Figure 65).

The linebacker is inside the inside man. On the snap he comes across, facing inside, so he cannot be blocked without being slipped. He can still cover any wide pass out to any of the wide eligible receivers.

The guards go into an automatic overshift set with the out guard moving to a linebacker position behind the tackle. From tackle to tackle they play slow to take care of any possible running play the opponent might run to keep the defense honest. In this automatic defense, the

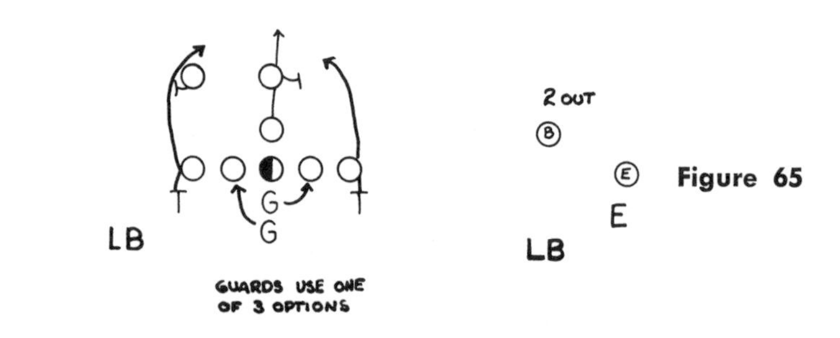

Figure 65

three deep are always in 3 deep zone playing their one third of the field (Figure 66).

It is important to take time in spring and early fall practice to look at these unusual spreads and learn the basic rules that apply to them. Continue a review, if only for a few minutes every week. There are many ways to lose football games, but the worst way is to give up an easy touchdown on some unusual formation that your team was unprepared for. This is one thing that will haunt a coach forever. Always include a spread defense in your repertory, and keep it on your defensive check list.

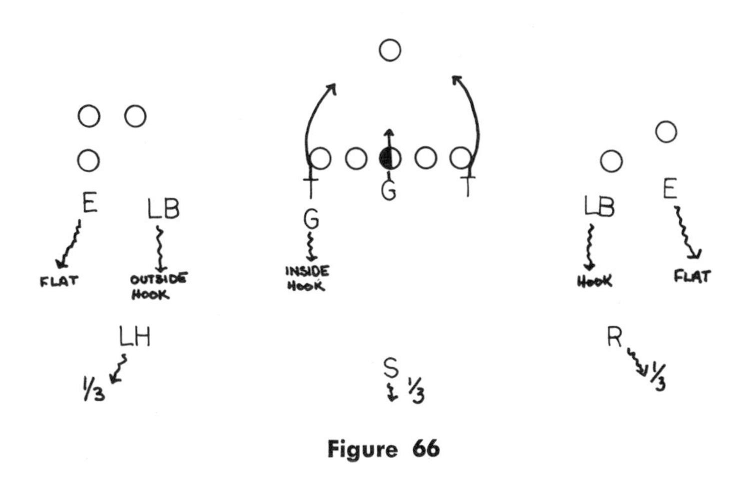

Figure 66

Defensing the Single Wing

Fifteen years ago it would have been unbelievable to think that the single wing would be classified someday as an unusual formation. Today it does fall into this class, and can cause you defensive problems if you are not prepared for it. Spending very much practice time defensing the single wing is unjustified if you play only one team a year that uses this formation. But in keeping with my defensive philosophy you should be able to *adjust* your basic defenses to the single wing.

5-4-2 versus Single Wing

First, let's look at the 5-4-2 adjusted to the single wing (Figure

67). Start with the perimeter. The Monster should always declare to the formation. The three deep are constant and maintain their regular three deep responsibilities.

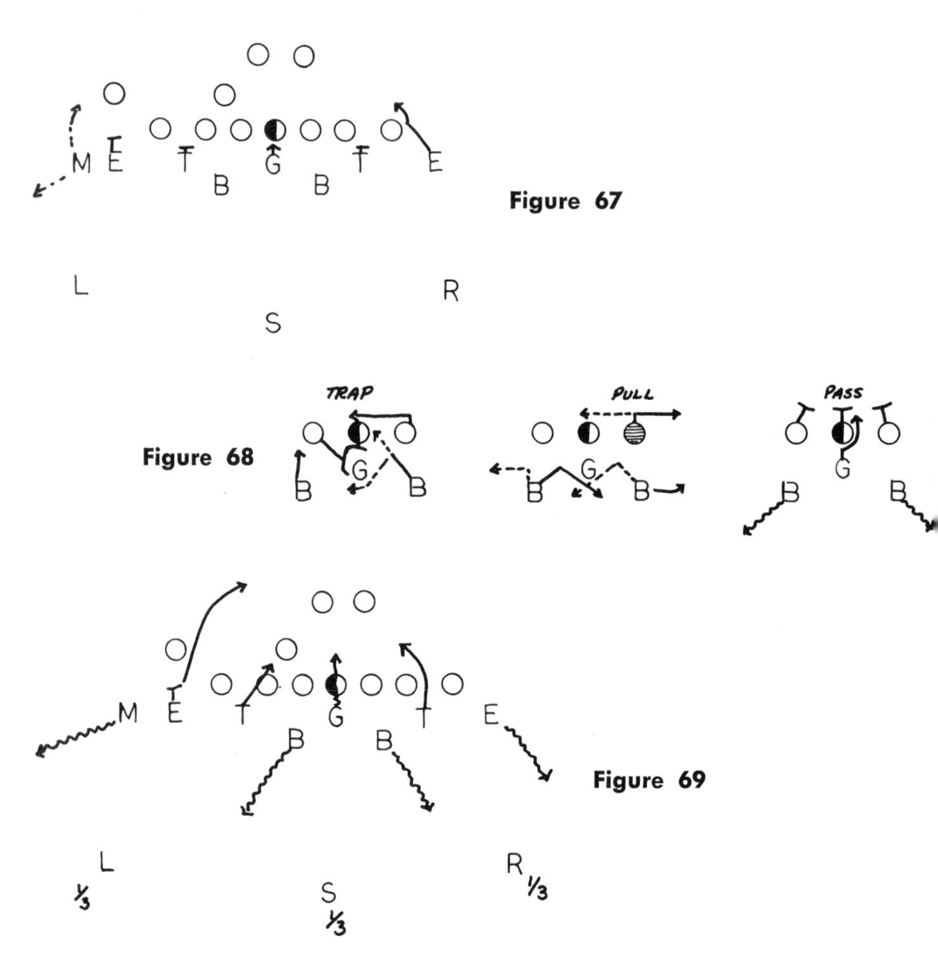

Figure 67

Figure 68

Figure 69

End Play. In playing against the single wing, it is necessary for the end play to be designated strong-side (to the formation) and weak-side (away from the formation). The *strong side end* lines up head on the wingback. He does not cross the line and has lateral pursuit angle on all running plays to his side. On plays away from the strong side the end becomes the chase man. On stand-up pocket passes he becomes the container.

Weak Side. The end lines up one yard outside of the offensive end. From this position he plays 60 Heads end play. He is responsible for the outside on running plays and drops off as a second safety if play is away from him.

Tackles. Both strong- and weak-side tackles lineup one-half yard from the line of scrimmage in the gap between the offensive end and tackle. On the snap they take a lateral step to protect them from the offensive end and play the play from this position. If the play is away, they become the chase man. On passes they become hard rushers in their lane.

Middle Guard. He lines up one-half yards off the ball and plays slow. He should draw two blockers on any trap. He is ready first for the draw play, then rushes the passer hard in his lane.

Linebackers. They line up one and a half yards off the ball on the outside shoulder of the offensive guards. They key the guards. If the guard on their side blocks down on the middle guard, they come in under control ready for a trap (Figure 68a). If the guard pulls to his outside, the linebacker goes with him. Should the guard pull behind the center, the linebacker takes one step in to slow down his pursuit so he doesn't overrun the play (Figure 68b). If the guard sets back on a passive pass protection block, the linebacker covers the strong hook zone (Figure 68c).

Monster. The Monster will always declare to the formation, left or right. He lines up one and a half yards outside his defensive end. On all running plays coming his way, he comes across on the snap and plays the first blocker (or blockers) he engages. If he meets a double team block from the blocking back and fullback, he must play the backside shoulder of the fullback or the deepest man. He has flat responsibility on all pocket passes and is the container on running passes his way.

(Figure 69 shows the 5-4-2 set for a pass from the single wing.)

Eagle Defenses Adjusted to Single Wing (Figure 70)

This is one of the best defenses against the single wing. Maryland first used it in the Sugar Bowl against a great University of Tennessee

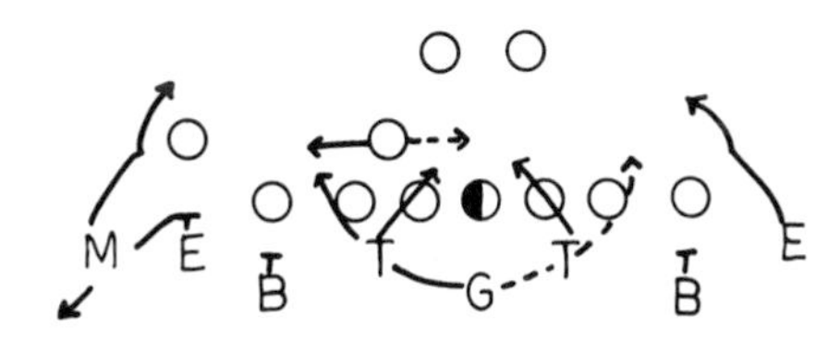

Figure 70

team in 1952, and stopped them cold. It is a well balanced defense against both the run and the pass.

The Monster declares to the formation as in the 5-4-2 the secondary has three deep responsibility.

Ends. The strong end lines up on the wingback and plays on the line with off-tackle responsibility against the run. On a drop pocket pass he holds up the wingback and becomes the container. On a running pass to the formation, he covers the flat zone. The weak end lines up two yards outside the linebacker, and has 60 Heads responsibility. With the exception that on passes he comes across and contains on all pocket passes. On running passes he covers the flat.

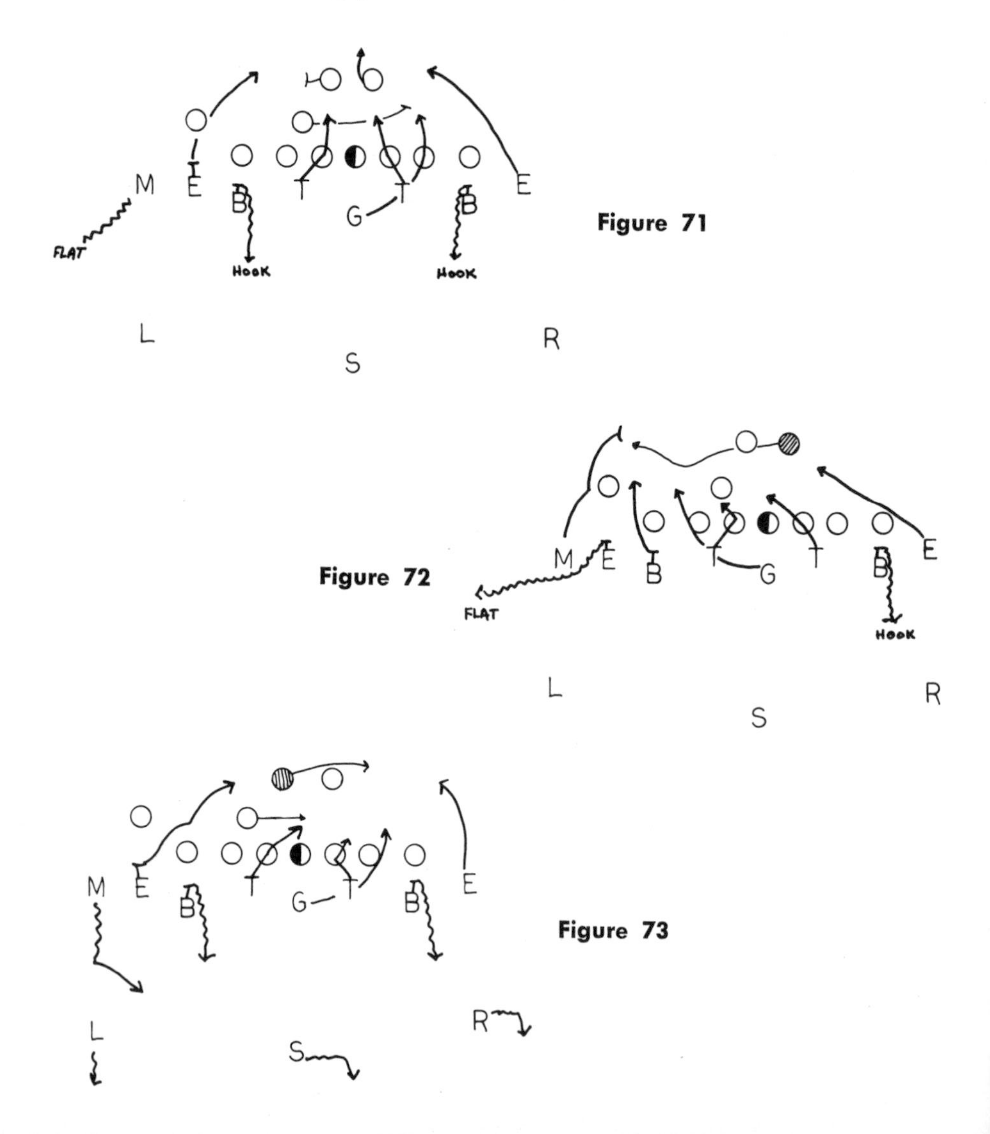

Figure 71

Figure 72

Figure 73

Tackles. The tackles line up at the gap between the offensive guard and tackle. On the snap they converge over the inside shoulder of the offensive guards. They are responsible for the middle on all running plays and become hard rushers up the middle on all passes.

Middle Guard. The middle guard is the key to the defense. He lines up at the offensive center one yard off the ball. He keys the blocking back and goes with him over the offensive tackle's position. He is the man who should be in every play from tackle to tackle. With the key you wind up with an eight man line toward the blocking back.

Linebackers. The *strong linebacker* lines up on the strong offensive end and plays him hard on the snap, forcing him to release inside. On pocket he plays the end hard and covers the strong side hook zone.

The *weak linebacker* lines up on the short side offensive end on his outside ear. He plays him hard on the snap and forces him to release inside. On all passes he covers the weak-side hook zone.

Monster. He lines up in rotated position on the line ten yards outside the defensive end. He is responsible for outside on all running plays. On pocket passes he covers the flat zone and on running passes he becomes the container.

(Figures 71-73, Eagle pass defense vs. three single wing passes.)

Unbalanced Line

A very popular offensive maneuver today is to place one of the offensive ends on the same side of the center as the other offensive end. Usually one of the ends is split out wide. Some coaches call this the "End Over formation," while others simply refer to it as an unbalanced line. The best offensive feature is that either end can be "swung" without changing any of the offensive blocking rules. This creates the same defensive problem as the single wing: if the offense unbalances, so should the defense.

Here are some simple rules to follow in defensing an "end over" or unbalanced line.

1. If you are in a Monster defense: declare Monster to the unbalanced side and keep the rest of your defense on the ball (Figure 74).
2. If you are in any kind of balanced front: move your defense over and align on the strong offensive guard as if he were the center (Figure 75).

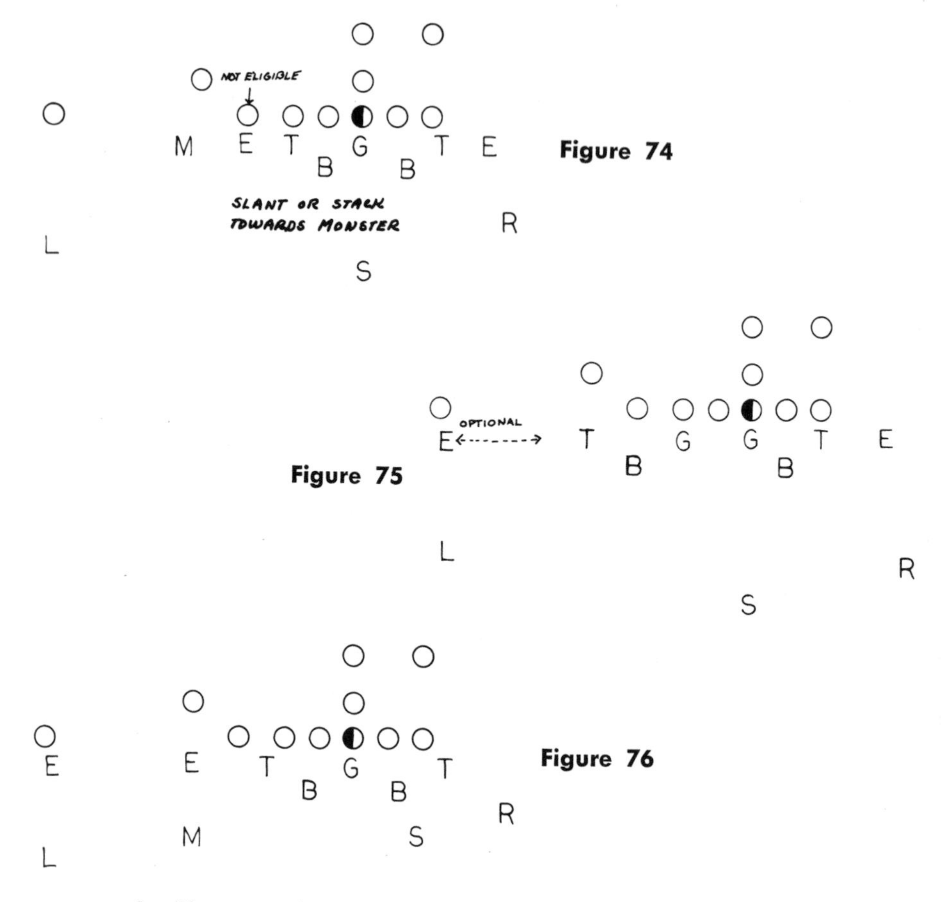

Figure 74

Figure 75

Figure 76

3. If you are in a four deep secondary: align your two defensive ends up in the middle as the offense breaks the huddle. Have each of your defensive ends line up on the end he would normally line up on. This means that if the offense has two ends on one side of the center, so will the defense and everything else is equal (Figure 76).

8

Goal Line Defenses

In any discussion of defensing the goal line, the first thing that should be brought up is exactly where you go into a goal line defense. Everyone knows a different style of defense should be employed when the defense in depth is reduced, but not everyone defines this area exactly. For example, first and goal at the eight yard line is a goal line situation, because the offense needs to make only two yards each down to score. The area in depth is only 18 yards, but depth is not the main reason for this being a goal line situation. Down and distance are the most important factors. Keep the two yard formula as a guide to go by. This dictates whether or not you should be in a goal line defense. For instance, second and six, third and four, fourth and two. If there is just one yard more to go, you should *not* be in a goal line defense. First and nine, second and seven, third and five, or fourth and three are long yardage situations and should be defended as such.

Every defensive repertory should carry one defense labeled "goal line," and it should be scrimmaged more than any other defense. We will discuss the three most widely used goal line defenses, the 8 - 3, 7 - 4, and 6 - 5. They are all good, and we have used them all. You should use the one that most closely fits your particular style of secondary play in your basic category. If you employ an 8 front with three deep as a basic defense, then you should use an 8 - 3, sometimes called Gap 8. Some three deep teams employ the 7 - 4 also. And last, if you are a pure four deep team, the 6 - 5 should be your goal line defense. This decreases the amount of new material that must be taught.

All these defenses have one thing in common—*penetration.* To keep an opponent to less than two yards a play, you must penetrate into his side of the line of scrimmage. Pursuit is not of much value, because the offense has already made two yards or more if you have to depend on pursuit to down the ball carrier.

Penetration is harder to achieve than generally believed. Offenses close down and feature "wall" blocking. So the next best thing to penetration is leverage. The forcing men (line) must not only drive for penetration, but must drive lower than the offensive blockers (Figure 77). This creates piles. MORE GOOD BACKS ARE TACKLED OR STOPPED BY THEIR OWN LINEMEN THAN ANY OTHER WAY. If your line does a good job, there just isn't any place to run. Of course, nothing can replace frenzy on the goal line.

Figure 77

GOAL LINE STANCE AND CHARGE

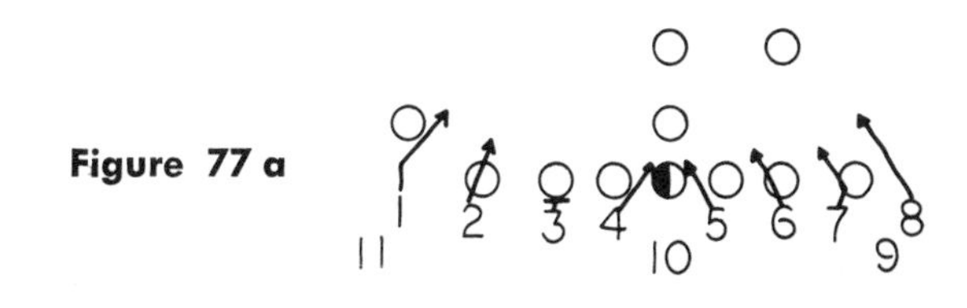

Figure 77 a

The 8-3 (Figure 77a)

Position Rules

1. *Monster*—Apply Bullets technique. You may cross fire with your anchor end or fire straight. It is most important that you force power plays and sweeps deeper and wider than they want to go, taking away lead blockers. Do not come up field too much, as this creates a hole inside you. (Adjustments are discussed right after these position rules.)
2. *Anchor*—Apply anchor rules. Cross with Monster when called. Use the three point stance and drive through the offensive end's outside shoulder if threatened by a close flanker. When in 8-3 goal line and flanker is close, play a little wider to flanker. Drive for penetration.
3. *Tackle*—You have two situations. First, if there is an offensive halfback in on your side and second, if there is no offensive halfback in your side. With the halfback in, charge under the offensive tackle, aiming at his inside knee. If no halfback is in your side (the ghost side) play head on the tackle and be able to take inside or outside.
4. *Pinch*—Align on guard's nose and dip charge the guard—center gap. You must prevent the sneak.
5. *Pinch*—Apply Pinch #4 rules.
6. *Tackle*—Apply Tackle #3 rules.
7. *Backside Backer*—Align in the middle with Monster. You will never be on Monster side. After declaring, align on inside shoulder of offensive end. Charge this position first to prevent the down block. On second step, square up if no pressure from the end (See adjustments below).
8. *Backside End*—Apply fire technique. Use rules as described under Monster #1. When cross charging with linebacker call "Razor" and apply Razor rules previously described.

9, 10, 11—Orange coverage (See adjustments below).

Adjustments for the 8-3 Goal Line Defense

1. *Wide Flanker* (Figure 78).
2. *Split End* (Figure 79).
3. *Wide Flanker and Split End* (Figure 80).
4. *Motion* (Figures 81, 82).
5. *Motion to Wide Flanker* (Figure 83).
6. *Motion to Split End* (Figure 84).
7. *Unbalanced* (Figure 85).
8. *Strong Set* (Figure 86).
9. *Pro Set* (Figure 87).

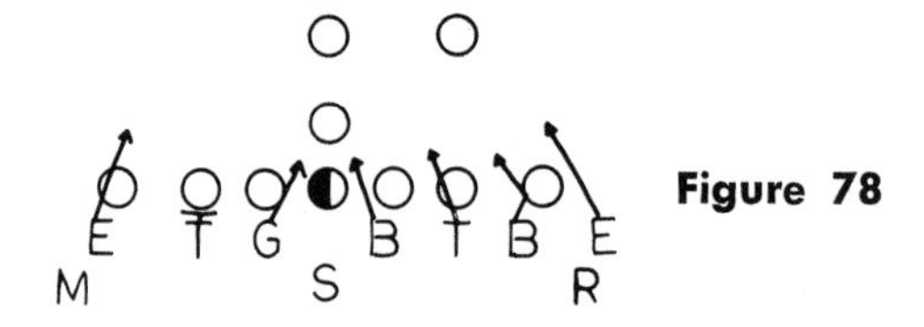

Figure 78

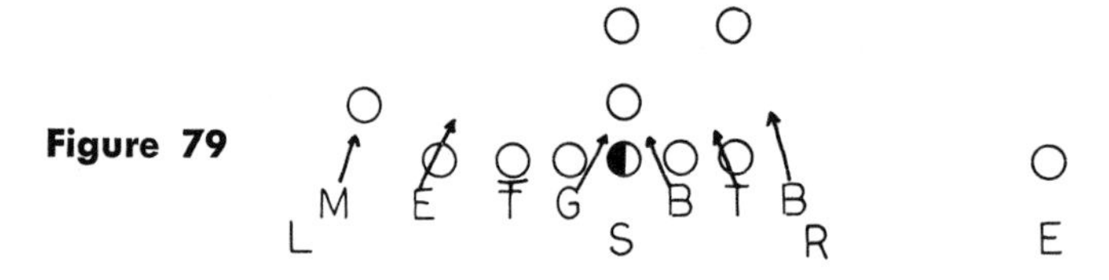

Figure 79

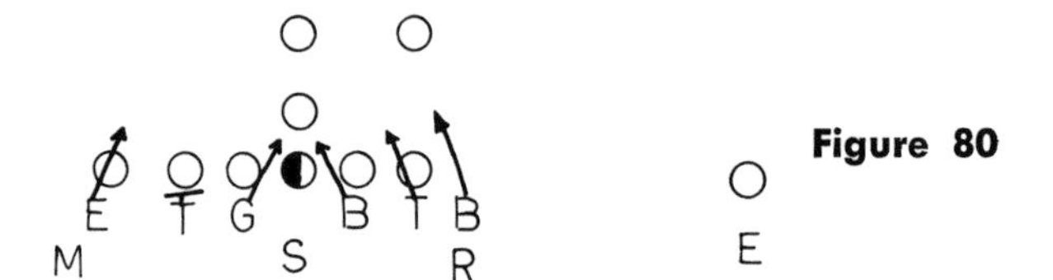

Figure 80

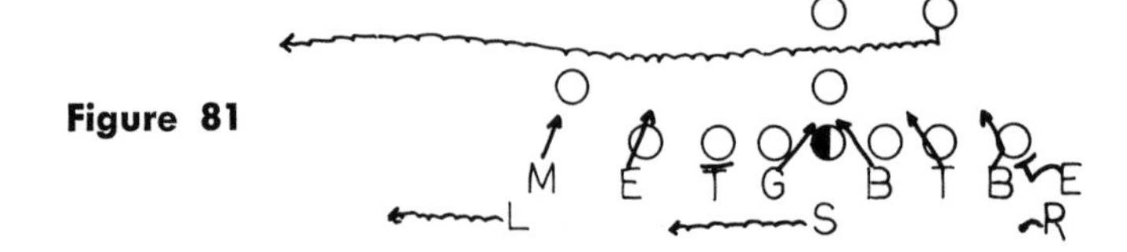

Figure 81

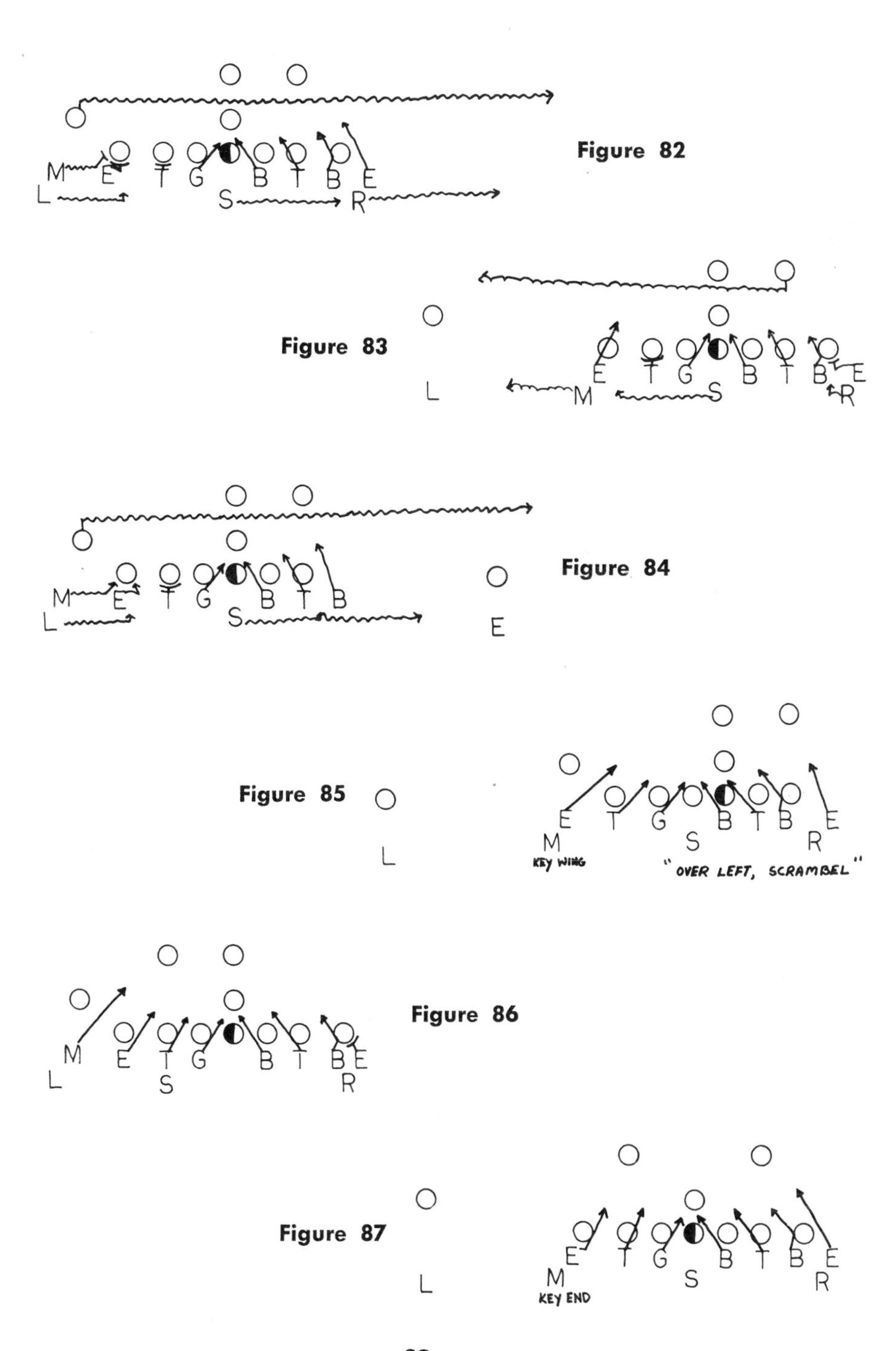

Figure 82

Figure 83

Figure 84

Figure 85

Figure 86

Figure 87

The 8-3 (Figure 77a)

Position Rules

1. *Monster*—Apply Monster rules with certain responsibilities removed. Use Regular motion rules. *Motion to Monster*—slant and cover with Monster. *Motion away*—rotate and cover with right half back. Keep outside zone if eligibles release.
2. *Inside Fire*—Apply Inside Fire technique previously described.
3. *Gapper*—Apply Gapper technique previously described.
4. *Tandem*—Align behind gapped tackle. Key offensive quarterback. *Ball action your way*—replace our end and assume contain responsibilities. *Ball action straight back*—take hook area. *Ball action away*—sprint to strong side (flow side) hook area. Keep sneak support in mind.
5. *Nose*—Align on center's nose, make a hard charge on center and control middle.
6. *Gapper*—Same as Gapper #3.
7. *Tandem*—Same as Tandem #4.
8. *Inside Fire*—Same as Inside Fire #2.
9. *Squirmed Corner*—Apply Monster rules as outlined in #1 above.

10, 11—*Twin Safeties*—Align just outside offensive ends. Key ends; if end blocks, support alley between our outside man and offensive end. If end releases, take inside zone. Play combination with corner.

Adjustments for the 7-4 Goal Line

1. *Wide Flanker* (Figure 89).
2. *Split End* (Figure 90).
3. *Wide Flanker and Split End* (Figure 91).
4. *Motion* (Figures 92-93).
5. *Motion to Wide Flanker* (Figure 94).
6. *Motion to Split End* (Figure 95).
7. *Unbalanced* (Figure 96).
8. *Strong Set*—3 Receiver Rule (Figure 97).
9. *Pro Set*—3 Receiver Rule (Figure 98).

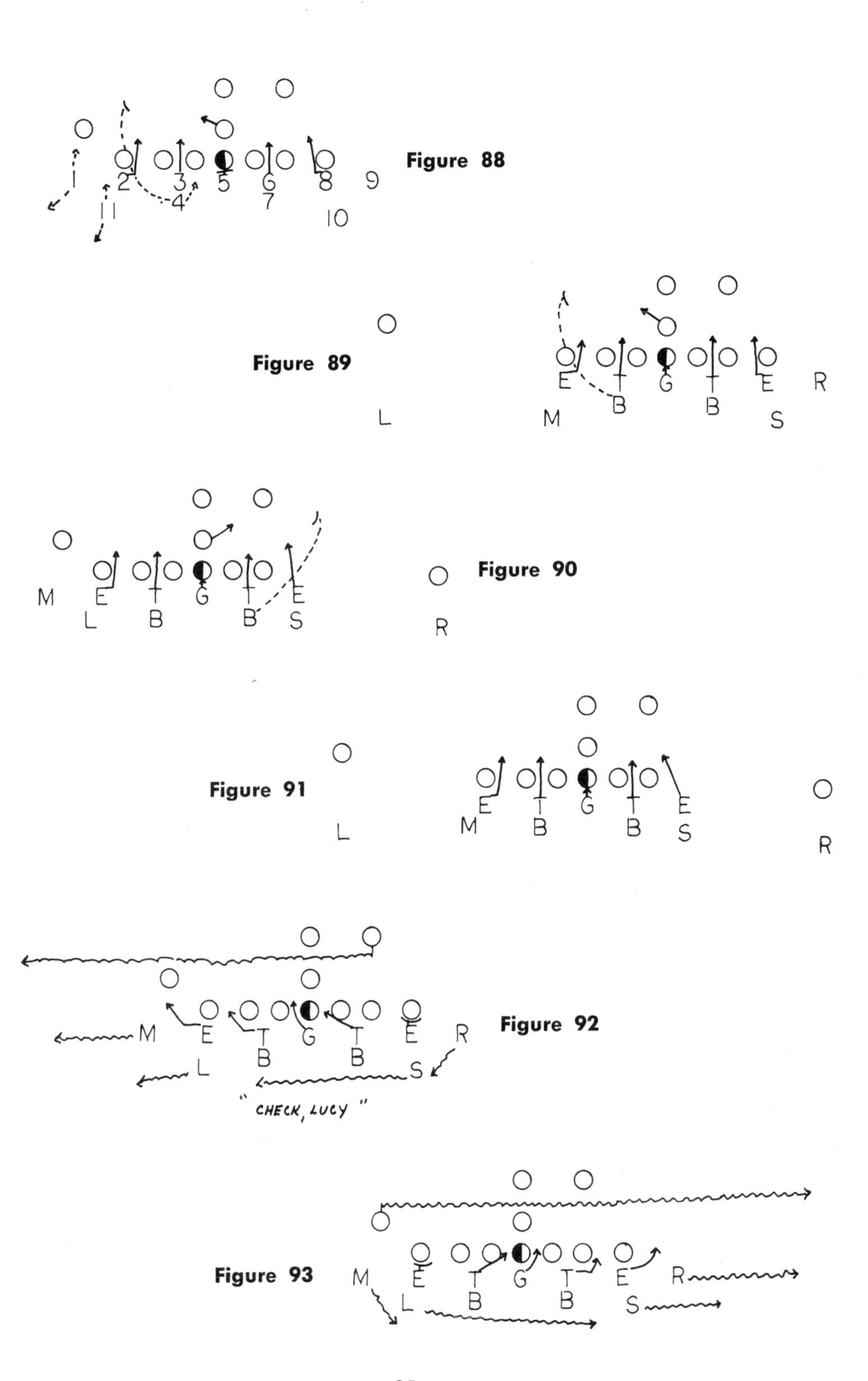

Figure 88

Figure 89

Figure 90

Figure 91

Figure 92

Figure 93

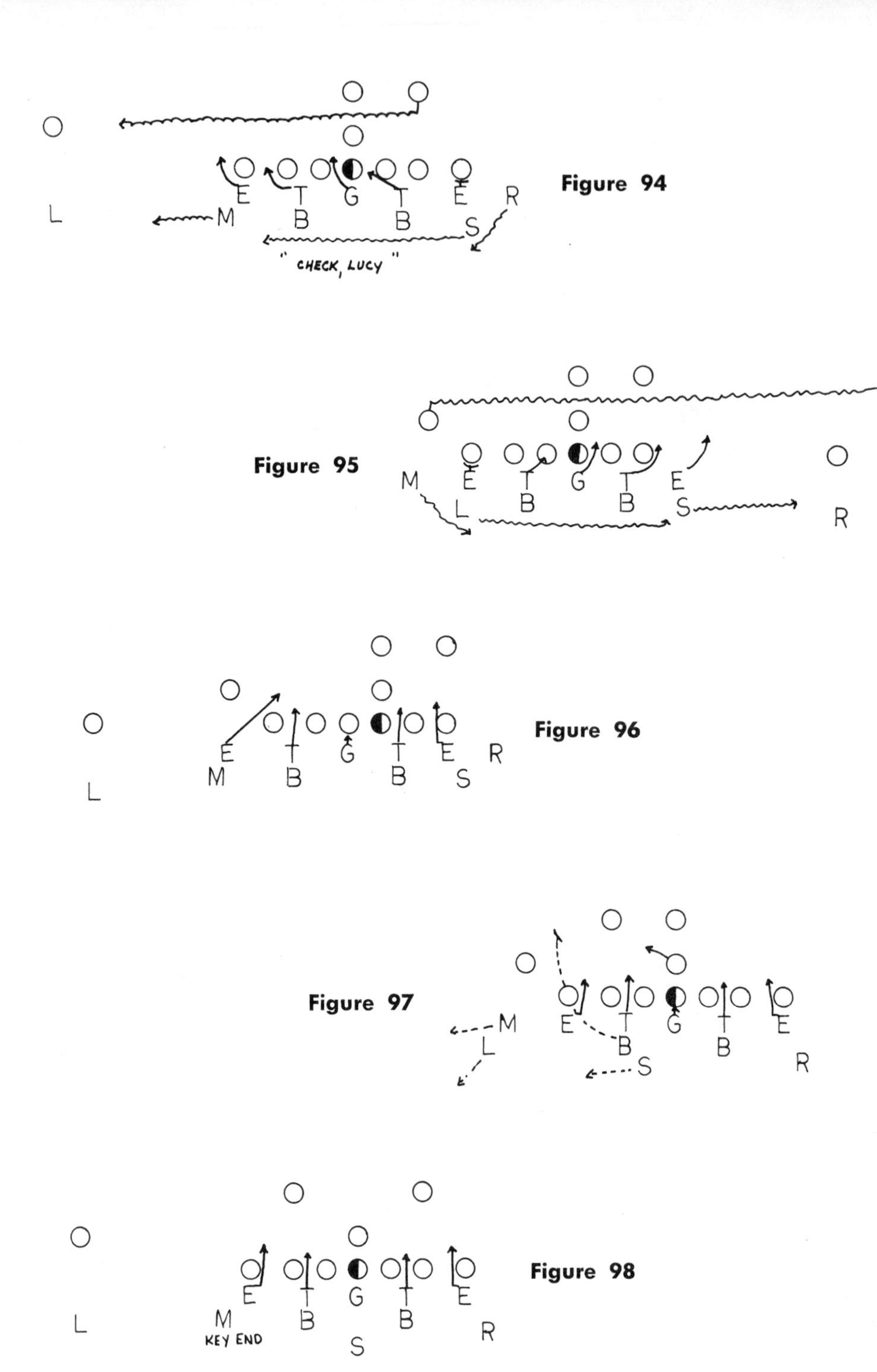

Figure 94

Figure 95

Figure 96

Figure 97

Figure 98

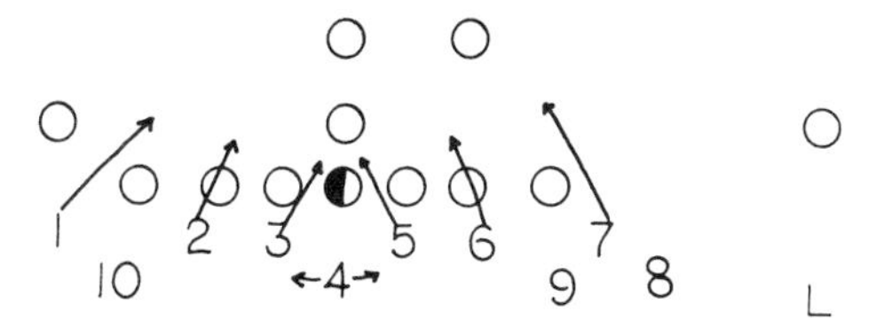

Figure 99

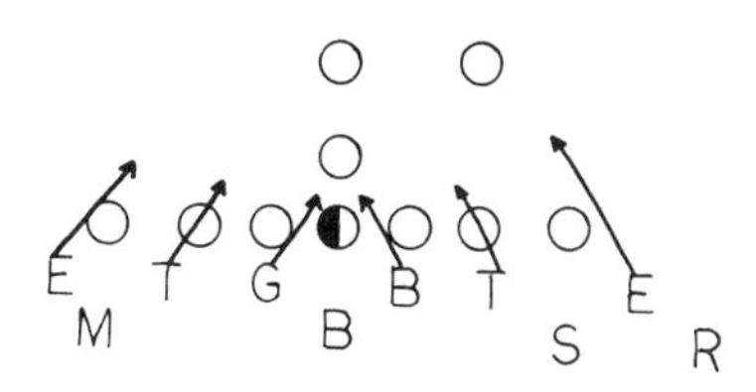

Figure 100

6-5 Goal Line (Figure 99)

Position Rules

1. *Fire*—Apply Fire rules.
2. *Press*—Apply Press rules as outlined previously.
3. *Pinch*—Apply Pinch rules as outlined previously.
4. *Rover*—Apply Rover rules when not in the "in" position. First concern, the guard—tackle gap.
5. *Pinch*—Apply Pinch rules.
6. *Press*—Apply Press rules.
7. *Fire*—Apply Fire rules.

8, 9, 10, 11—Black coverage.

Adjustments to 6-5 Goal Line

1. *Wide Flanker* (Figure 100).
2. *Split End* (Figure 101).
3. *Wide Flanker and Split End* (Figure 102).

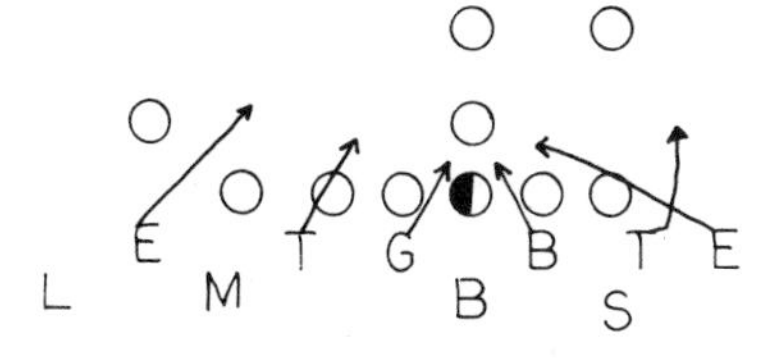

Figure 101

R

Figure 102

L

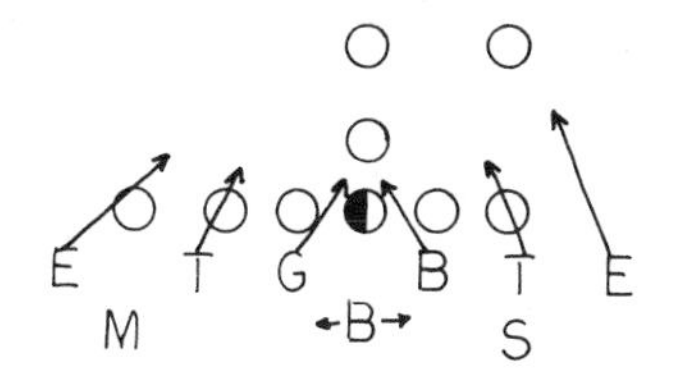

R

4. *Motion* (Figures 103-104).
5. *Motion to Wide Flanker* (Figure 105).
6. *Motion to Split End* (Figure 106).
7. *Unbalanced* (Figure 107).
8. *Strong Set*—3 Receiver Rule (Figure 108).
9. *Pro Set*—3 Receiver Rule (Figure 109).
10. *Pro Set Alternate Coverage* (Figure 110). By using middle backer in pass defense, you can keep man-to-man coverage. Call Rover 5.

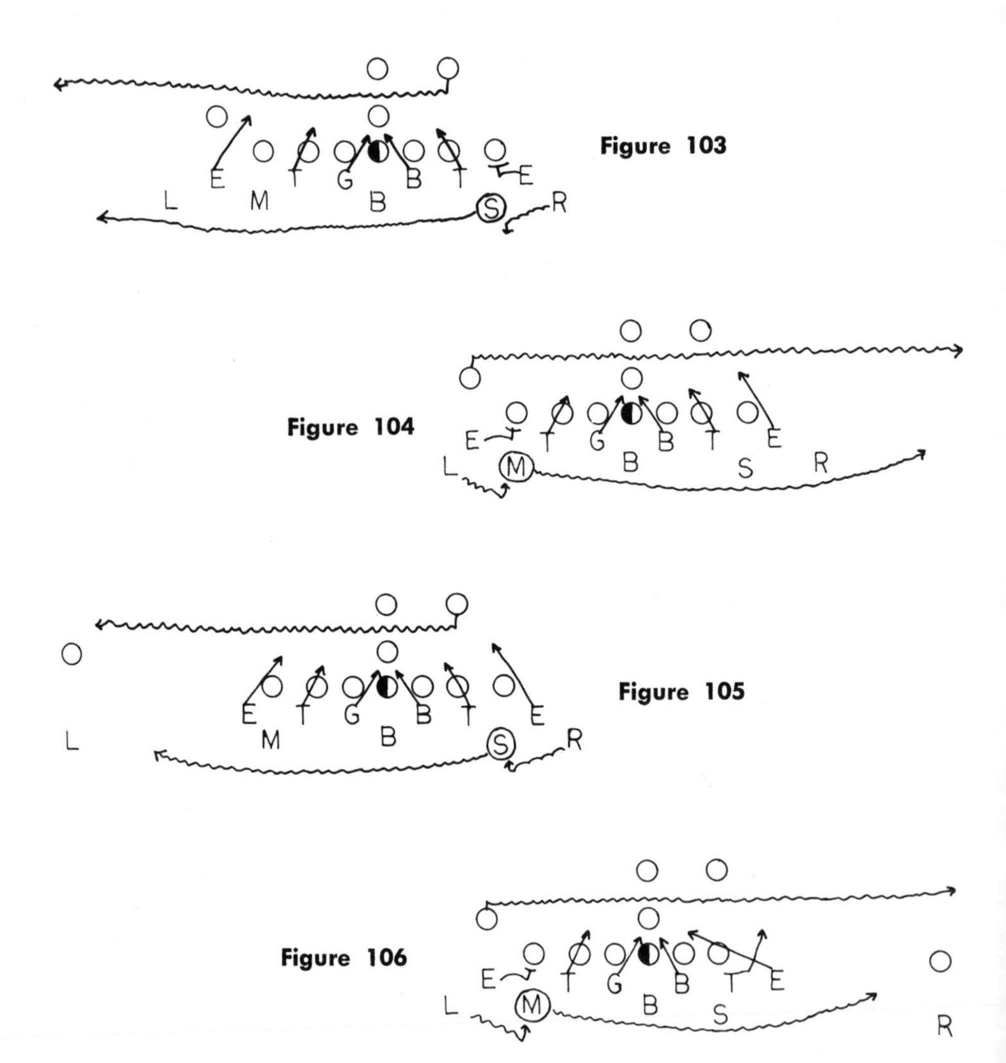

Figure 103

Figure 104

Figure 105

Figure 106

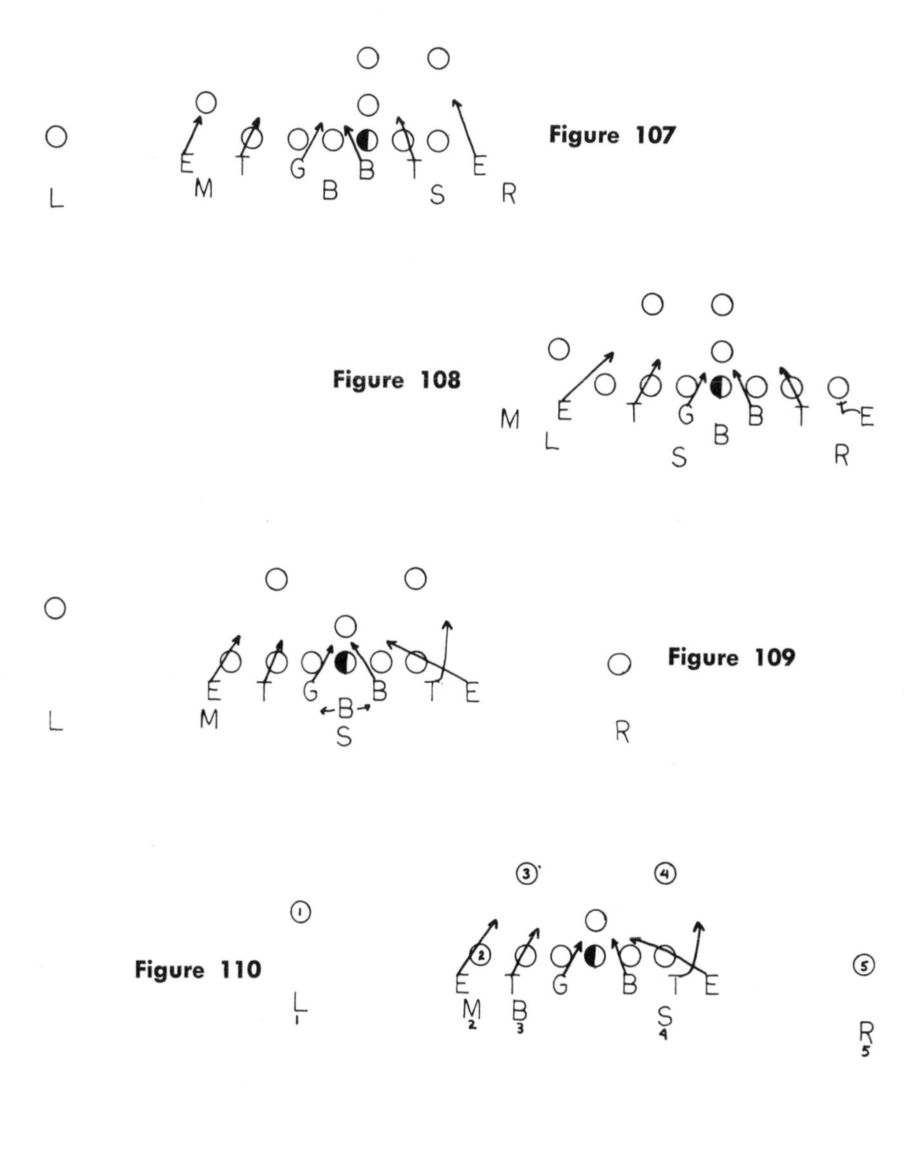

Figure 107

Figure 108

Figure 109

Figure 110

9

The Monster Secondary

Pass defense is the most critical phase of defensive football because a long pass can score in a few seconds' time. Because of the danger of the forward pass, secondary coverage are the most varied. Coaches are constantly looking for easier ways to combat the modern passing game. There are no easy ways to a sound pass defense; it requires hard work and a lot of dedication to develop security in the secondary. Up-front defenses have changed back and forth from 6 front to 5 front alignments over the past 15 or 20 years, but the most drastic change on defense has come in the secondary coverages since the mid '50's.

Before the mid '50's, the basic philosophy of zone pass defense was, "never allow the long pass." The 3-deep zone, made famous by Bob Neyland and his disciples, was the most popular coverage. Being a student of Neyland's, I used the zone defense both at Georgia Tech and at Florida, but we feel that the days of cushion and zone are out as far as a basic coverage is concerned. One reason for the success of the zone defense was the tight formations necessary for a strong running attack that were used by the offensive teams. Most defenses were geared to the 6 front and stopping the running game so popular prior to mid '50's.

Another reason for the popularity of zone pass defenses was that during a ten game schedule you might face only one or two quarterbacks with the ability to beat you with the forward pass. Today, we play almost every week a quarterback who can beat you with the passing game.

Here are a few good reasons why our thinking has changed regarding pass defense. First, offensive football has begun to use formations to spread the defense. This caused defensive coaches to seek methods for making sound adjustments to (a) formations, (b) motion, and (c) shifts. The perimeter has to be flexible enough to make these adjustments, and it is easier to make these with a four deep secondary. Second, professional football and television have caused colleges to improve their pass offense. Third, high schools are developing better athletes and colleges are recruiting quarterbacks that can pass. Let me mention some of the finest quarterbacks to play modern day football—Florida has had to defense all of them—Jim Sidle of Auburn, Billy Lothridge of Georgia Tech; Larry Rakestraw of Georgia, Steve Tensi of F.S.U., George Mira of Miami, and Joe Namath of Alabama. When you have to play against quarterbacks of this caliber you have to develop a good perimeter.

Basic Philosophy

The basic philosophy at Florida is not to give up any passes, because with today's passing game, any team can march up and down the field with short completions. We play a man-for-man type zone defense and a true man-for-man.

Secondary calls are coordinated with up-front defensive calls. We feel that this is a must in order to have sound overall defensive objectives. The two categories of defenses, to summarize what has been mentioned, are "Reading" defenses, using a zone type coverage (Blue or Orange), and "Pressing" defenses, using a man-for-man coverage (Black).

Since the Monster defense is our base, we will begin with "Blue" coverage, which is used with the three monster defenses. The "Monster" defenses (54 Slant, 54 Stack, and 54 Split-Stack) come under the "Read" category of defenses. The other 54 defenses are reads unless the word "Fire" is used. When we are in the read defenses we use a zone type coverage in the secondary. We call this coverage "Blue." These defenses are basic defenses so they should be perfected. Most of our perimeter time is spent using "Blue" coverage.

In most instances we will declare our monster to the strength of the formation. In the illustrations and diagrams we will use such declarations. It is necessary to mention that we refer to "Blue" coverage as man-for-man zone coverage. Although we are in a zone type perimeter, we have a defender directly responsible for any receiver that comes in his zone. It is the defender's responsibility to jump on the first threat in his area. We do not believe in giving up any passing yardage. As was explained, the modern quarterback will pick a secondary apart if the receivers are played with a cushion. Keep this philosophy in mind as we explain our man-for-man zone or "Blue" coverage.

Blue Coverage (Figure 111)

Monster Position

The Monster will remain in the middle of the defensive perimeter until the offense breaks the huddle and declares the formation to be used. In most game plans Monster will declare to the strength of the offensive set. The Monster lines up on the line of scrimmage two yards outside the offensive tight end, close enough to the defensive end to prevent a hole. He must also be in a position to prevent the wingback from releasing outside quickly. If the wingback splits more than a normal wingback's position, employ the same rule that an end would, and play head up on him up to five yards. If the flanker gets further, consider it a wide out and make other adjustments to be explained under wide-outs. If the wingback is in a wider position the important thing is to prevent the crack back block on the monster.

Key. The Monster keys the direction of the quarterback, not the flow of the backs, because he will receive a false key by watching the remaining backs. If a run is toward him, he should play the right shoulder of the fullback with his right shoulder (Figure 111). He should force the ball carrier inside, closing the cavity between him and his defensive end, and play as deep as the ball. If he can't force the play inside, he must force the ball carrier as deep as possible to allow the L.H. to make the tackle. The Monster has the pitch on the option, but remains on the line until the quarterback pitches. If the run is away from him, he should take a step back, face inside keeping everything inside him, and rotate to the L.H. position.

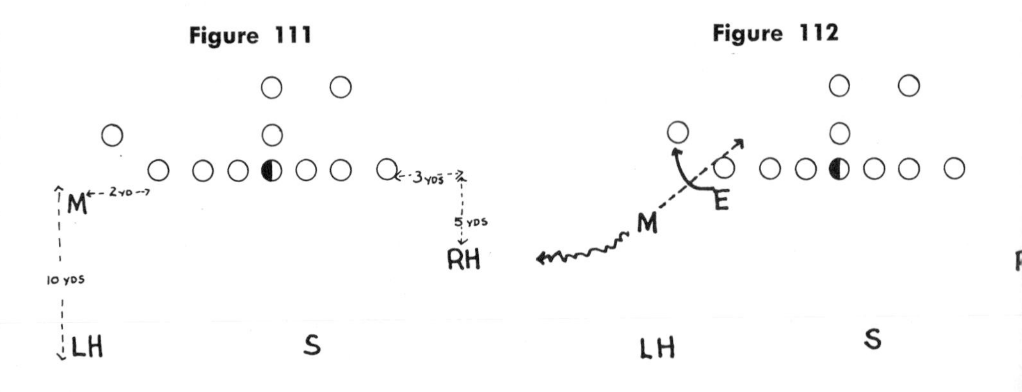

If pass action comes toward the Monster, he has to contain the quarterback only as deep as the ball. When action comes his way, he must hold up the wingback and not let him release outside. At the same time the anchor end is holding up the offensive end. This causes both receivers to release together and gives the L.H. a chance to cover both men. The L.B. on the Monster side is also breaking to the area of these receivers to play the hook. In a long yardage passing situation, we can slant toward the Monster in order to release him to cover the flat. We also have a switch call between the Monster and the Anchor End. This call is used in a long yardage situation to strengthen our pass defense.

Switch Call. The end widens slightly to a position where he can get up field to contain the passer and the Monster deepens slightly. The Monster *now* keys the offensive end. If the end releases, he plays the flat. If the end blocks, he fills in where the defensive end has left to contain (Figure 112).

When the quarterback shows drop back pass action, the Monster is in the flat. When flow of the quarterback is away from the Monster, Monster takes a step back, faces inside, and rotates to L.H. position covering the receivers in his area.

L.H. Position

Line up behind the Monster 9-10 yards deep (Figure 111), and key the flow of the quarterback. You do not have to commit yourself because you have the Monster on your side. If run action is toward you, you should be in a position to tackle the ball carrier if the Monster forces the cut-back. Never cross the line of scrimmage until you are sure of making the tackle. If the option is coming your way, be in position to tackle the quarterback if he keeps. When he pitches, help the Monster tackle the halfback. If a run is away from you, take a step back and rotate to the position of the safety man and maintain an inside out position on the ball-carrier.

If the flow of the quarterback is toward you on a pass, you have the deepest receiver in your zone. You can cover both receivers when they are forced to release together. If the quarterback shows drop-back pass action, you have the deepest 1/3 of the field. When the quarterback's action is away from you, rotate to safety and be aware of both tight ends for they can split a zone and run by you.

Safety — Position

Line up over the offensive guard unless the ball is on the hash mark in from the sideline and key the offensive left end and L.H. Be aware of the flow of the quarterback. If the offensive L.E. blocks, fill to the line of scrimmage, and your play is exactly as the L.H.'s play was when flow was his way (Figure 113). Stay on the line until you are sure of making the tackle, and be in position to take the cut-back or the quarterback if he keeps on the option. If the run is forced deep, be able to make the tackle inside-out. On a run away from you rotate to L.H.'s position and stay head on the ball carrier. Go to the ball when you are sure of making the tackle.

When the quarterback's action is toward you on a pass and the halfback is in the flat, you must get to a position to cover the end deep. *Never* cover the end on a hook route because the L.B. covers the hook, and the halfback could run the sideline route and beat the R.H. deep (Figure 114).

A coaching point regarding play action passes: if the fullback or halfback fakes up the middle, the Safety and L.H. should take a step back to diagnose the play. By doing this, they will avoid coming up and allowing the receivers to get a jump on you (Figure 115).

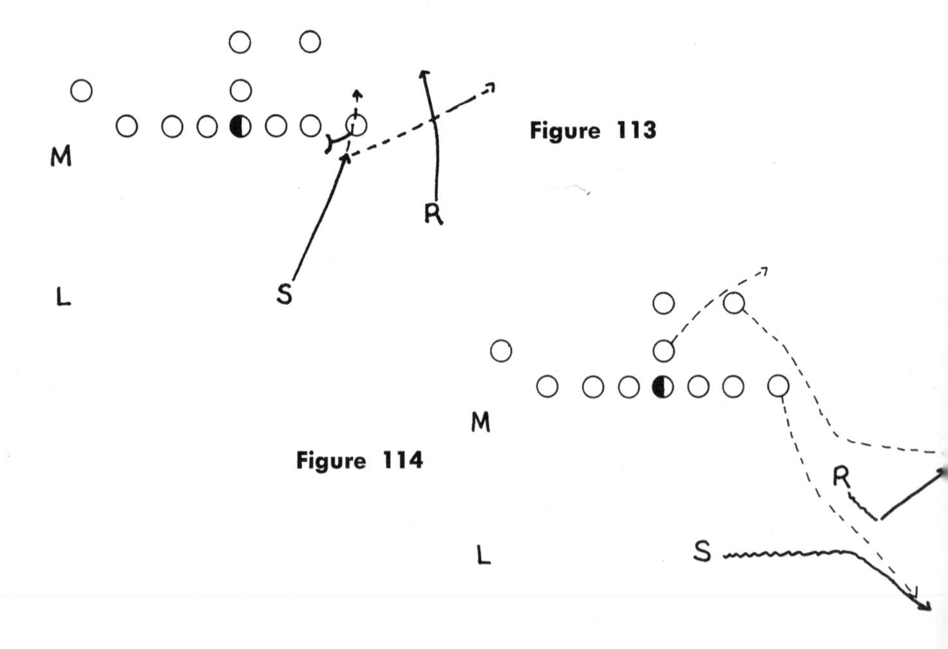

Figure 113

Figure 114

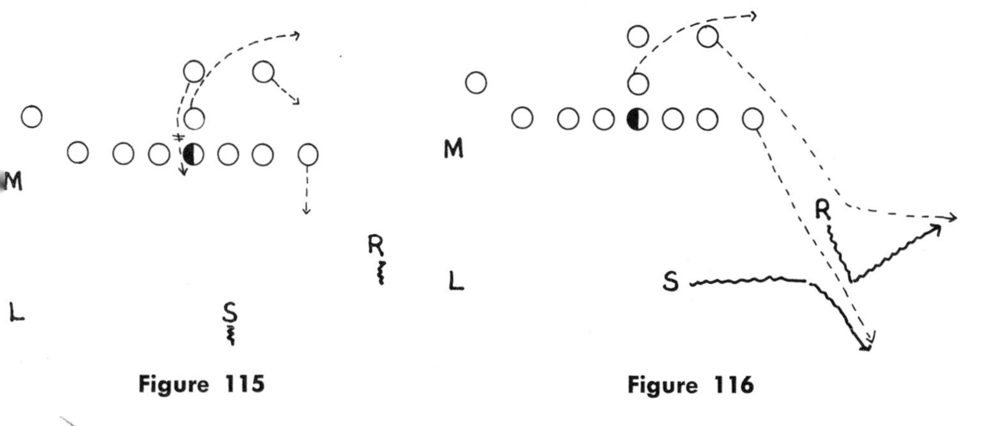

Figure 115

Figure 116

When the quarterback's action is drop back or toward the Monster, the safety *always* plays the middle zone.

R.H. Position

The R.H. will be referred to as the Squirm H.B.. We align our Squirm H.B. three yards outside the normal offensive end and five yards from the line of scrimmage (Figure 111) and he keys the offensive end and the back on his side. When the offensive end blocks, the R.H. comes up as deep as the ball and plays as nearly like the Monster as possible. The R.H. should be ready to play the left shoulder of the lead blocker with his left shoulder.

The R.H. should force the ball carrier inside or, if this is not possible, make him take a deep course so the safety can tackle him. He is a corner back and has the pitch on the option. When the run action is away from him, he takes a step back, faces inside, and rotates to safety, making sure not to overrun any receivers coming back his way. He continues to an inside-out position on the ball carrier to prevent a long touchdown run.

When the offensive end releases and the halfback is in the flat (Figure 116), normally the quarterback's action is toward the defensive right side.

When this situation occurs, the R.H. must make the offensive quarterback think he is covering the end up to eight yards deep. He should follow the end in, but back out on the same plane in which he aligned himself prior to the snap of the ball. By covering the end up to eight yards he accomplishes two important tasks. First, he prevents the end from catching the quick look-in pass. Second, he buys enough time for the Safety man to get over in a position to cover the end if he is trying to out run him to the flag. After the R.H. has covered the end up to eight yards, he breaks up on the receiver coming to the flat and covers him closely. If for some reason the offensive pattern doesn't have a man in the flat, he should stay with the end deep.

When the quarterback's action is straight drop back or away, the Squirm H.B. plays the receiver in the deep 1/3 of the field. He should never play the hook or an end crossing shallow.

Adjustments to Motion (Figure 117)

Motion to Monster. When we get motion toward the Monster (Figure 117), our linebacker will yell "check Lucy" which means we now slant to the Monster and free him to cover the motion man. The Monster will adjust cautiously, on the same plane as he lined up, and in a position to play the remaining wingback in the flat as well as the motion man. The L.H. widens, but does not deepen until forced to do so. Only one receiver remains to our *right* so we bring our safety over to compensate for the three receivers on one side as well as to fill where our L.H. moved over. The rule for the safety is to be aware of either tight end splitting the zone up the middle. The R.H. or Squirm H.B. should adjust to two yards deeper and come in one yard and key the end, playing him man-for-man. If the end blocks, the R.H. comes up to outside and plays the run.

Motion Away from Monster. Motion away from the Monster should be treated the same as the quarterback's pass action away from the Monster, because you end up with the same areas covered (Figure 118). As soon as the motion wingback passes the offensive F.B. the

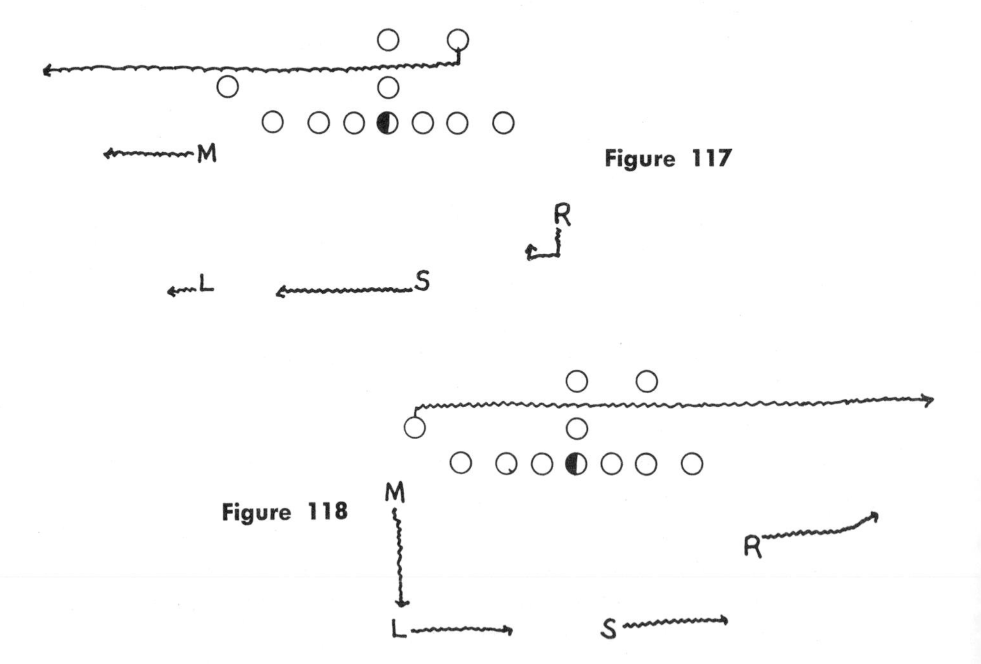

Figure 117

Figure 118

Monster should immediately jump back to the L.H. position and key only the offensive right end. If he blocks, the Monster should come up to outside and play the run, and if the right end releases, he should cover him closely, almost man-for-man. He should not follow him if he crosses shallow. With three receivers on one side, the L.H. should move to head on the offensive tackle, keeping in mind that both tight ends can split the middle zone. The safety now becomes the R.H. and is responsible for the deep outside 1/3 of the field. Technically, the R.H. has now rotated up to become the Monster. He still stations himself to cover the motion man and the remaining offensive L.H. in the flat. What has taken place with this type of motion is that we have completely rotated from monster left (before motion), to monster right.

Blue Variations

We prefer to have one sure way of making adjustments to motions and the various offensive sets. One of the trends in modern offensive football is the wide use of spread passing formations. Today's football forces us to have in our defensive repertory various ways to defend and cover the passing sets. We mentioned that the Monster defenses were basic and that we spend a great amount of time using Blue coverage in our perimeter, but the wide sets force us to go to variations in order to cope with a strong passing attack. We will now discuss the spread formations against our "Blue" coverage.

Blue Coverage Versus One Wide Receiver (Figure 119). The L.H. is aligned head up to flanker and not more than seven yards deep. He keys the flanker, and plays him man-for-man.

With a flanker or a wide out toward our Monster, we normally slant toward the Monster in order to free him, or we can play a 54 Regular Defense with our ends wider to relieve our Monster of contain responsibility. By having a flanker, the offense has reduced the strength of a sweep play and therefore we can align our Monster in a position

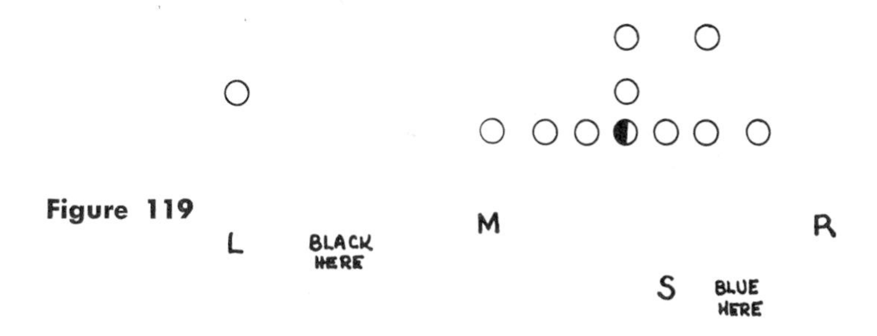

Figure 119

off the line to strengthen our secondary. We prefer to play our Monster man-for-man on the tight end, which gives us a chance to cover the backside with normal "Blue" coverage. If the tight end blocks, our Monster will fill just outside our defensive left end, and is responsible for the run outside. The end has the quarterback on the option, and the Monster the pitch man. With the quarterback's pass action away from Monster (Figure 120), the Monster should cover the tight end through the safety, which allows us to squirm and cover the flat. The safety and R.H. play normal Blue coverage.

The adjustment to motion toward the Monster is the same (Figure 121). The safety should be sure to play the offensive right end close.

Blue Coverage Versus 1 Wide Out (Split End) (Figure 122). The split end side is really where the most concern is concentrated regarding

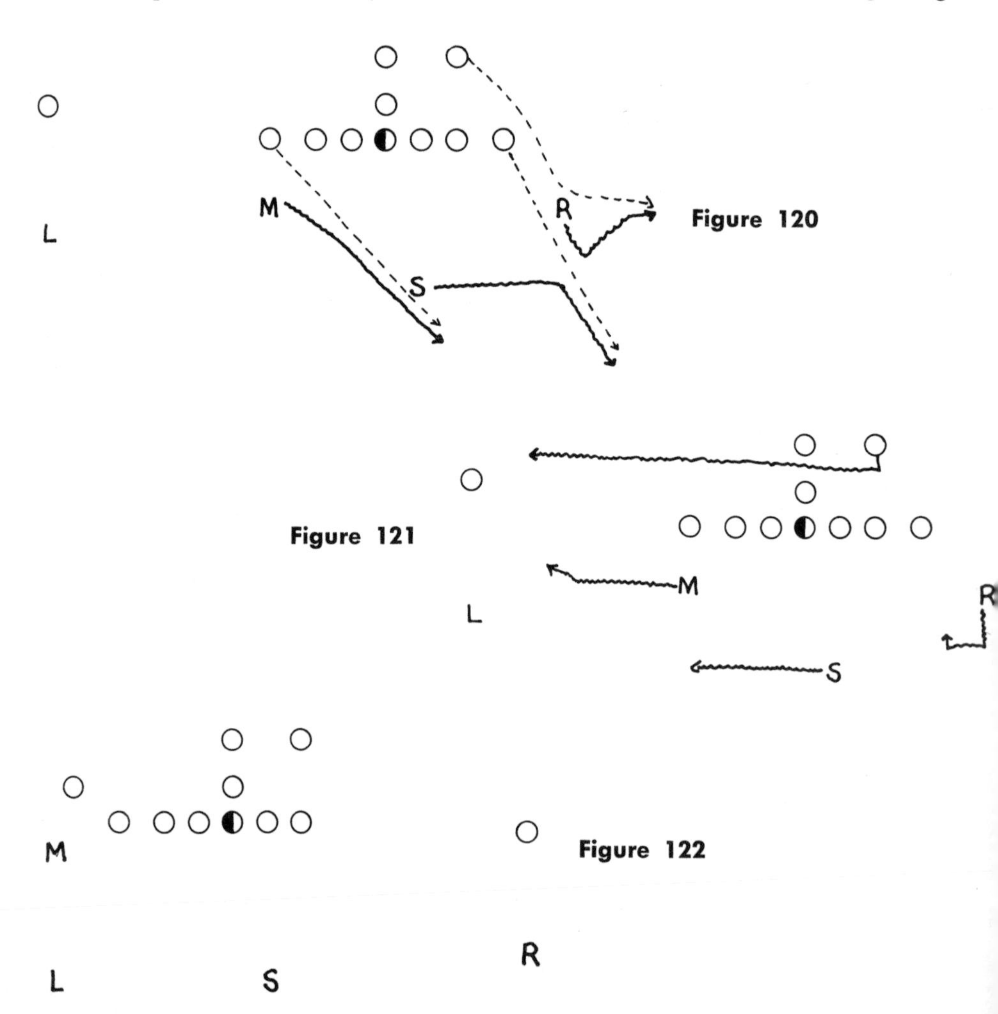

Figure 120

Figure 121

Figure 122

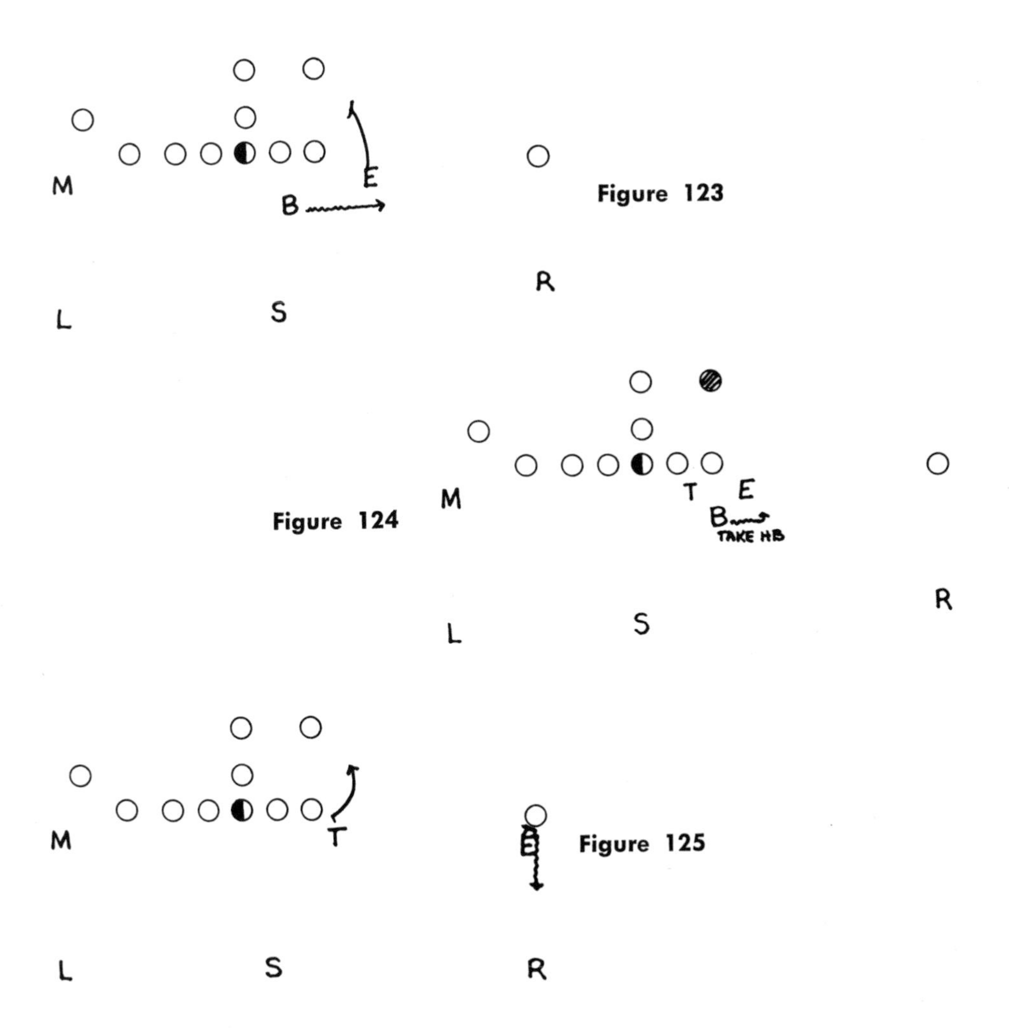

Figure 123

Figure 124

Figure 125

the Monster (Blue coverage) defense. At Florida, we have five ways to handle the opponents split end offense.

1. The Monster and L.H. play normal "Blue" coverage versus this offensive formation (Figure 123). As previously mentioned, our concern is the split end side, and how to cover the halfback on his various maneuvers.
2. We can play the safety in the middle and have him play the ball, and cover the halfback with the L.B. (Figure 124). We can eagle the backside and put the L.B. in a better alignment to cover the halfback.
3. We can give up some of our rush and run support by doubling the offensive end with our defensive end and zoning the split end area (Figure 125).

4. If we have a 54 Slant called, then we have the halfback covered with our defensive end since he is slanting toward that area. We prefer this to happen (Figure 126).
5. If we are playing 54 Regular, then our defensive end has to contain the quarterback, so we must use our safety to cover the offensive halfback man-for-man since we do not want to give up the flat.

In each of these examples, except when we use our end to double cover, we play our R.H. on the split end head up and man-for-man. In each example, the Monster and L.H. play normal "Blue" and react to the quarterback's direction.

Motion toward the Monster is the same as normal "Blue." Motion away from Monster versus a split end varies somewhat (Figure 127).

The Monster and L.H. make their normal motion adjustment. Instead of the R.H. rotating up and safety out, we invert our safety to a position where he can cover the motion man and the remaining offensive halfback in the flat. The safety should be alert for the crack back by the offensive split end. The R.H. can loosen slightly because he has a man covering the flat in front of him.

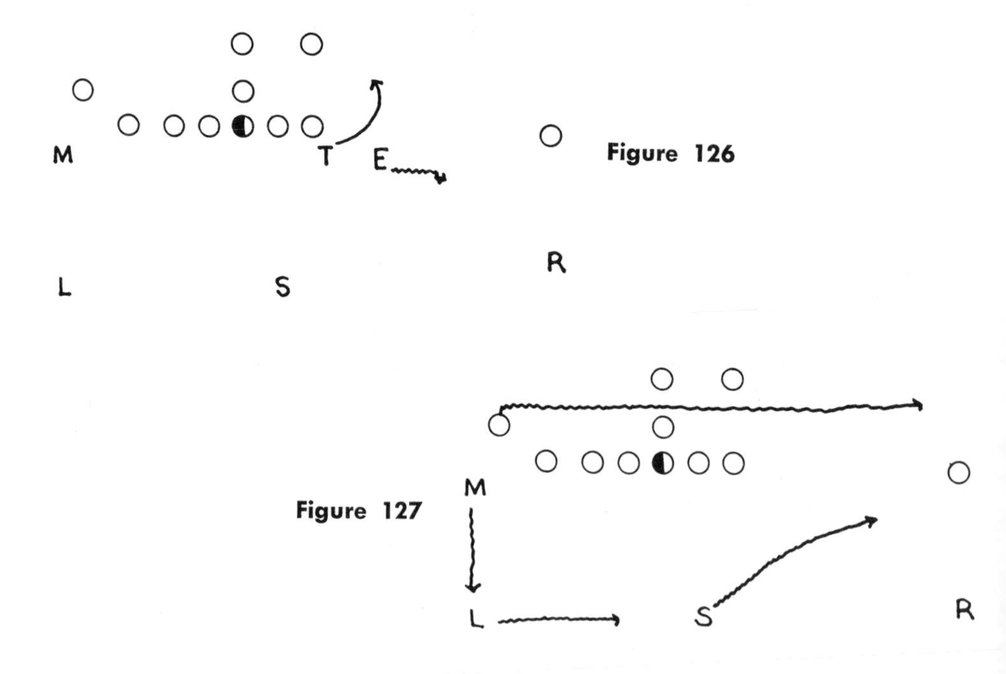

Figure 126

Figure 127

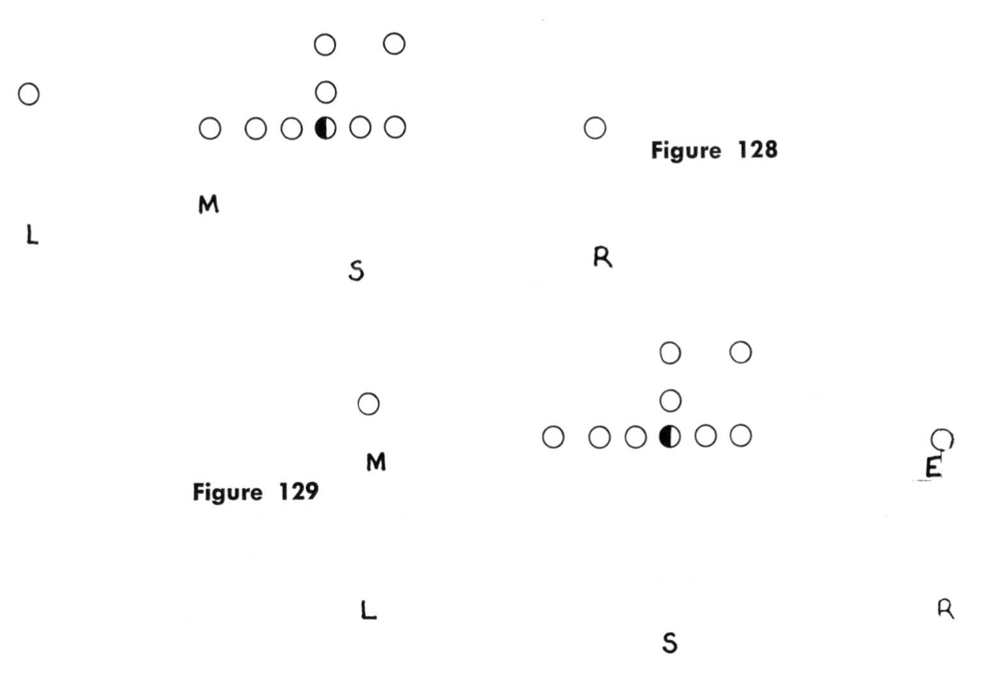

Figure 128

Figure 129

Blue coverage vs. two wide outs (Figure 128). Basically, the offense forces us to play man-for-man by employing two wide outs. Again, remember that we want to properly cover the split end side of the formation. We have already shown how to do this with five variations which we use at Florida. Motions either way are covered as already shown in Figures 117 and 118.

We can use true zone coverage by doubling the split end and playing the Monster in the flat, but we feel that this is not in the best interest of our perimeter (Figure 129). We double cover with the Monster and defensive end in a long yardage situation or save-the-game situation.

Black Coverage

When using the second category of Florida defenses, the Press, we use Black coverage in our secondary. Black is true man-for-man coverage. It is necessary to remind you that when we are "Pressing," our defense is exerting as much pressure on the offense as possible. The pass rush should get to the quarterback before the receivers can get downfield thirty yards. Our defenders can adequately cover the offensive pass receivers up to that point. When the safety man, who calls our secondary coverages, hears one of the Rover or 54 Defenses called, with the word "Fire" attached, he calls "Black" to give us man-for-man coverage. Our goal line defenses get a "Black" call in the secondary, but vary slightly (See the chapter on goal line defenses).

If we are in a "Press" defense and are exerting pressure, trying to force an offensive mistake, we can play "Black" in the secondary and prevent the quarterback from dumping the ball to a receiver quickly. We play the receivers close, and as soon as a pass shows, we cover the pass receiver as closely as possible (Black alignment—Figure 130).

Positions

L.H. Position. Line up three yards outside the offensive end and three yards deep.

Key the wingback. When the wingback blocks, come up and play the lead blocker's right shoulder with your right shoulder. Force the run inside. If this isn't possible, make the ball carrier take a deep course so the Monster can make the tackle. Be sure to limit the hole between you and your defensive end.

If the wingback releases off the line cover him closely (Techniques are covered in Chapter 8).

Monster Position. Align yourself on the outside shoulder of the offensive right end and five yards deep.

Key the offensive right end. When the right end blocks, come up to line of scrimmage and fill inside the L.H. and be in a position to tackle the ball carrier on his cut-back, or take the quarterback on the option keeper. If the ball carrier is forced deep and outside, be able to tackle him. When the right end releases off the line for a pass, cover him closely.

Safety Position. Line up on the outside shoulder of the offensive left end and five yards deep.

Key the left end. If the left end blocks, fill inside the R.H. and be in a position to tackle the ball carrier on his cutback. You must take the quarterback if he keeps on the option. If the ball carrier is forced

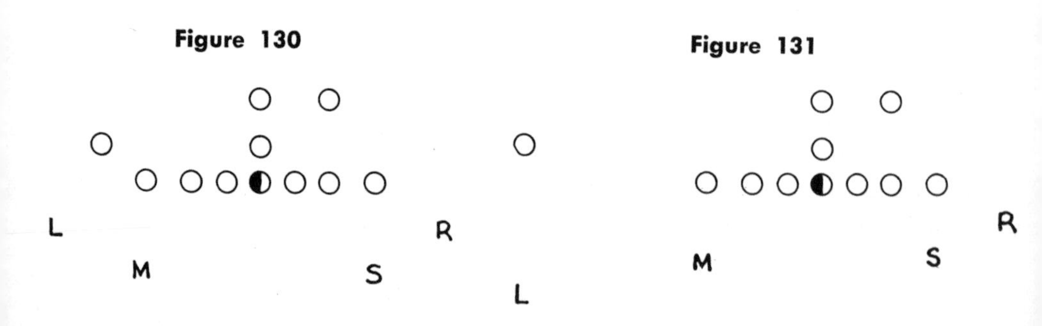

Figure 130

Figure 131

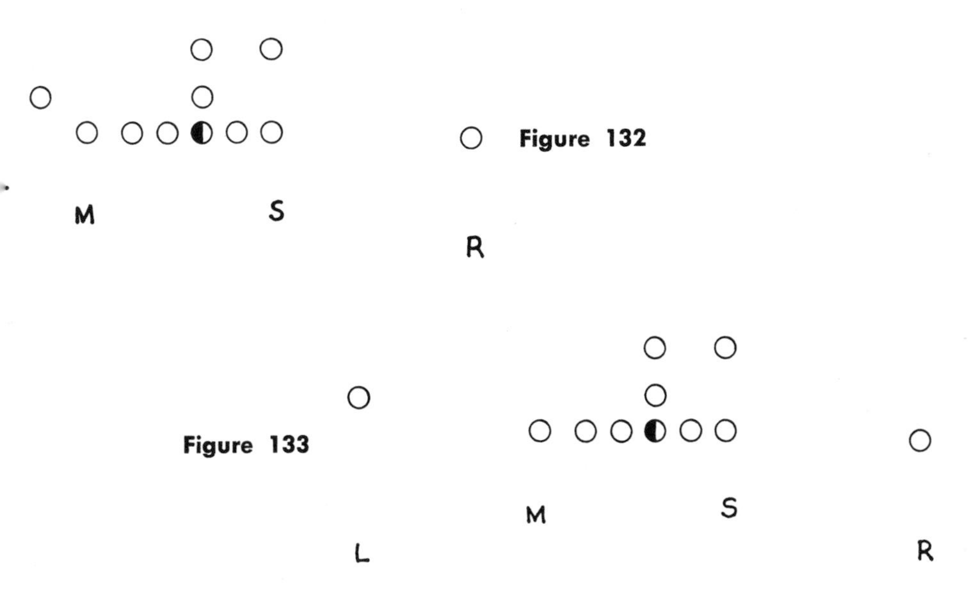

Figure 132

Figure 133

deep and outside be able to tackle him. If the left end releases for a pass, cover him closely.

RH Position. Line up three yards outside the offensive left end and three yards deep.

Key the offensive left end and the offensive L.H. If the left end blocks, come up to outside and play the lead blocker's left shoulder with your left shoulder. You must force the run inside and reduce the hole between you and your defensive right end. If you can't force the run inside, make the ball carrier take a deep course so the safety can make the tackle. If the L.H. comes out on a pass, cover him. If the offensive L.H. blocks or goes away from you, key the offensive left end. If he releases, help cover him. When he blocks come up and play the run.

Black Coverage Versus One Wide Receiver (Figure 131)

The alignments and keys are the same as above.

Black Coverage Versus One Wide (Split End) (Figure 132)

The only difference in keys and alignments is the safety and R.H. change receivers. If the safety man's HB blocks, he is free to play the ball.

Black Coverage Versus Two Wide Outs (Figure 133)

Keys and alignments are the same as above.

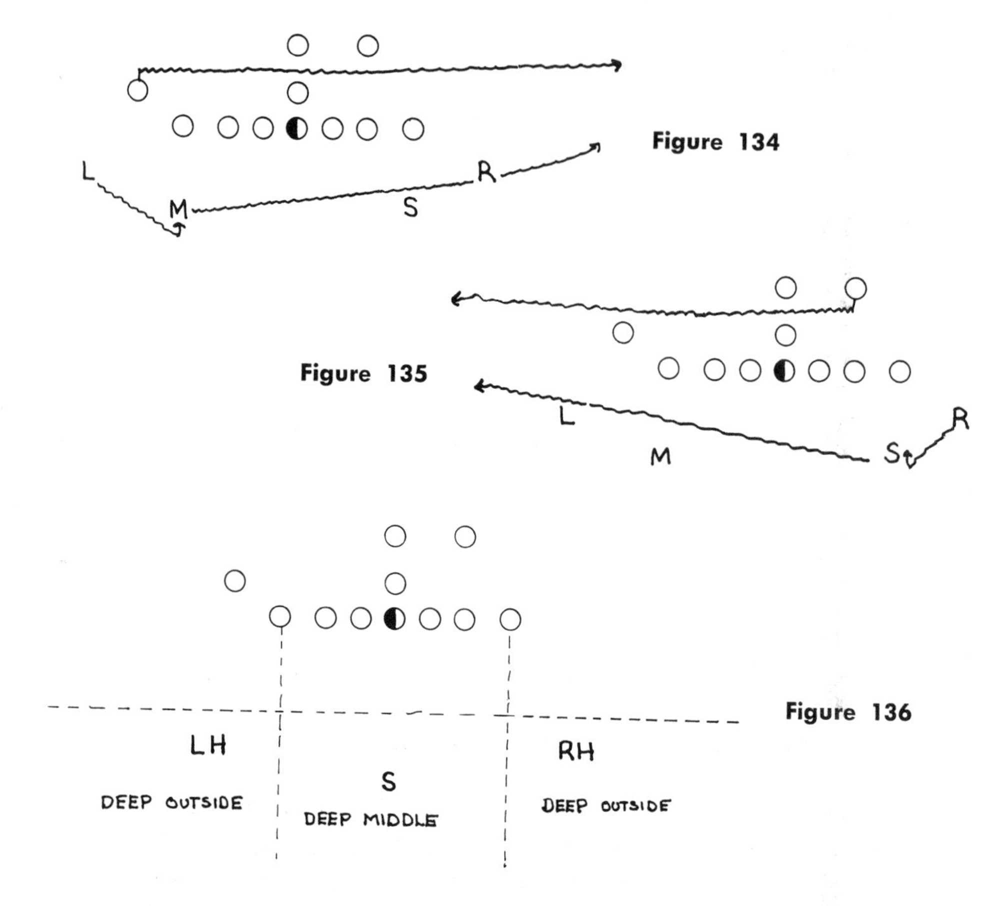

Black Adjustments to Motion (Figure 134)

Versus Motion Right. When the wingback goes in motion, the Monster goes with him all the way rather than have the L.H. go with him (Figure 134). The L.H. adjusts to a position where he can cover the offensive right end as soon as his halfback leaves. If the end blocks the defensive L.H. should come up to outside and play the run.

Versus Motion Left. When the offensive L.H. goes in motion the safety goes with him. As soon as the defensive R.H.'s man leaves, the R.H. adjusts to a position where he can cover the offensive left end. If the left end blocks, he should come up to the outside and play the run.

Orange Coverage

This is our basic three-deep zone secondary (Figure 136). Since we are not a three-deep team, we do not try to teach everything a three-deep must do, as if that were the only secondary being used. Three-deep teams must employ pass defense help from their ends and line backers. This takes so much training that it should be the only secondary plan used. We use the three-deep zone mainly as a "prevent" defense. We do not ask our ends and and linebackers to learn anything different. The two main times we will use Orange are when we are rushing with eight men, and when we are double-covering both sides at once, which is a save-the-game defense. All we hope to get out of this coverage is that no one breaks deep on us for a score. Put simply, all we want our three-deep men to do is divide the field into thirds and get as deep as the deepest man in their zone.

10

Concealed Yardage and the Kicking Game

Having been closely associated with the late General Neyland of Tennesse and Bobby Dodd of Georgia Tech, I have always been aware of the importance of the kicking game in college football. If all the major teams in the nation lumped their losses together, sixty percent of these losses could be traced to failure in some phase of the kicking game. This involves protecting, covering, and returning as well as the actual kick itself.

It also provides for the term "concealed yardage." Success or failure in this area doesn't show up in game statistics, but it greatly influences a team's overall effectiveness. A better than average kicker, with good protection and coverage, will force the opposition to gain over 100 yards, the hard way, to offset no gain on kicks returned in a single game. During an entire season, this is approximately 1000 yards that never shows up statistically as a part of your overall effort, even without considering such assets as good field position, etc. Of course, there are ways to actually win a game by kicking alone: field goals, extra points, and opponent fumbles in handling punts and kickoffs than can lead directly to a score.

Practicing the Kicking Game

Everyone acknowledges these facts. The thing to do is show how to improve all phases of the kicking game. In a normal game, there are altogether about 120 plays, by both teams. This includes an average of twelve punts, six kickoffs, four extra points and two field goals. This is about twenty-five kicking plays. Therefore, if practice time was in the same ratio as game plays, at least one-fifth of practice time would

Figure 137

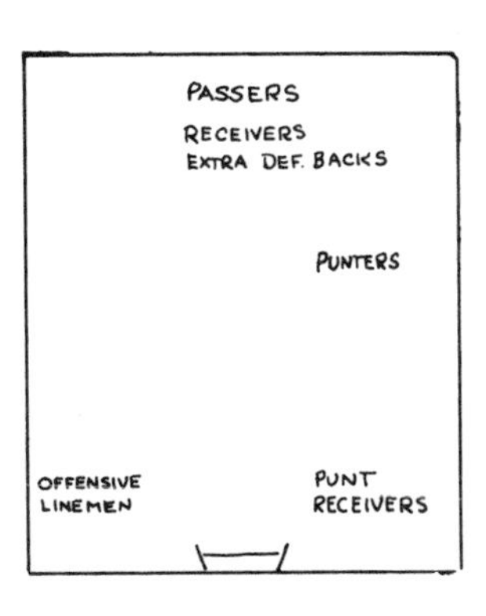

be spent on all phases of kicking. But not many coaches give that much time to the kicking game. Here is a plan that devotes that much effort to this vital area of football. Every practice starts with what is called the Specialty Period, in which everyone involved with the kicking game works on it (Figure 137).

The punters, with one center, work on their punting. They use the part of the field that forces their receivers to receive at about the ten yard line. This gives the receivers practice in fielding and making decisions on which punts should not be handled. The practice group includes punters, center, and the three deep on punts. At the same time another center works with a place-kicking group. On another part of the field the passers, ends and flankers work on their "cuts." The extra defensive backs are with them and work on man-to-man coverage. Offensive and defensive linemen split up and work slowly on special phases of football in which they may need extra help. The centers rotate in order to practice their different long snaps. This period usually takes about 15 minutes. Then we split up into offensive and defensive teams and work on kick-offs and covering kick-offs for ten minutes. Then we go into a regular practice schedule.

Team punting and covering take part of the offensive team time, while punt returns are executed by the defensive team during their team time. These things are done every day. As a final kicking workout, we ask the centers to stay out after practice and work on their long snaps when they are tired.

How to Teach the Long Snap

This phase of the kicking game is becoming more and more of a problem. Few high school centers can make a swift, accurate fourteen yard snap. Today's spread punts are based on just such snaps. Actually, with a quick, two-step kicker and a really good center who can rifle back a snap, there is no need for sustained protection. The front nine

Figure 137 a **Figure 137 b** **Figure 137 c**

can release almost right away. When we have great centers and kickers, we try to see if a rusher, unhindered, could block the kick. Surprisingly, the rusher must get a "jump" at the start and be unusually fast, and even then cannot block all attempts. So the center's job is quite important.

Training the snapper starts with his stance (Figure 137a).

The snapper must reach for the ball. His right hand grips the ball as if he were throwing a forward pass. The other hand is on top of the ball. This hand guides and helps give the ball rotation for a good spiral. When the snapper is ready, he picks the ball up (Figure 137b) and throws it back between his legs with a fast, long sweep of his arms (Figure 137c). He employs the same wrist snap as a golfer hitting a golf ball. Speed is the object. Even if other things are wrong, such as poor spiral or poor trajectory, never allow a slow snap. When the ball is picked up, the long axis of the ball should not be tilted up or down, but remain parallel to the ground. The trajectory should be straight at the kicker's hands. We've had a lot of snappers who throw back a "rainbow", and this is just too slow. The speed of the hands and arms of the snapper must be emphasized. He must throw it back as hard as he can.

Snappers should pair off with each other and throw overhead two-handed passes to each other from about ten yards apart as part of their warm up. Next they should snap to each other from about eight yards apart, gradually increasing the distance up to fifteen yards. They should make ten to twenty long snaps after every practice. The best way to do this is to make sure there is one coach on your staff who is assigned to coach these players and work with them. When they practice by themselves, they tend to get sloppy. Heavy balls are O.K. from a psychological standpoint, but should be used on shorter snaps only.

Incentives

Incentives are discussed in another chapter, but it should be mentioned here, particularly, since most teams do not emphasize these so-called fringe areas. A good idea is to keep charts showing yards returned on punts, places where kickoffs were returned, etc. These should be made available to your players so they can take pride in these areas. One season a few years ago our opponents were averaging only one yard per returned punt. This made kick coverage drill fun, because the players all wanted to keep this record. The players were kept posted each week, and they all were shooting for a better record. The old Army expression, "That which is not inspected will be neglected," applies to these often overlooked areas of football.

Position or Possession?

There has always been a lot of discussion about "position or possession" football. Everyone, except an experienced coach, deplores a team that plays for field position rather than ball possession. The rabid fan just cannot be happy unless his team is striking for the goal line from anywhere on the football field. This is a natural emotion, and is therefore understandable.The fact is, however, that the percentages are against any team that consistently opens up its offense inside its own 35-yard line. To prove this beyond a shadow of a doubt, the following statistics should help quiet even the sharpest of critics. These figures were gathered over a two year period, 1963-64. Every Florida opponent's offensive "start" was plotted on graph paper: the yard line of the "start," how far the drive went, and what stopped it. These are unusually accurate because our defensive teams over these two years were unusually similar. Each team ranked nationally (ninth both years) on defense. They both allowed about the same number of yards per game: the 1963 defensive team gave up 194.1 yards per game, and the 1964 edition gave up 194.4. In order to make these figures more understandable they are plotted here on a football field. The striped end zone is our goal and the plain end zone is our opponent's goal (Figure 137d).

It is interesting to notice that we were almost as charitable as our opponents in the critical area. The undisputable fact is, that for every touchdown our opponents made opening up their offense inside their 35-yard line, we got two.

Maybe the old boys were not too far from the truth. Remember the old expression, "Drives of over 80 yards are seldom successful"? Well, I'll tell you how seldom. Out of 80 starts our opponents made from their 20 or back (over a two year period) THREE scores resulted! *That's 27-to-ONE odds.*

Kicking Assignments

With these facts at hand, let's go into the actual assignments on all phases of the kicking game.

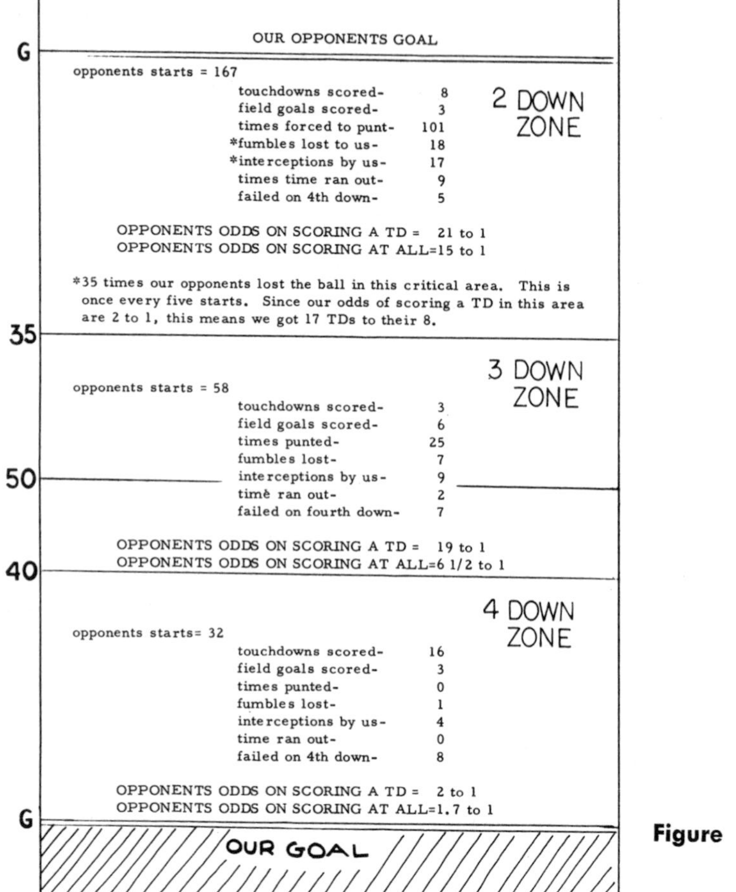

Figure 137 d

1. Punting (Figure 138)

The nine men on the line must line up one man apart. That is, the distance apart that one man would fill if he were lined up in the gap. Everyone but the center uses a two point stance with their hands on their knees. The blocking rule is "inside"—"over"—"outside." This means each man's responsibility is to his inside first, over next, and lastly, outside of him. If a team puts stacks or a large number of men on one side, the blockers call "loaded" to alert the outside men and the fullback. Since there is some angle blocking, each blocker must get a "square" bite on the proper opponent. This means that those facing angle blockers must hop sideways on the snap. Also, it is a good idea to get each blocker to point to his man prior to the snap.

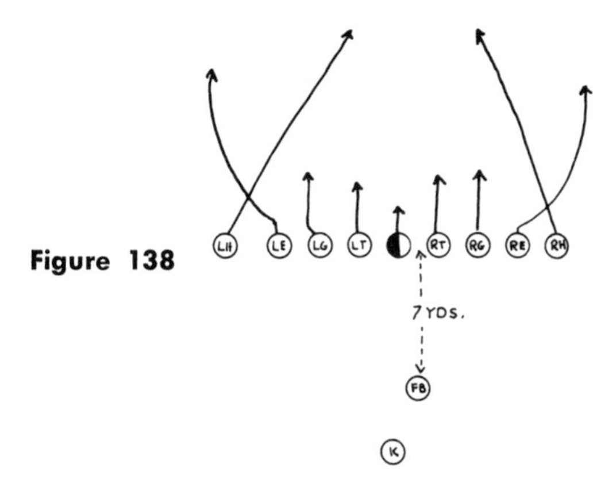

Figure 138

Just as soon as each blocker has gotten one good "square" bite on a rusher, he releases to cover the kick. The two outside men are two halfbacks and go immediately to the ball. The next two men inside are the ends and they cover outside and become containers. The next two men inside are the guards. They widen and then stay in that lane. The two next to the center are the tackles and they cover in straight lanes. The center makes his snap and is not counted on as a blocker unless he can't avoid contact. He covers straight to the ball. The full-back picks the side of the return and covers to the ball. The kicker becomes safety man. All punt coverers should be taught to come to "collection" when close to the ball.

2. Extra Points and Field Goals

Offensive blocking for extra points and field goals is the same. The only difference is that field goals must be covered as if they were punts. Each man on the line takes a comfortable stance snug against the man on either side. They use the same stance as described under punt protection. On the snap they take a slight hop backwards and get into a hitting position. They remain high and resist getting moved in any direction. If it is necessary to lean inside or outside, they must keep an anchor foot, which never moves. The two wingbacks stay behind their ends and block inside out on the first man outside their own end. They too must keep an anchor foot. Everything must be forced outside the kicking area.

The holder signals to the center when he is ready. He is on both knees and must be able to "field" bad snaps. He extends his right arm and catches the snap with both hands. The left hand guides the ball to the tee as the right hand goes to the point of the ball. After the kick, all front nine men expand and cover the kick. It is a good idea to let them "cover" on extra points just to stay in the habit.

3. Kickoff Returns

Middle Wedge (Figure 139). This is the easiest one to teach and has one very good fundamental: the return gets straight up field as soon as possible. Very often side returns get nailed before they start gaining ground forward. The center is the focal point for all blockers. When the ball is kicked, the center "eyeballs" the kick and follows its flight. He knows he is to "set" the wedge so he must pull up sooner on short kicks, etc. When he pulls up and turns around to face the kick coverers, he comes to collection and waits for the wedge to form. As soon as all blockers close to the center they turn and pick out the nearest opposite color. Timing is the important ingredient—too soon or too late and you don't have much of a return.

Middle Cross (Figure 140) Again timing is of great importance.

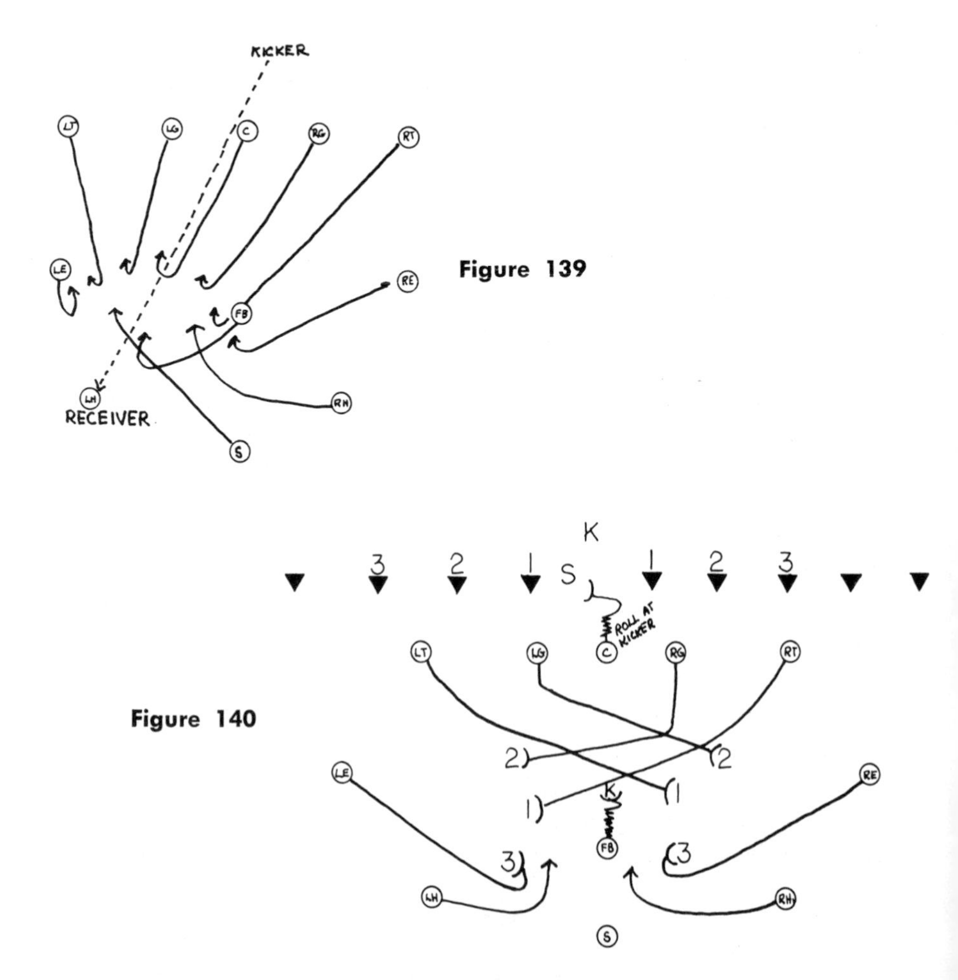

Figure 139

Figure 140

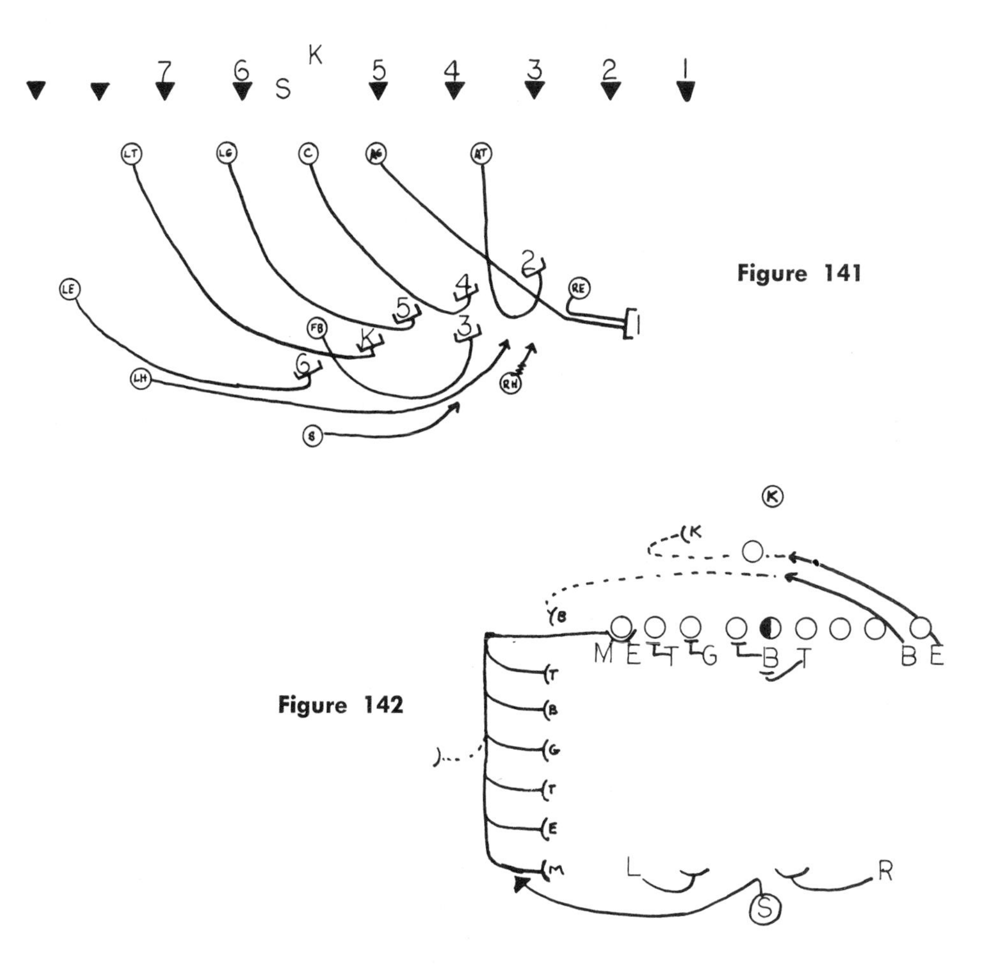

Figure 141

Figure 142

The blockers should be taught to pace themselves so they do not block too soon.

Side Line Return (Figure 141) By swapping the assignments, this return can be run to either sideline.

4. Punt Returns and Punt Rush

80 Load Left, Return Left (Figure 142) Alignment is in the gaps. Stress a good hold of two full seconds. The "wall" leader sprints to make the "corner" block. All blockers space at five yards apart. The middle guard looks for a "leaker" outside the wall. Be sure the wall is formed close to the sideline. If the kick is to the opposite side of the field, the halfback on that side returns straight away, getting all he can on his own. The three deep are lined up with the two blockers in front of the one safety. The blockers will take side kicks only. Their prime responsibility is blocking—they must protect the reception. "Load right, return right" is just the reverse in responsibilities.

80 Load Left, Return Right (Figure 143) Again the reverse is true on 80 load right, return left.

80 Load Left, Rush (Figure 144). 80 "Load right, rush" is the same, just reversed. All rushes including special rushes require an automatic right return.

80 Right (Figure 145) This is different from the load series, and as before, the return 80 left is reverse from this.

80 Pick (Figure 146) Very often when an opponent is kicking from his own end zone you want a quick return either way. Also, this is good if a kicker were to "squib" one off his foot. You have a straight shot with blockers up either side.

80 Part (Figure 147) This will prevent everyone from flying to the outside on all your punt returns.

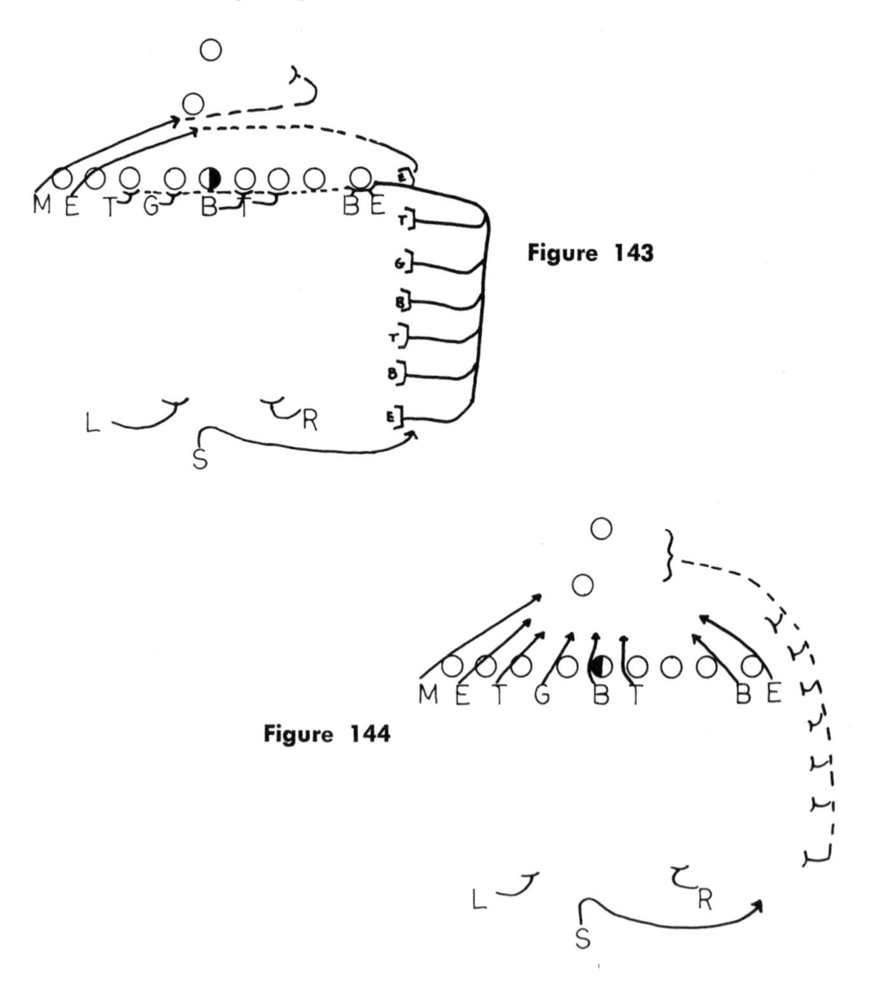

Figure 143

Figure 144

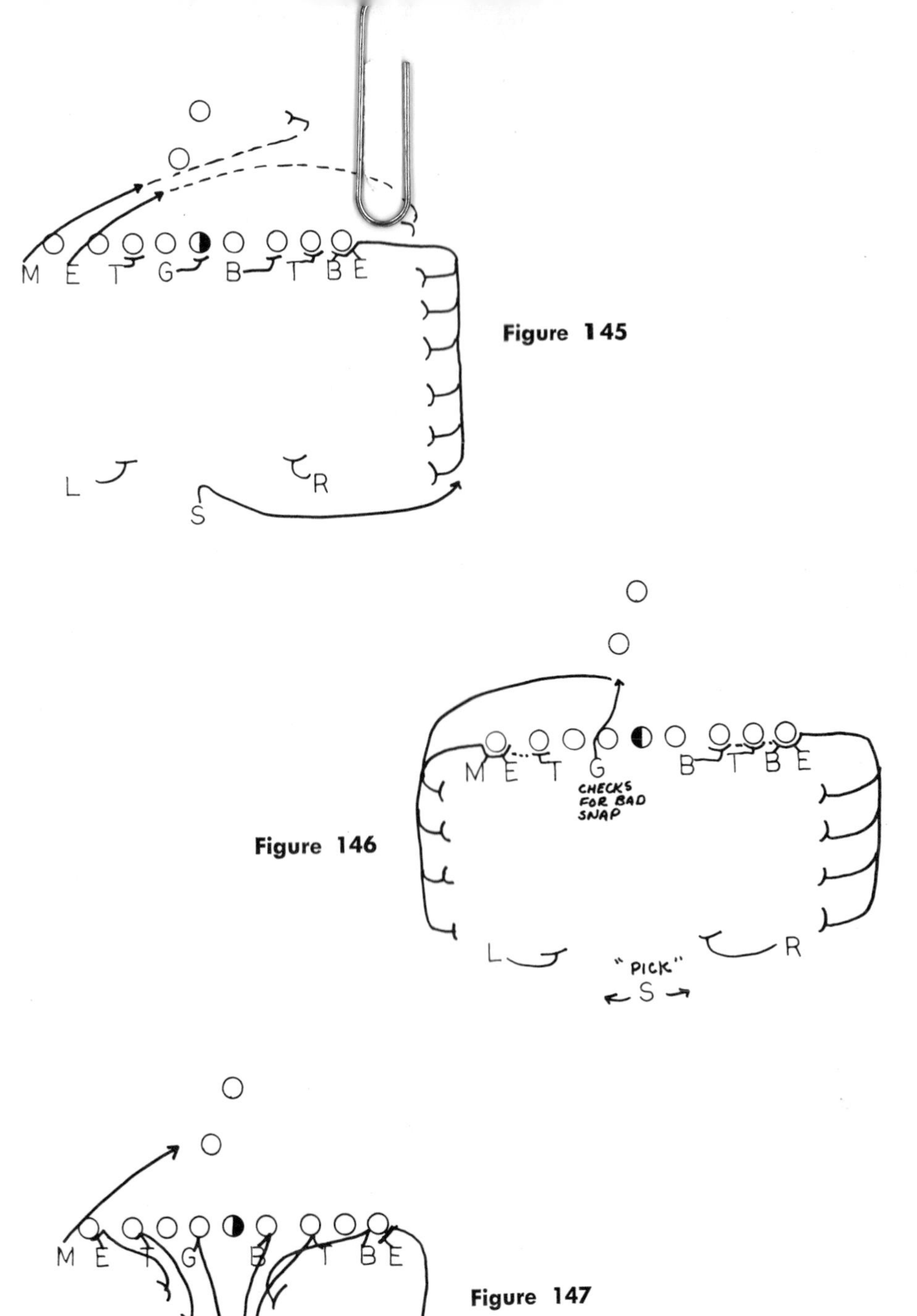

Figure 145

Figure 146

Figure 147

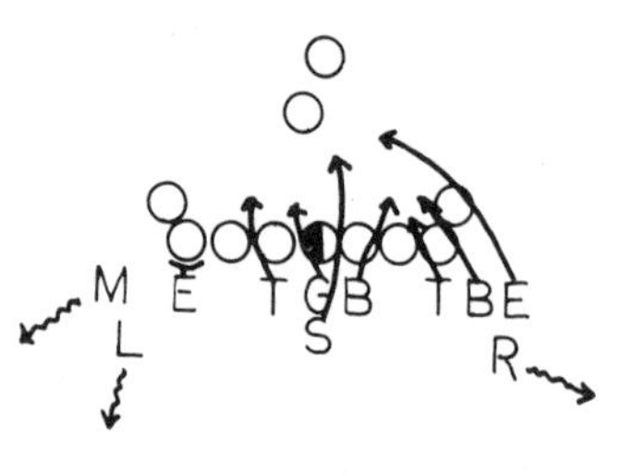

Figure 148

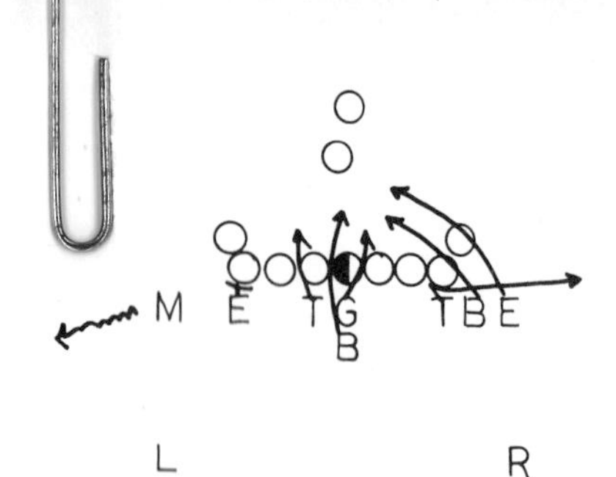

Figure 149

5. *Extra Point Rush (Figure 148)*

You can rush as many as you dare, considering your opponent can still attempt a pass from extra point formation for a two-point play. Scouting should tell you if the holder or kicker is a passer. In order to get a reckless rush you should come from one side only. This prevents injury to your own players and gives the rushing side confidence that they won't have a head-on collision with a rusher from the other side.

6. *Field Goal Rush (Figure 149)*

Discipline in these assignments is necessary. Sometime ago we lost a game because the man assigned to cover the screen area to our right decided, on his own, to rush. The snap was fumbled and the kicker picked it up and ran our right side for a score.

7. *Kickoff Coverage*

Middle Kick (Figure 150)

Cross Field Kick (Figure 151) If you have an accurate, high place kicker, this kickoff has a lot of merit. The ball is placed down on the hash mark and kicked diagonally across the field. The aiming point is between the 20 yard line and the 10 yard line, but is still successful if not exactly in this area. The idea is to place one or two unusually fast men on your left flank and kick a high "mortar shot" down in front of them. Because of the distance the ball travels, and the distance the sprinter runs, you can have a tackler almost waiting on the reception. Using this kickoff, in 1963 we started Alabama off on their own six yard line. Of course there is the risk of the kicker kicking too far and kicking the ball out of bounds. That is why you should select a high kicker.

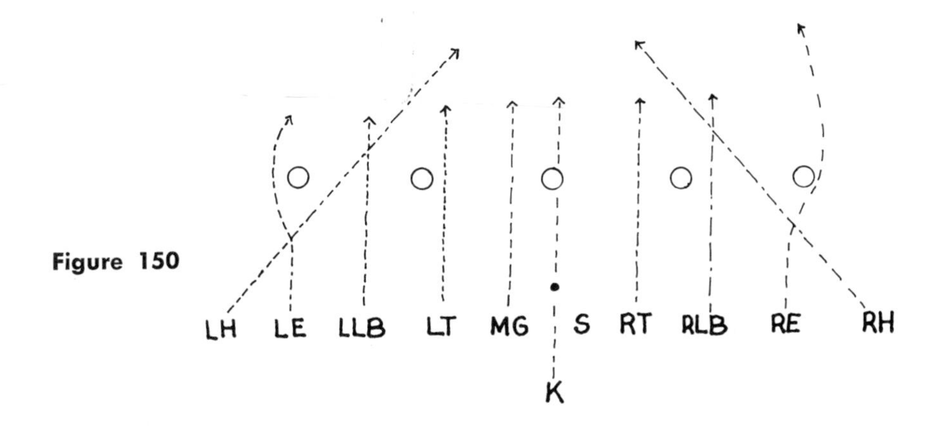

Figure 150

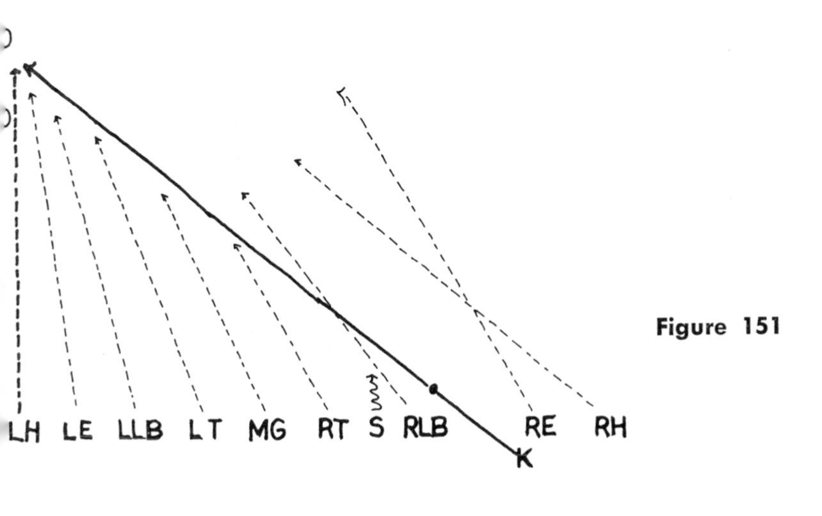

Figure 151

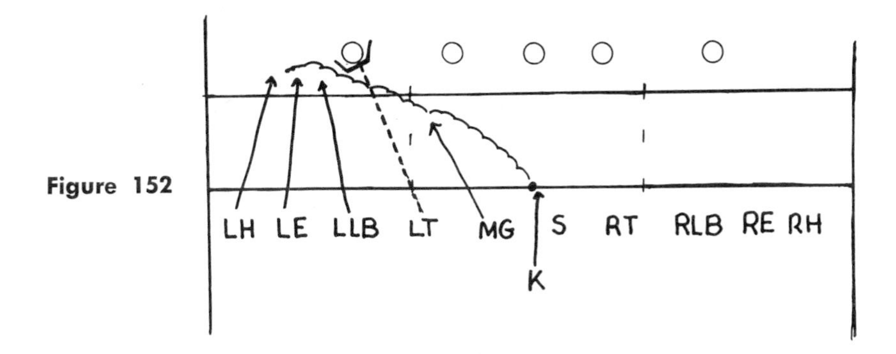

Figure 152

All kick coverers line up in a straight line across the field facing in towards the kicker. They all have their hands on their knees and drive off their back foot when the kicker passes them.

Short Kickoff (Diagram 152) There are only two fundamentals in recovering an on-sides kick. One is a kicker who can hit the ball on the side and place it it front of your covering left side. The other involves the designation of one blocker who blocks the one man on the receiving team who can fall on the kick and the other members of your team who can go for the ball.

Part III

How to Teach Defensive Football

11

Middle Guard and Tackle Play

Selecting the Middle Guard

The best defensive lineman on the team should play middle guard. Some teams call him simply "the nose man." Size alone will not qualify a player to play middle guard, but it does give you a little more security to know your middle is not light. Quickness and speed are essential because of the nature of the position. Being in the middle provides the middle guard with the opportunity to pursue plays either way with equal chance of being in on the tackle. If you play an odd front defense, your three middle men (middle guard and two inside line backers) should always be your three leading tacklers.

The slant-and-gap defenses take the middle guard away from this middle position somewhat, but the premium of quickness still pays off; the middle guard is still somewhere close to the middle of the offensive formation.

In addition to quick footwork, the middle guard must be able to master the hand shiver as well as the forearm flipper. Later on in this chapter the shiver will be explained, along with other agility drills.

The starting point for coaching any athlete (in most sports) is his initial stance. The middle guard and the two tackles should be on one knee after getting their defensive signal. This keeps them in a "ready" position; it also enables the Monster and safety to see the offensive huddle break, and more quickly determine their declaration. Nothing can blot out the scenery better than three wide interior linemen standing up. As soon as the offensive center touches the football, the middle guard hollers "BALL." This signal should snap everyone on the defensive team into their stance. For the middle guard and two tackles this amounts to putting one hand on the ground and coming up off the knee that they were resting on.

The Stance

The coaching points on middle guard's and tackles' stance are given below and illustrated in Figure 153.

1. *Head*—set down into shoulders, looking up. Imagine there is an ever tightening drawstring attached to the top of the head and the end of the spine. This will also help keep the back flat.
2. *Shoulders*—parallel to the line of scrimmage and completely straight across; neither shoulder point is lower or higher than the other.
3. *Arms*—The arm on the side of the foot stagger is straight down to the ground. With shoulders straight and arm straight, a center line should look like an inverted "L." The other arm should not be resting on the "up" knee; this makes the shoulders lose their straight line and puts the stance in a resting position. It should be almost straight and *in front* of the up knee. It should be slightly crooked with the fist clenched. By reaching and straightening this arm, you could make a four point stance out of this.
4. *Hands*—We've already said the dangling arm should have a clenched fist. This is not too important, but it does stress readiness. The hand of the supporting arm is naturally in contact with the ground. There are two ways this hand can support, both acceptable. One is a

Figure 153

five-finger spread, the other is a tripod consisting of the thumb and first two fingers bent so the weight is on the area between the first and second joint. We teach the short-armed player to use the five-finger spread and the rest use the knuckle base.

5. Back—Flat as is humanly possible, like a coffee table. As mentioned before, the ever tightening drawstring idea will keep the back flat, and square to the line of scrimmage.

6. *Feet and Legs*—The feet should be at least as wide apart as the width of the shoulders, but not too wide. Feet are too wide when they have to be brought back together in order to be able to run. The build of the player should be considered. If he has long legs, he will need a wider base, but long-legged players often get too wide. This can be corrected by increasing the amount of stagger. A normal physique should have a toe-heel stagger and slightly wider-than-shoulders spread with the feet.

Short-legged players must keep their spread and stagger down to the minimum. This is particularly true with a smaller lineman. He has a chance if he utilizes all his quickness and power by keeping a narrower, more square stance. The heels must lean to the outside of the stance, giving the player an appearance of being slightly pigeon-toed. The weight now should be on the toe of the staggered foot, and on the ball of the "up" foot. Don't let the player's knees lean inside. They should be out in line with the feet.

Selecting the Tackles

Selection of the two defensive tackles is usually an easy one because of the size factor. The tackle position requires strength; you cannot get by with a small tackle. He is the most often double-teamed man on the defense. Also, his position is such that if he gets knocked back from the line, he clutters up all the pursuit lanes. An ideal tackle is one that has size and strength and can move like a big cat. Unfortunately, there aren't too many around like that. The big, tubby kid is always placed at tackle in high school. Most of them stay that way. It is very rare that a youngster weighing over 235 pounds becomes a top flight college tackle. There are many kids around playing high school football in the 250 pound weight classification, but only two or three have played for us. Of course, these are the kids everyone recommends. The zealous alumnus or interested fan always pushes just such kids, in the mistaken idea that they are college material. The really fine college tackles are all mostly in the 215-to-235 pound range.

The stance of the tackles is the same as for the middle guard, except that they should always have their inside foot staggered back. If they are taught this way from the beginning they can learn the right side, which requires the left hand be on the ground and the left foot back.

Regular Style Play of the Three Interior Linemen

This is our reading defense. All three players read the offensive blocker's head. The middle guard reads the center and the tackles read the offensive tackles, or in the case of an Eagle Regular, the offensive guards. We are aware of influence blocks or false head keys, but until we get hurt doing this, we will continue to let the blocker establish our direction of pursuit.

The big selling job in this style of defense is to get the defender to strike a legal blow *while* he is reading. Most kids start off reading and not moving. It must be sold as an aggressive maneuver. As soon as the blockers head indicates a right or left signal, the defensive man moves in this direction keeping "leverage" or "position" on the blocker. Very often this involves a cross-over step using the inside arm as a lever. The answer is beating the blocker by just a half-a-step. Whenever the blocker indicates no direction at all, the defender gets lower and looks for a double team. The middle guard must feel which guard is coming down on him and then tunnel under the power, or beat it laterally if he is quick enough. The tackle's job is easier since his double-teams always come from the outside.

Drills

One of the first drills we do every day is this reading drill (Figure 153a).

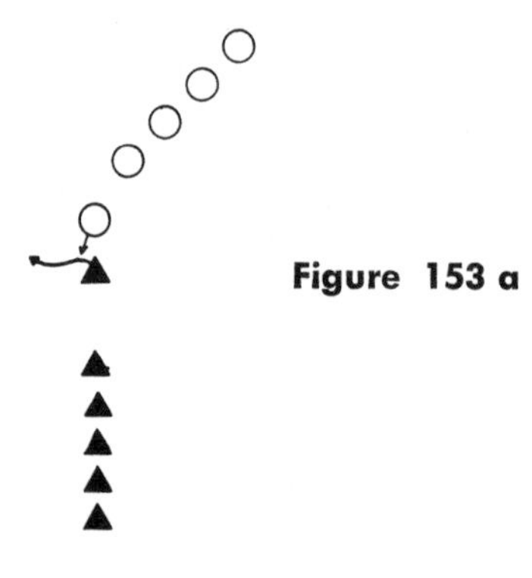

Figure 153 a

We use a line of five or six alternating blockers. Against them, one at a time, we have our six varsity interior linemen. The blocker drives for the inside or outside leg on his own count. The defender must move on the blocker's movement. All the defender should do is beat the blocker to the inside or outside; or in the case of the middle guard, the right or left. This drill now graduates into a seven-on-three drill (Figure 154).

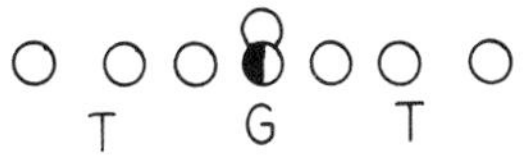

T G T

Figure 154

We now can throw double teams and traps, pass blocking, etc., at the middle three. Tackles should be taught to "flatten out" the defensive tackle if he tries an inside release.

This drill is the basis for all our interior drills. By calling a technique such as Regular, Fire, Press, Eagle Fire, Slant, Stack and so on, we can direct every possible game condition type block the defender will see. For example, the coach calls "Regular." He indicates the offensive left tackle, left end and right guard are alive and the defensive right tackle is also alive. He now stands behind the defensive right tackle. By quick signals to the blockers, he puts on the tackle hook-in block, the double team, the trap, the turn out, etc. This tackle gets six or seven full-speed situations using his Regular technique. The coach moves down the line and applies the same thing to the middle guard. Then on to the left tackle. Then back to the number two kids in all three spots. He then can change the technique such as Roger or Lucy (slant) giving the defender the same set of blocking situations, of course, not in a predictable order. This makes for recognition which we believe is one of the most important phases of defensive play at any position.

Once the players understand this drill, you can run off all your techniques with two sets of interior linemen in about twenty minutes, because you don't have to do much individual coaching. We have found that they learn by watching the other player, and you shouldn't have to do too much talking after the first couple of times. Usually the first time you do this, you can only cover one technique, but after a while you can zip through your whole repertory.

Techniques

The basic techniques of the interior linemen are shown in Figure 155 and described below.

Figure 155

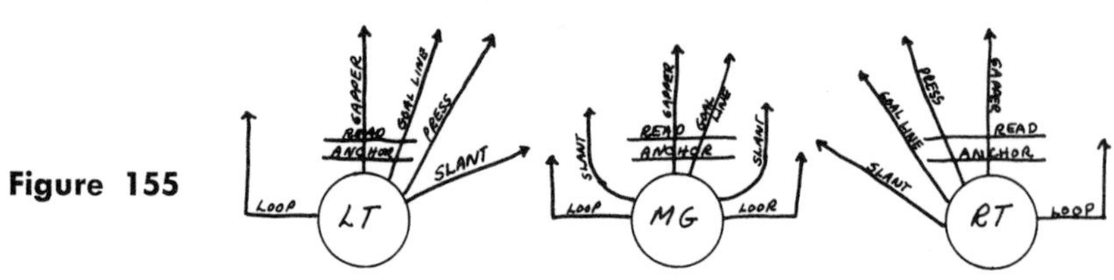

Slant Technique

The middle guard executes a quick around on the center. This can be done either by cross-over or lead step. The lead step is safer. The idea is to beat the center, no matter which way he is blocking. If your middle guard is quick, he should be able to defeat the center even if the center is leading him to the side or gap the middle guard is taking. By getting to the center's head, the middle guard can get penetration, since the center didn't get enough "bite" on him to block him. Should the center lay out quick enough to get a solid piece of the middle guard, then the middle guard can flatten out and is still in better pursuit position. When the middle guard pops clean the big plays are usually made approximately two yards behind the line about even with the off tackle hole.

If your middle guard isn't breaking clean, he is either too slow or too high. Should the play be going the other way, the center will lay out away from the middle guard's "quick around." This means the middle guard must feel the flow, collect, and pursue around the center. Very often he can catch a play from behind. Should it be a pass, the middle guard will always find one or the other offensive guards picking him up. He must bounce fight his way through them and get his hands up.

The tackles have two techniques on Slant. One is the slant and the other is the loop. They always slant to the inside, and loop to the outside. When slanting, a tackle must keep in mind his relationship to his middle guard. This means he should not go up field on flow away. He must never rush a pass to the outside of any blocker. We teach the cross-over on the first step and aim at the neck of the offensive guard. This makes him harder to keep out of middle plays and plays away from him. If he used the lead step, he would be able to break off his slant quicker and pursue around the offensive tackle and help out more on plays to his side; however with a Monster, anchor end, and scrape-off line backer, he shouldn't be needed to that side as much.

This technique is hard to do incorrectly. Looping is more difficult to do properly. You must take a completely lateral step first, then step forward with the base foot next. Most players cut down on the lateral step and make a sort of slow slant out of it. We make our linemen go across the field and back, every day, using the push off and lateral step. The looping tackle is looking for the end's inside shoulder. He hits under it with a good sharp flipper.

While on the subject of flippers, let's take a closer look at how this maneuver is done. Most high school kids come to us with the

PROPER USE OF THE FLIPPER

Figure 155 a

idea that this is a blow struck by completely bending the arm at the elbow and then swinging the elbow. While this may have its points, it is neither legal nor effective. This type flipper is easy to get under; it does not protect the defender's body. The best flipper is one that will keep the body protected. This is accomplished by swinging the arm, as part of a shoulder charge, in a slightly bent position. The forearm takes the blow and the whole arm acts as a lever. No arm can stop a good offensive charge. The defensive man must meet the offensive blocker at least shoulder to shoulder. The flipper then comes up and "lifts" the blocker, at the same time keeps his shoulder from getting to the body or legs of the defender (Figure 155a).

Eagle Technique

This is the same as Regular, with one man removed to the inside.

Eagle Fire Technique

For middle guards and tackles, this involves the cross and the anchor. When the middle guard crosses with one of his tackles, he must execute a loop step first. This gives his tackle time to get in front of him. The middle guard times himself to fire through this area just as the tackle passes in front of him. The closer they cross, the more effective the stunt. The tackle executes a slant technique into the center. The middle guard will try to run a circle around the tackle. This delays him considerably, and split seconds count. He should drive off his lateral or loop foot before the tackle is actually by him, and he should drive straight, not run an arc.

Gapper Technique

Both tackles and the middle guard must learn the Gapper technique. It is somewhat similar to a goal line technique, but calls for recognition of pressure and adjustment to it. Just driving for penetration is not enough. Everyone will try to "overblock" a gap stack. That is, the offensive blocker coming at you *away* from the play. It is somewhat reverse of the normal offensive "angle." Usually, offensive teams seek to get "down" blocking angle, but "overblocking" is more or less blocking "up hill." The main feature is that for the offensive man to lay out across the gap, and count on the defensive man to make a blind charge and falling over the blocker. Consequently, we teach the gapper to drive low into a crab position and be ready to *react in the direction of the pressure*. This can only be taught by doing.

Press and/or Bang Technique

These are the same: tackles *Press,* but middle guards *Bang.* This is a hard shoulder charge through an offensive blocker's shoulder. There is an element of reacting, but in general, we don't expect anything but penetration and pressure.

Anchor Technique

Several different positions are required to use an anchor technique. Where it applies to tackles and middle guards, it takes on the character of playing a waiting game. We call this "Spy." We feel that stunting or firing line backers are safer if there is an "anchor" to hang the stunt on. If one guard gaps, or fires, on a 60 Front defense, the other should anchor his stunt and spy. If the middle guard and tackle cross charge on an eagle front, the other tackle should spy. When you execute this technique, you do not penetrate or pursue fast, but hang and prevent the long gainer. If you must retreat, retreat back through your own position.

Agility and Running Drills

Quickness, reaction, movement and running ability can be taught and always can be improved. If you are not careful, you'll do these drills for a while during early season and then drop them when you get interested in defensing a special team. Running and movement drills also get boring. The best way to make sure you keep this in your practice schedule is to always start end practice with some form of movement drill. The following are some of the many agility drills we have used through the years. They are a collection of drills picked up from other coaches, the U. S. Army, clinics, books, and personal experimentation. Naturally, we don't use all of these drills anymore. It is hoped that you will find some that can fit into your particular program.

1. Form Running Drills

a. Make a big circle with any number of players. Have them all do a right face and look back to the middle where the coach demonstrates. Put them in the following positions: feet apart, toes in, leaning forward at the waist with elbows tight against the side, and fists clenched. Have everyone reach out with the right hand and arm and grab onto an imaginary handle. At the signal everyone pulls back on the "handle" hard enough for their arm to show past their body. Alternate hands and arms. Reach, grab, pull; Reach, grab, pull. Start the circle in a dog trot stressing arm action.

b. Having a single file line of players come straight at a stationary coach stressing base, body lean, getting off the heels. Add a simple fake. Plant one foot, fake with upper body over the planted foot, then drive off of this foot in the other direction. Stress an even speed.

c. Add to the above drill by finishing up with a forward body roll to the ground and coming up to collection. Then add a player facing the runner to meet him with a shoulder and flipper as he comes up off the ground.

d. Shoots, cages, or other gimmicks are good for linemen, because they stress running in a forward leaning position. Be sure, however, they are not too low for proper running position. You don't want to teach waddling like a duck (Figure 155b).

CORRECT RUNNING FORM

Figure 155 b

2. Agility Running Drills

Dizzy Izzy—Have about two or three lines of five men each. On signal the lead men run a circle, tightening it down as they run. Runner looks to the inside, pumping his arms with elbows tight to his body. Try to get the runners to "get some sand in their hip pockets." If they fall, they land on one hand and regain running position.

Switch—Players run away from the coach looking back at him over the shoulder. On command "SWITCH" they turn while running and look back over the other shoulder. Runners never turn their backs to the coach. About 30 yards.

Grapevine—This is a side running drill. Players face 45 degree angle from running direction. Step with lead foot sideways. Cross over with other foot and leg in front of lead foot, then another lead step, and then cross with next step behind the lead step. The crossing leg goes in front, behind, in front, behind. Runner must utilize hip action and foot work.

Wave Drill—Runners start running in place and break on coach's arm and hand signal of "right," "left," "forward" and "back." The same drill can be done from the crab position.

Zig Zag—Have a line of runners start off, one at a time from a place on a marked football field where the yard line intersects the side line, Runners are running across the field toward the other side line. They run at a 45 degree angle toward the next five yard line. When they reach this place, they plant and pivot back to the inside and run back toward the yard line they started on. This makes a zig-zag pattern as they cross the field.

3. Reaction Drills

Quick-Quick—This is a group exercise where the group imitates the leader. Leader's movements are exaggerated and overly quick. Such normal exercises as side straddle, touch alternate toes, touch toes, belly, and up, push ups, chase the bunny, etc., are done by watching and reacting. Always get the group to strike a football position first, then react.

Face Drills—Two players face each other in a football position. One is designated leader. He attempts to make the other lose him by quick movements such as lateral running and stopping, body rolls, etc.

4. Gym Drills

Run, Jump and Roll—Two lines face each other in single file. The first man out on one line is designated as a roller. The man in front of him jumps over him as he rolls. The jumper then rolls and the next man comes out and jumps over him and so on.

Tumble Drill—This is similar to the above drill. Use three men, two on their hands and knees and one standing. The standing man jumps between the two kneeling men and rolls under the far man, who jumps and rolls under the close man, who jumps and rolls under the starter.

Rocking Chair—Two men stand back to back and lock arms. One man leans forward pulling the other man back. The other kicks his feet in the air. He then drops back and rocks forward bringing the first man back who is now in the air. This rocking process is repeated.

Rooster Fight—Two men face each other with both arms behind their backs standing on one foot. They butt at each other, trying to make each other lose balance.

Relays—Any number of relay games can be made up. Horseback ride, wheel barrel, backwards run, sprint to a place and do any number of different physical things such as push ups, quick-quicks, etc.

Guerrilla Drills (done in a walking circle)

Duck Walk—hands on hips, full squat walk.

Bear Walk—walk on all fours, hand and foot on same side move together.

Elephant Walk—semi-squat-walk dragging both hands in front.

Crab Walk—backward leaning rest, walk feet first. This is the reverse of normal crab position.

Squat Jump—hands on head, full stagger squat. Jump up and reverse feet.

Russian Dance—two men face each other in a full squat. By holding on to each other by one hand they can do the Russian dance without falling over backwards.

Football Tie-in Drills

Tackling Drills—Use any form of agility, roll, or obstacle drill resulting at the end in a form tackle on a live ball carrier.

Oklahoma Tackling Drill—Have tackler lie on the ground on his back with his head pointing towards the intended ball carrier. Ball carrier has ball, but is turned around so he is backwards to the tackler. On signal, the tackler scrambles to his feet, the ball carrier whips around and the tackler makes a head-on tackle.

Hamburger Drill—Place two flat dummies on the ground two paces apart. Have a blocker in the middle of the two dummies with a ball carrier three yards in back of the blocker. Place defender in front of the blocker (or on either shoulder). On signal blocker tries to knock defender out of the hole and ball carrier tries to run to daylight through the prescribed area. Defender must whip blocker and make the tackle. In the case of beginning linemen, make one phase dummy and the other alive. For example, make the blocker dummy and the ball carrier alive or vice versa. When defenders get better, then make the whole thing alive.

Pass Rush Drills—Have five blockers and one passer against five rushers. Give the five blockers five plays to protect the passer and add up the number of seconds. Switch the lines and find out which line can whip the other. Another pass rush drill is with the Middle Guard and two tackles against five interior blockers. Have passer try to throw to either hook area. Stress the defenders getting their hands up and jumping at the thrown ball (Figure 155c). Teach the proper time to jump. If rusher is clean he doesn't jump but makes a "down" tackle on the passer. Most youngsters jump too soon. Jumping is done only when the ball is thrown and can be done when rusher is two to six yards from the passer. Never tackle passer low.

JUMPING FOR THE PASS

Figure 155 c

Fumble Drills—Use a hamburger set up, but feature loose balls rather than making a tackle. Defender hits blocker and recovers. Another fumble drill, featuring competition, is to have two lines of equal number coming up two at a time. Coach throws out a loose ball and one player from each side tries to recover the ball. You can make this a team game or use elimination to find out the best ball hawk.

Form Tackle Drill—This is our favorite and it is done everyday. Two lines are designated as ball carriers; tacklers face each, one at a time. The ball carriers run at an angle to the tacklers about half speed. Tacklers measure him, and get head in front, as they tackle they clamp their arms and lift (Figure 155d). It isn't necessary for either man to hit the ground. We usually give every player about three tackles with each shoulder every day.

IN-LINE TACKLING ILLUSTRATED

Figure 155 d

Hand Shiver Drills—Put a lineman down on all fours and line the rest of players in the front of him in a single file line. Have each player come up, one at a time, and "shiver" the man on his all fours. Teach a two-handed jab, locking both wrists and both elbows. This is a "under and up" motion and is designed to raise the offensive blocker's charge (Figure 155e). When used in a game, one or both hands may hit the opponents' head gear. This is particularly true when the blocker is pass blocking. The most common fault is allowing the elbows to point outwards, which has no strength at all. Another fault is not locking the

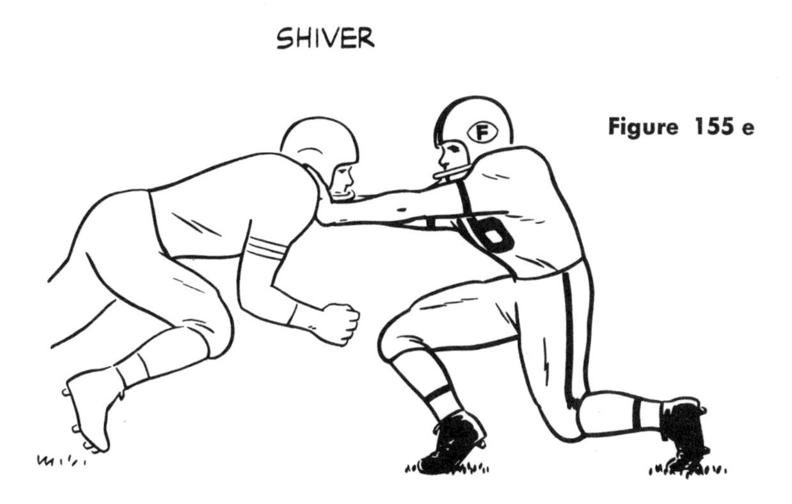

Figure 155 e

elbows. When the arms get bent back into the defender's body defensive leverage is lost. As soon as contact is made, the defender should push off in the direction of the play. A shiver can not be held for long, so quick reaction is a must. Thsi can be practiced against two-man and seven-man sleds. Always stress stepping in with the back foot and moving out quickly.

12

Defensive End and Linebacker Play

It seems today everyone is trying in one way or another to get wide with their offense. Perhaps the advent of the sprint-out pass has placed more responsibility on the defensive end than any one offensive maneuver has in a long time. Couple this with the "I" formation quarterback sweep, and the modern defensive end has his problems. This is especially true if you line your end up in an Oklahoma 54 position all afternoon.

This is why we believe in multiple defenses. We want to give our opponent the same initial look, but on the snap we try to get a different style of end play. Our ends are taught to play the Oklahoma 5-4, wide tackle six, and Monster slant. Their charge is varied from a reading-reacting style to a pressure-charging technique. Every defense has a weakness, and if you stay in it long enough you're going to get "picked." If your opponent is going to use different methods to attack your perimeter—why not give your perimeter more than one way to stop them?

One of four basic principles in teaching defense is the elimination of mistakes. In other words, even though we are a multiple defense team, we still stress simplicity. We feel that by teaching our ends three basic techniques, we can play any style defense we wish. We call these three techniques 'anchor,' 'blood,' and 'regular.' These will be explained in more detail later.

In discussing end play, or any defensive position, certain factors are important. *Defense is a) morale, b) position, c) recognition and d) reaction.*

a. *Morale*—Without the desire to get the job done no defense is worthwhile. We stress pride in our ability to be the best. We keep a running chart of tackles and assists readily available in our dressing room. We let our boys know where they stand in the nation on defense each week and we name an outstanding defensive lineman and back for every game. We recognize outstanding plays, such as a tackle for a loss, a batted down pass attempt, or an interception. We have a defensive honor roll which we recognize each year with a plaque, and place a picture in our defensive staff room of the chosen players. This is our way of attaining morale—a most vital asset.

b. *Position* is self-explanatory, but not always easy to get. A split by a lineman, a flanker, or a slot formation will invariably alter the end's position. Constant attention to proper alignment is a must. A good scout report will be an invaluable aid here.

c. *Recognition* is one of the basic differences between playing offense and defense. In the majority of our defenses we cannot perform our responsibilities until our opponents give us keys or clues as to where they are going to attack. We must react to their movement. It takes painstaking study to find these keys, and then time to teach them to the players. This is where size and physical character are sometimes overcome by the small, smart boy. Our players study their opponents; they have outstanding ability to recognize the intentions of the offense. Do not neglect this phase of your coaching. Later in this chapter we will discuss the drills that we use to teach recognition.

d. *Reaction* is the ability to make the defensive play after position and recognition have been employed. Reaction can be taught and it can be constantly improved. We would rather have quickness than size—football is a game of movement. Rather a 5′ 10″, 180 pound end at the point of attack and waiting, than a 6′ 3″, 220 pound end who is almost there. It's amazing every spring how our older boys are so much more advanced in their ability and quickness. It's equally amazing how, after two or three weeks, you can see the vast improvement in our young freshmen. Reaction, quickness, can be taught. We will discuss drills for improving reaction later in this chapter.

End Play

Stance—The Beginning (Figure 155f)

Before we can accomplish any of the preceding we must have a beginning stance. Our ends assume a stance with their feet approximate-

END STANCE

Figure 155 f

ly shoulder-width apart, knees flexed, and arms dangling by their sides. The stagger of their feet varies from toes parallel to a toe-heel stagger, depending on whether the end is using an anchor, blood or a regular technique. This is what we call a fundamental hitting position. The stance is the same for our ends, linebackers and secondary, except for the stagger of the feet. At the beginning of each practice we work on our stance, using the "Quick-quick" drills, which require "breakdown"—assuming the fundamental hitting position.

Variance of the foot stagger depends upon the technique to be employed by the end. If the end is using an "Anchor" technique, his feet are parallel. This is important because of his responsibilities. The end uses this technique to keep the offensive end off the linebacker, or from getting downfield fast. Therefore he needs lateral movement, for which a parallel stance is best.

When our ends use a "Blood" or a "Regular" technique, they stagger their outside foot back. This stagger depends on the physical make-up of the individual player. Here the end jab-steps into the offensive end first. A stagger stance gives him a stronger base by allowing him to drive off the back foot. The initial steps of the "Blood" and "Regular" techniques are the same, with the following exception. In using the "Blood" technique the end takes an opening step with his outside foot and then a cross-over step to gain the wide tackle six position.

Figure 156

In the "Regular" technique (the Oklahoma 5-4), his play is a jab-step and hold position (Figure 156).

Alignment

The alignment of our ends depends first on the defense called, and second, on the formation the offense employs. To simplify the discussion, we will first go over his alignment, assuming the offense is in a "Dead T" formation and the line is normal.

1. *Anchor* (Figure 156a). The anchor end lines up eighteen inches off the ball nose on the offensive end. His eyes are focused on the offensive end and he is in a good hitting position. His feet and shoulders are parallel at all times.

2. *Blood* (Figure 156b). The blood end lines up with his inside foot on the outside foot of the offensive end. He should take all of the ball he can get without being offside. His eyes are focused on the offensive end but he must also see the near back. On the snap he takes a jab step with his up (inside) foot and, using his hands, jabs the offensive ends head into the "out" charge of our defensive tackle. His next step is an opening step with his outside foot, then a cross-over and hop step. This maneuver puts him in a wide-tackle-six end position. This is a position from one-and-a-half to two yards from the offensive end.

Figure 156

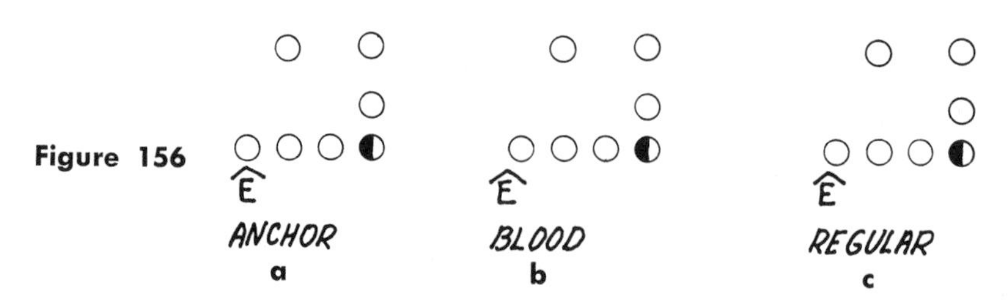

Remember, he should keep his shoulders parallel to the line of scrimmage and stay in a good hitting position at all times.

3. *Regular* (Figure 156c). A "regular" position is an alignment of the inside eye on the outside eye of the offensive end. This may seem like hair-splitting, but by being this specific, we think we can impress upon our ends their responsibilities in using the various techniques. Again, the defensive end should take all the ball he can get and stay in a good hitting position, with shoulders parallel to ball.

Because we see very little of the Dead T Formation today, we will describe how to play the slot, close flanker, wide flanker and split end using the three basic techniques.

4. *Anchor End versus a Close Flanker* (Figure 157a). As soon as the anchor end is attacked by a close flanker (wingback) he assumes a three-point stance instead of the normal two point. He should cheat out to where he lines up his inside eye to the outside eye of the offensive end.

5. *Anchor End versus a Slot Formation* (Figures 157b, c). Here again the anchor end is attacked by an offensive man wider than he—so

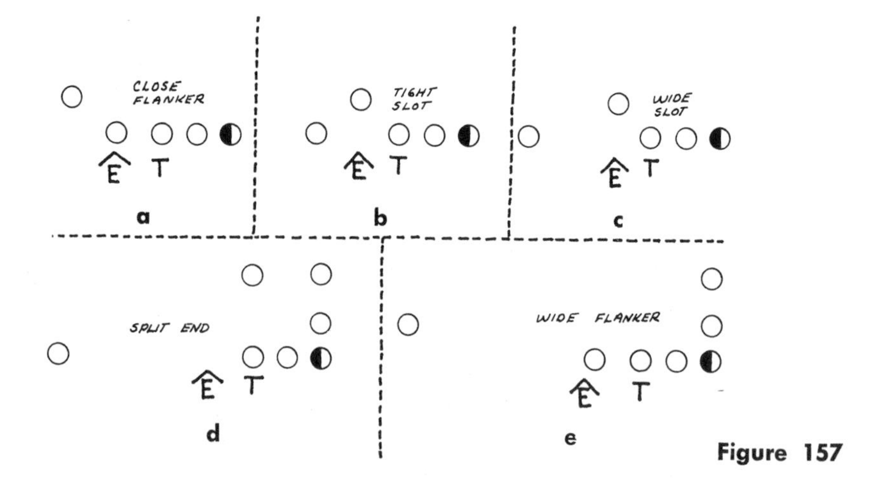

Figure 157

he again assumes a three-point stance with the inside foot back, providing this is a normal split. If the slot back is wider than normal, the anchor end will come back to the position where a normal offensive end would play.

6. *Anchor End versus Split End* (Figures 157d, 158a). The anchor end on the split end side should line up on the split end up to three yards. If the split is greater than this, he should come back and line up in a position where a normal end would be (Figure 158b).

7. *Anchor End versus a Wide Flanker* (Figure 157c). Here the end should line up with his inside eye on the outside eye of the offensive end and about eighteen inches off the ball.

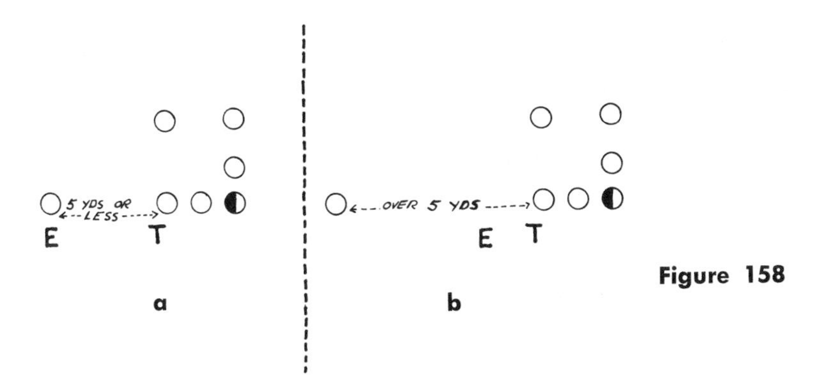

Figure 158

8. *Blood End versus a Close Flanker* (Figure 159a). We do not like to have our blood end in this position but, because our slant defense requires us to slant to and away from monster, there will be times when this situation will arise. The blood end when attacked by a close flanker will cheat out and split the difference between the end and the wingback on the snap. The blood end will step a lateral step with his outside foot and then an "up" step with his inside foot, playing through the outside shoulder of the wingback.

9. *Blood End versus a Slot* (Figures 159b, c). The blood end will line up on the outside shoulder of the offensive end, taking as much of the ball as he can get. If the slot is a wide one, and the slot back is wider than normal, the blood end will play head up on him.

10. *Blood End versus a Split End* (Figure 159d). This situation is more common for the blood end. The blood end respects the split end in the same manner as a flanker—playing him nose up until he has split

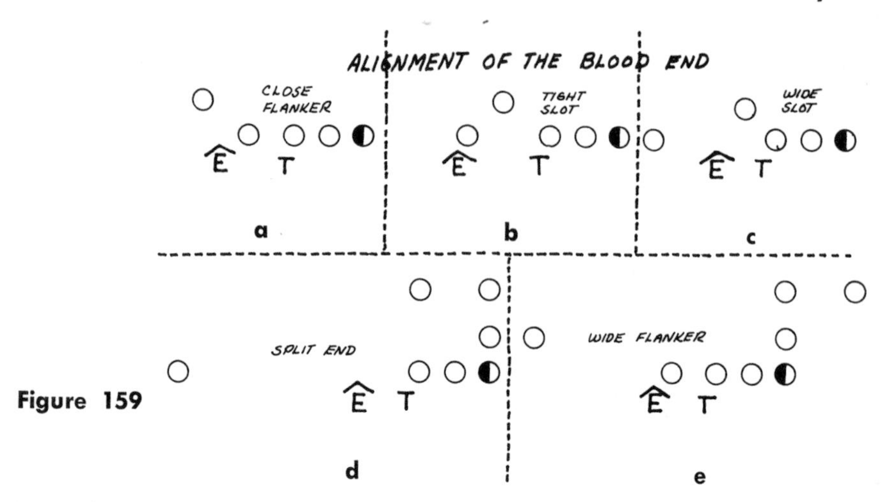

Figure 159

farther than five yards. If the offensive end splits more than five yards, he should come back and play normal.

On occasion we will double-cover a split end or play in the walk-off position. However, this is not normal coverage and depends on a specific game plan.

11. *Blood End versus a Wide Flanker* (Figure 159e). Most of the time our monster plays to the other outside. But on occasion we will change off to keep from giving the offense a pattern.

When the blood end has a flanker back his side wider than a normal wingback (one yard wide and one yard deep) he will respect him up to five yards. This means that he will play nose on the flanker, to take the "crack-back block" away. We can do this because our "loop tackle" is slanting out.

12. *Regular End versus a Close Flanker* (Figure 160a). The regular end uses the same alignment as a blood end.

13. *Regular End versus a Tight Slot* (Figure 160b). The regular ends alignment versus a tight slot is on the inside shoulder of the offensive end. Since we are attacked by a man who has an outside position on us, we use a three point stance.

14. *Regular End versus a Wide Slot* (Figure 160c). When a regular end has a wide slot his side, he will line up with his inside eye on the outside eye of the slot back.

15. *Regular End versus a Split End* (Figure 160d). We will respect a split end up to five yards. If the split is greater than five yards, the regular end will come back in and use his normal play. On occasion

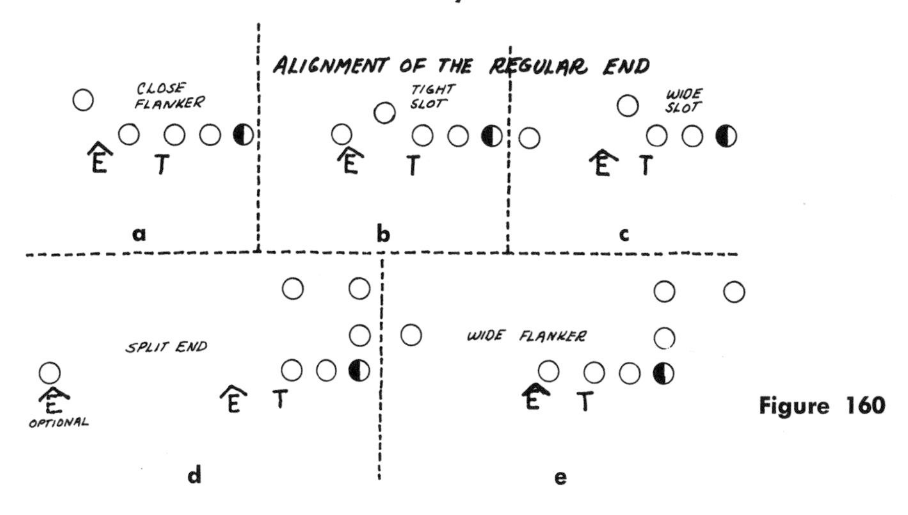

Figure 160

we double-cover the split end, or play in the walked-off position (Figure 160).

16. *Regular End versus a Wide Flanker* (Figure 160c). The regular end respects a wide flanker up to three yards, using two-point stance and dividing the difference.

These are our basic rules for alignment against the most common formations. We do not always play these formations exactly this way. Game plans and team strength will alter some of these rules. However, if our players have a basic rule to follow when they come up against a formation that we have not prepared for we feel that they will be able to play a sound defense (until we can find a better way to play it).

Play When Ball Is Snapped

1. *Anchor End versus a "Dead T."* When the anchor end is not attacked by a close flanker he takes a two-point stance eighteen inches off the ball, in a nose up position. His center of concentration is on the offensive end. On the snap, he uses a forearm flipper and steps with the inside foot, keeping the offensive end on the line of scrimmage. He should not be in a hurry to release the offensive end. He is responsible for keeping the end off the linebacker and from getting deep fast. If the flow is his way, and it's a running play, he is responsible for the off-tackle hole. He should not cross the line of scrimmage after he has held the end up, or he will be exposed for a trap block. If the play goes outside of him, he should back up the Monster.

If the flow is his way and it's a pass, he anchors on the offensive end and keeps him from getting deep fast. After doing this, he shuffles down the line and backs up Monster. The anchor end should attempt to get into a position between the passer and the receiver in the flat.

If the play is a straight drop back pass, he "anchors" the end, then rushes the passer. When the flow is away from him and the play is a run or pass, he must still hold up the offensive end. After he has done this, he closes down toward center one step, then chases as deep as the ball. The anchor end must be responsible for all reverses and counter plays. The most common fault for anchor ends is not holding up the

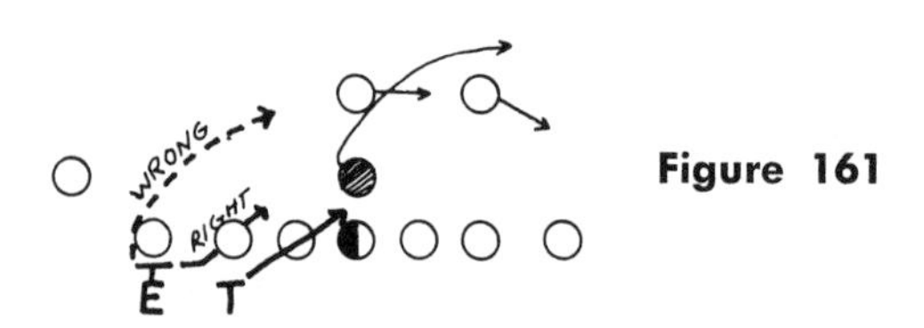

Figure 161

offensive end long enough. They must not be in a hurry. The second most common mistake is that the anchor doesn't "spy" long enough and gets in a hurry to get up field. When this happens, a big hole opens between the anchor end and the slanting tackle (Figure 161).

When flow is away the anchor end must close down.

2. *Anchor End versus a Close Flanker.* Following the rule for flankers, the end assumes a three-point stance with his inside foot back. He lines up with his inside eye on the outside eye of the offensive end. On the snap he steps with his inside foot, using a flipper on the offensive end. The anchor end must have the wingback and offensive end in his vision. As the anchor end steps he must be aware of the flanker back's intentions. If the flanker doubles down on him, his next step is with his outside foot driving his shoulder under the flanker's block. He should create a stalemate, not be driven off the line, and cut off the linebacker and the pursuit.

To recap the play: the anchor end must see both the end and the flanker. He uses a three-point stance because an offensive man has a flank position on him. On the snap he steps with the inside foot using a flipper on the offensive end. If the flanker blocks down, he steps with the outside foot, driving the shoulder under the block. If the flanker does not block down, then the anchor end's play is the same as for the "Dead T" formation. He simply keys flow.

3. *Anchor End versus a Tight Slot.* Using a three-point stance the anchor end lines up "nose on" the slot back. On the snap, step with inside foot, driving low for penetration. If the end blocks down, drop your outside shoulder and get under the end's block. Do not be caved in, leaving a large hole between you and Monster. If the end and slot-back do not double-team you, then look to the inside for a trap. Do not allow the slot back to get downfield fast. If the slot back tries to block on linebacker, close down with him.

When the flow goes away from you play the same as aganist the "Dead T."

4. *Blood End versus a Close Flanker.* The blood end cheats out and divide the distance between the flanker and offensive end. He uses a two-point stance. On the snap he takes a lateral step with his outside foot, then an "up" step with his inside foot, playing through the outside shoulder of the flanker back. While taking these steps he is conscious of the action of the next nearback and flow of the ball. If the flow is his way, and it's a running play, the blood end is responsible for the outside. If it is an option, the end is responsible for the quarterback. He should not come up field perpendicular to the line of scrimmage unless the quarterback takes the ball deep. He must limit the off-tackle hole. If the play is the Texas Power sweep, he should force the ball carrier outside so the squirm halfback and the safety can make the tackle. If the offensive end attempts to turn him out, he should fall back over his inside shoulder, giving ground, so that he can help on lead or drive plays.

If the flow is his way and it's a pass, he gets up-field fast and limits the quarterback's throwing area. By keying the nearback the blood end can get a tip on the type pass to be thrown.

When the flow goes away, he checks for bootleg and reverses, then falls off the inside shoulder and retreats through safety's position. The blood end is responsible for the flat on straight drop back passes. If the flow is away, and it's a throwback type pass, the blood end covers the flat, or any swing route by a back to his side.

5. *Blood End versus a Tight Slot.* The blood end lines up on the outside shoulder of the offensive end. On the snap he jab steps into the end and comes across the line of scrimmage approximately a yard and a half at a 45 degree angle. If the slotback and end double down on the loop tackle, the end sets for the block of the near-back. He should be in a good hitting position with his shoulders parallel. By doing this

he will be able to close the hole to his inside, forcing the ball carrier outside (Figure 162).

The blood end must contain any action or sprint-pass to his side from this formation. When the end and slot back release, the angle of the near back and the quarterback's actions will tip off "pass." The blood end should put on a quick contain. If the pass action is straight back, the blood end again covers the flat. All other situations for the blood end are identical to his play against a close flanker.

A point to remember: a spread by an offensive man forces the

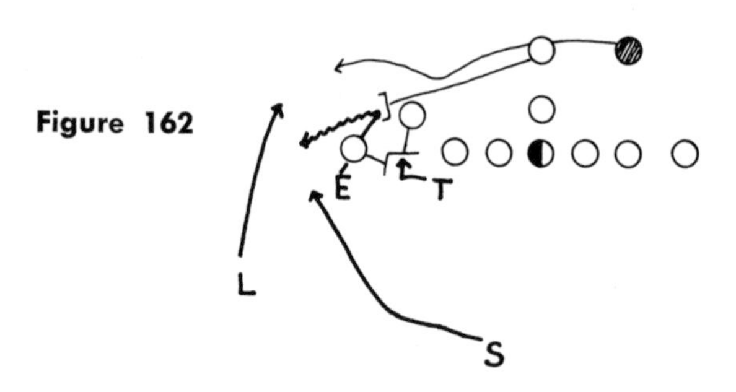

Figure 162

blood end to line up wider than normal, and eliminates the necessity of his shuffle to the wide end position. Refer back to the alignment portion if this is not clear.

6. *Blood End versus a Split End.* Respect a split end up to five yards. If the split is greater, come back into normal position. On the snap, key the near back and the ball. Take your shuffle steps to the

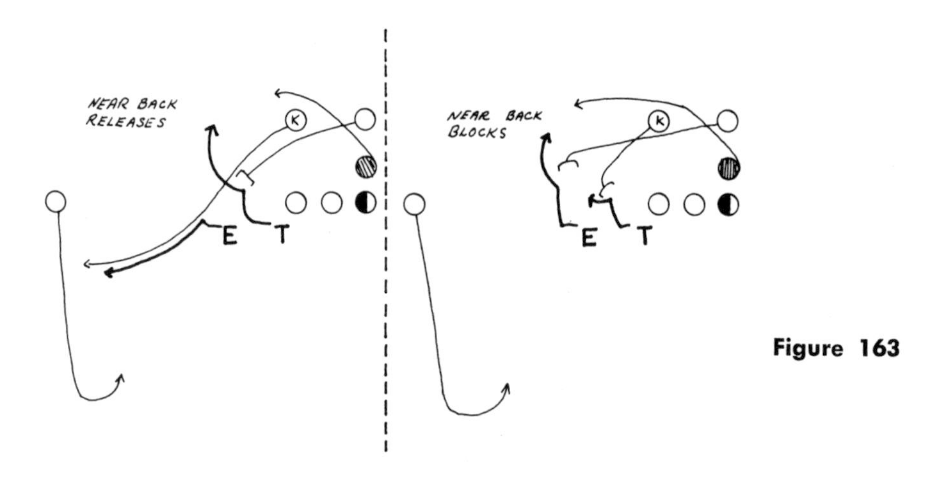

Figure 163

wide tackle six position when ball is snapped. If the near back blocks on the line of scrimmage, come across to limit off tackle hole or contain run, and pass. If the near back releases into the flat, drop off and cover the flat zone. We are able to do this because the loop tackle will be able to contain the passer (Figure 163).

We have two stunts or change ups to keep the offensive from picking on us. The first is a "TX" stunt which we use to put on quick pressure, and the second is the "Combo Stunt" we use to help on the *Lead* or *Drive* plays (Figure 164).

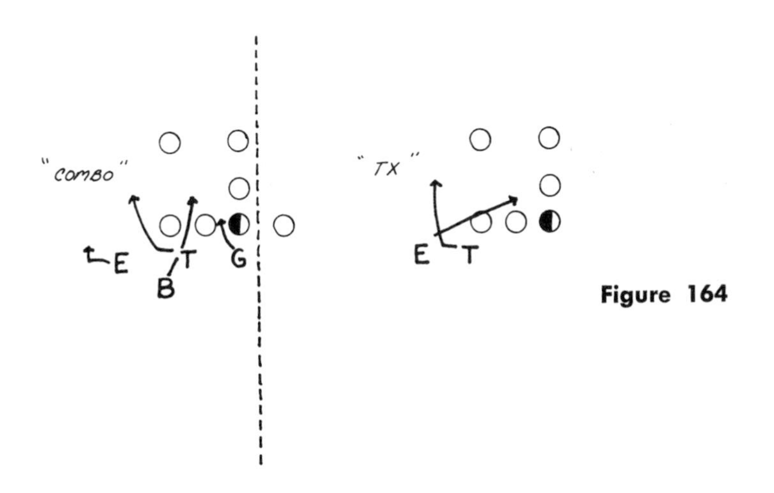

Figure 164

These stunts are vital to the soundness of this defense. Anytime our blood end is committed to a rush, he must communicate to the safety man and L.B. This is important because the safety man must now cover the remaining back, man-for-man. Also, the linebacker must not let the remaining back hit the seam between the safety and the defensive halfback (Figure 165).

> NOTE: *It should be pointed out that we have purposely not mentioned any particular defensive play, such as 54, Slant or Slant executed. As mentioned earlier, we teach techniques first and then our players learn what techniques to use on the various defenses. The ANCHOR and BLOOD techniques are used in the Slant and Slant Executed. The regular technique is used in the 54 Regular, 54 Eagle, 61 Rover.*

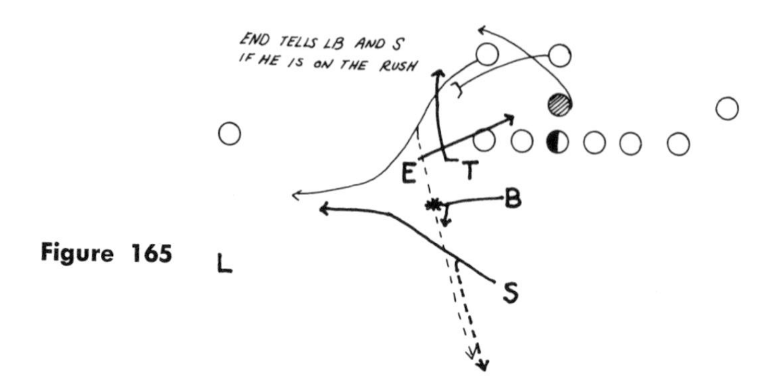

Figure 165

There is one other technique we teach our defensive ends when we call a "Fire." As previously mentioned we divide our defenses into "Press" and "Read" categories. Most of the discussion on defensive end play has centered around "Reading" style play. But when there is a need to put pressure on the offensive (in an attempt to make up for yardage yielded or to gain an advantage), we will add the word "Fire" to our defensive calls. This simply means we are bringing our ends tough and firing one or both linebackers.

We cannot fire an Anchor end but we can fire a Blood or Regular end. When a Regular or Blood end hears the word fire he simply widens his alignment slightly and fires for a position a yard and a half deep and a yard outside of the remaining halfback's shoulder. From this position he plays his regular keys and responsibilities. If there is no remaining halfback, then he fires to the point where he would if there was a remaining halfback.

7. *Regular End versus a Close Flanker.* The regular end will line up in a three-point stance dividing the distance between the end and flanker. On the snap he will step to the flanker, then back to the end. His first step will be with his outside foot, using a flipper on the flanker, then a step with his inside foot into the end. If the flanker and end do not double-team him, he gains collection, keys the near back and ball. In using the regular technique here the regular end should strive to stay in a low hitting position keeping his shoulders parallel to ball at all times. If the flow is his way and it's an option, he takes the quarterback. If the end doubles down on the tackle he sets for near back's block and limits the off-tackle hole. If the offensive end tries to turn him out, he fights pressure to his inside. If the flow is away, he is responsible for the containment of all passes.

The important point to remember in playing the regular technique is whether the defense called is a reading type (54 Regular) or a pressing type (61 Rover). If it's a reading style, his play is on the line of scrimmage, never getting depth until he has read the offensive play. If the defense is a pressing style he applies his keys.

8. *Regular End versus a Tight Slot.* The regular end lines up on the inside shoulder of the offensive end in a three-point stance. On the snap he steps with his outside foot into the end, then with an inside step into the slot back. If they are attempting to double team him, he fights for penetration and tries not to be caved in to the inside. If both release, his play is the same as that of a regular end against a "Dead T" or close flanker when they release. He must still check for bootlegs, reverses and counter plays before he starts his chase route.

Drills for Defensive Ends

Most of the drills have been covered in earlier chapters but there are two that we use especially for ends.

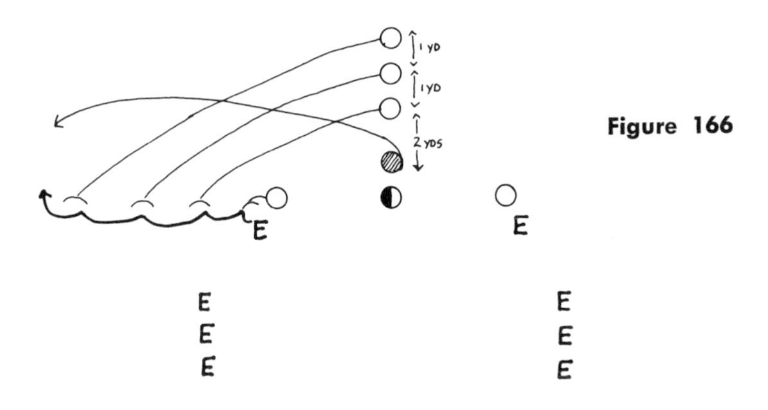

Figure 166

Ward-off Drill (Figure 166). In using this drill it is important to time the blockers until they become accustomed to its use.

Run the Bag Drill (Figure 167). This is one of our best drills for ends. Start this drill at half speed until the players gain confidence.

Linebacker Play

Our linebackers play many positions. They play the "Slant," which involves the "Scrape-off" and the "Shuffle" linebacker positions, the

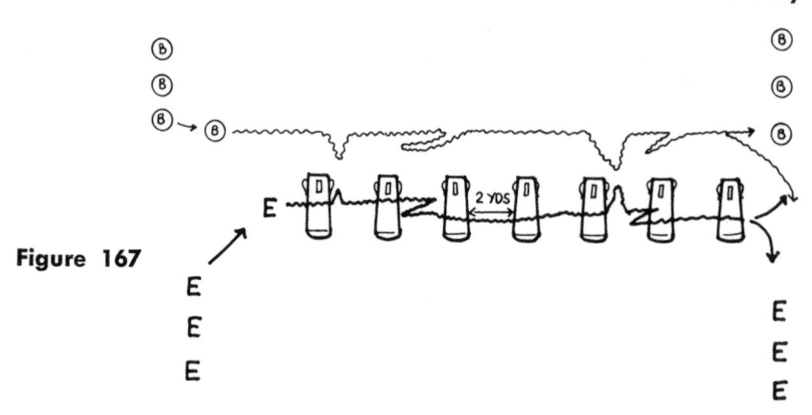

Figure 167

Slant Executed, 54 Regular, 54 Eagle, 61 Rover, 65 Goal line and many variations of these. Therefore we need a reliable and "heady" performer at this position.

Stance (Figure 167a)

The linebacker's stance is identical to the end's. The feet are shoulder width apart, with knees flexed, back straight, head up, arms relaxed and dangling by the sides, and weight on the balls of the feet. Here again the description is of a good "hitting" position. The stagger

LINEBACKER STANCE

Figure 167 a

of the feet will vary from parallel to toe-and-heel. We use the parallel stance in all defenses except the "54 Eagle." Here the linebacker should use a jab step into the end, so he uses the stagger. From this position he can deliver a more explosive blow.

Alignment and Play on Snap

Scrape-off Linebacker. The scrape-off linebacker lines up in a good hitting position nose up on the offensive guard approximately two yards deep, with his feet parallel. Our keys vary but for the most part the scrape-off linebacker will key the ball. On the snap, if the flow is his way and it's a running play he is responsible for the area vacated by

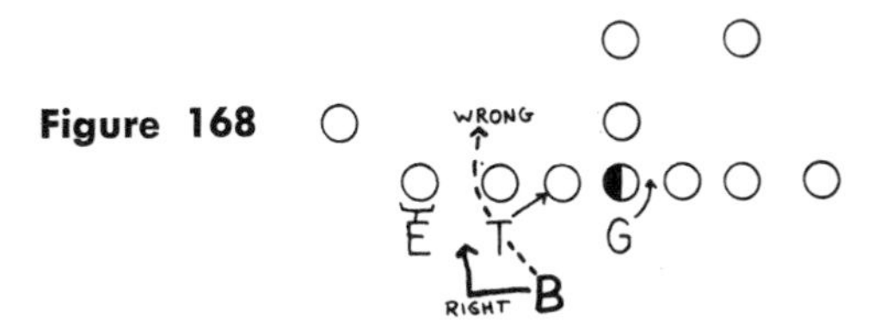

Figure 168

the slanting tackle. The important point here is to make sure the scrape-off linebacker squares off and does not angle to his responsibility (Figure 168).

If the play is hitting wider than the scrape-off linebacker's responsibility, and he can go through to make tackle, he does. If it is too congested, and he cannot get through, then he should shuffle down the line keeping leverage on the ball.

Anytime the ball stays behind the center the scrape-off linebacker should take a step to his outside with his outside foot, keeping the inside foot planted. This prevents committing too fast on counter plays. If the flow is away from the scrape-off linebacker, he cautiously pursues down the line keeping leverage on the ball. He should keep his shoulders parallel to the line and gain depth as the play gets wider.

If the flow is his way and it's a pass, the scrape-off linebacker should start the same step to his scrape-off position then, as he reads the pass, start back to his hook area. If the quarterback pulls up, he pulls up and gets to a depth of ten to twelve yards. If the quarterback sprints on out he goes with him, "bracketing" the ball.

If the flow is away, and it's a pass, the scrape-off linebacker starts for his throw back zone. When the quarterback pulls up he should pull up and go ten to twelve yards in depth. As he is doing this the scrape-off linebacker should be looking for the end or back coming into his zone. He should never allow a receiver to cross in front of him. If the quarterback sprints wider, he should bracket the ball as he sprints to the off-side hook.

On occasion we "fire" the scrape-off linebacker. When we do this he keys the ball the same way. If the flow is his way he fires over the offensive tackle's outside shoulder. If the flow is away he plays the same as for "Slant" regular.

Some important points to remember in coaching the scrape-off linebacker:

1. Make sure he squares off and does not angle to his responsibilities.
2. He should step up into the hole with shoulders square and in a good hitting position.
3. If flow is away he should not take a false step to his outside. He should only do this when ball is delayed behind the center —thus indicating a counter play.
4. When getting back to his hook zone his first step is the outside, then a cross-over step turning toward the hook zone, keeping his head and eyes on passer. If the quarterback pulls up, the scrape-off man should get depth and square up so he can break on the ball.

Shuffle Linebacker. The shuffle linebacker lines up on the outside shoulder of the offensive guard in good hitting position with his feet parallel on the heels of the middle guard. This is approximately a yard and a half off the ball. On the snap, he keys the remaining halfback to his side and the flow. He is responsible for the area from outside the offensive guard to the outside of the offensive tackle. If the remaining halfback drives straight ahead, the linebacker should step up into the hole to meet a drive play. If the remaining halfback indicates

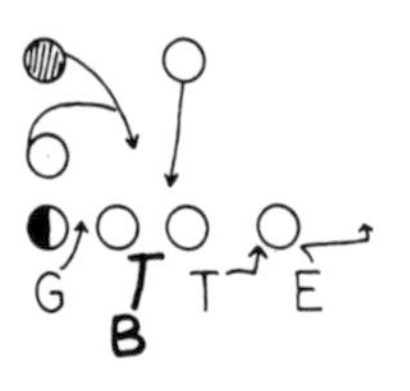

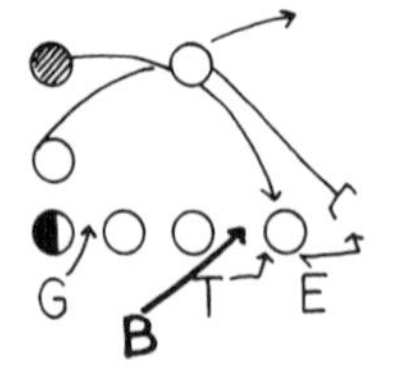

Figure 169

an off-tackle play, the shuffle linebacker should angle to the play through the offensive tackle (Figure 169).

The shuffle linebacker should take a lateral step to his outside any time the ball lingers behind the center. We consider this a tip-off for counter and reverse plays.

Pass responsibilities for the shuffle linebacker are the same as those for the scrape-off linebacker. The major difference is in their footwork. The shuffle linebacker is not required to take a lateral step first. He can start back to his hook zone sooner. Other than this, his play is the same (Figure 170).

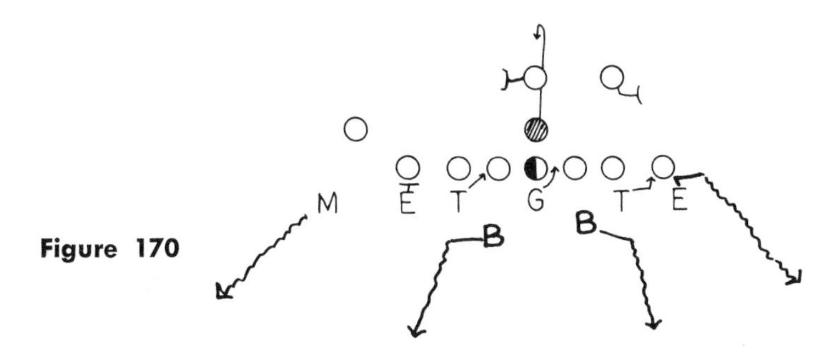

Figure 170

Because of motion and shifts we are forced to change our "Slants" after the initial call has been made. It is important that the signal caller make these changes fast and that everyone hear him. The linebackers, as well as the defensive ends, must then make their alignment adjustment quickly. This should be practiced constantly.

Regular Linebacker

We refer to this style of linebacking play when we are in a true 54 Oklahoma defense. The stances and the olignment are the same. The only difference lies in our keys. Both linebackers key the ball, because we are stronger on the lead (drive) plays, since our tackle is not looping out. We do not change our alignment because this would be a tip-off to our intentions. Any time a team uses the slant as its basic defense, it must be able to slant both ways as well as play straight up. This gives the defense an edge on the offense's blocking patterns.

Pass responsibilities for a regular linebacker are identical with those of a shuffle linebacker. His stance and footwork are the same.

Eagle Linebacker

In our scheme of defenses this is our best pass defense. Not only are we able to defend better, we also get a better pass rush.

The stance for the Eagle position is basically the same as for the others. The only difference is the stagger of the feet. We line up with our outside foot on the inside foot of the offensive end, taking all the ball we can get. On the snap, we jab step into the end using a flipper, watching the offensive tackle to our inside. If the flow is our way, and it's a run, we are primarily responsible for the off-tackle hole. If the end does not block down on the Eagle linebacker, then he is conscious of the offensive tackle's block. If the tackle blocks down, the linebacker sets for a trap or a block by the near back. If the end turns out on our defensive end then we are ready for a turn-out block by the offensive tackle. The important point the Eagle linebacker must remember is, do not come across the line of scrimmage. His play should be on the line and his shoulders should always be parallel to the line of scrimmage.

When the flow goes away and it's a run play, the eagle linebacker should step back with his inside foot gaining a little depth, then take his correct pursuit angle.

This is a better pass defense because the linebacker is out on the end and directly in front of his hook zone. Thus he is able to get back on this zone quicker. Secondly, because he is on the end, he can feel the end releasing and can keep him to his outside, thereby knowing where he is at all time (Figure 171).

Other than his initial alignment the pass responsibilities are the same. However, on some occasions we will use the eagle alignment when we want the linebacker to cover a remaining halfback man-for-man.

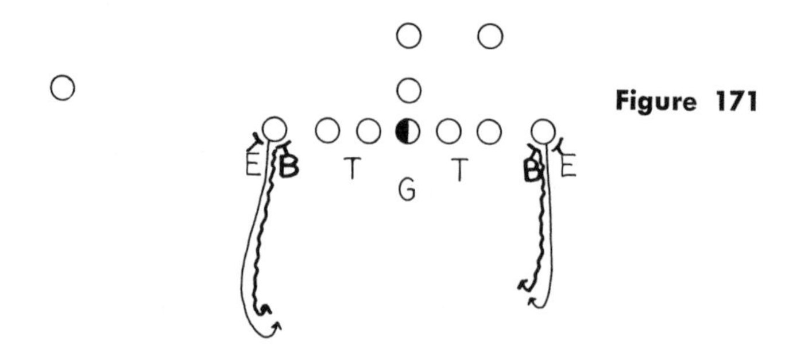

Figure 171

In early chapters we explained that adding the word "Fire" commits our linebackers on the rush. This applies to all our defenses, especially the 54 Eagle alignment. Over the years this has been our most consistent pass rush. When "Eagle Fire" is called the linebacker and end should line up just as for the "Eagle Regular." On the snap the linebacker will fire over the outside shoulder of the offensive tackle. It is important to remind him to stay in his rushing lanes to prevent a hole from developing between him and his tackle. Because we don't want our opponent to pick this rush up we have a variation called "Razor". This is merely a cross between the end and the linebacker—they simply exchange responsibilities (Figure 172).

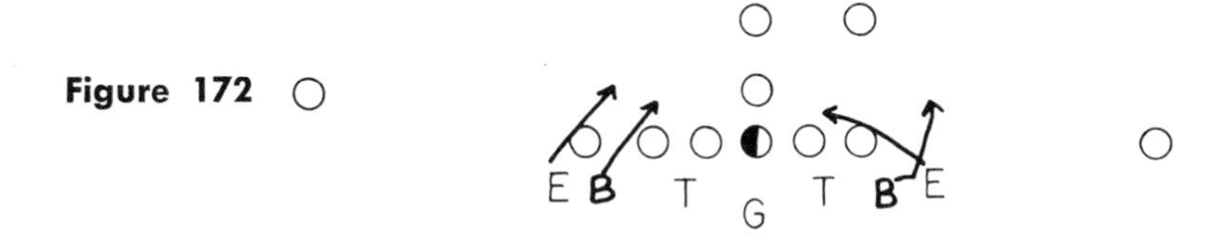

Figure 172

Any time we get exaggerated splits by the offensive line we give our linebackers the right to fire on their own. This is true not only for the eagle linebacker but the scrape-off, shuffle and regular linebackers as well.

Middle Linebacker

We refer to this style play when we are in our 61 or 65 Goal line defenses. The stance is the same, with feet parallel and in good hitting position. The alignment is head up on the offensive center and two yards deep on normal down and distance. As this is also our short yardage defense, the depth will vary. The basic key is the offensive fullback. The middle linebacker has no definite run responsibilities; rather he is the clean up man. He should make tackles from end-to-end, since no offensive blocker can get a clean shot at him. We do insist that he keep his shoulders parallel to the line of scrimmage and shuffle down the line, instead of turning his back and running. The weakness of this defense is counter plays. The middle linebacker has a better chance to get back if he keeps leverage on the ball and has a parallel position.

Since we are usually in man-for-man pass coverage in this defense, the middle linebacker goes into the hook zone, to the side of the flow.

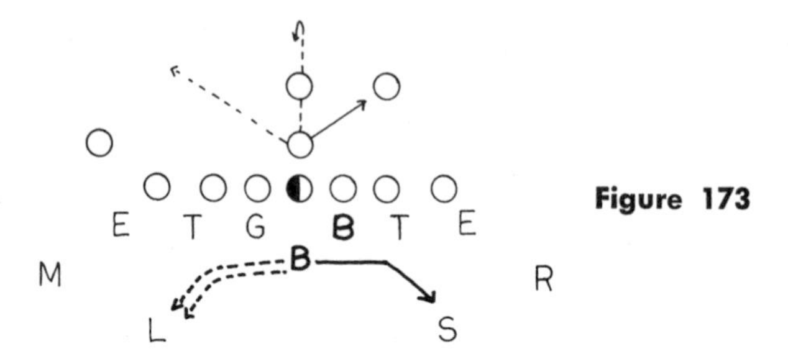

Figure 173

If the pass is a straight drop-back type, he will normally go to the first back outside (Figure 173).

The 61 Regular defense is only a part of our 61 category which also includes the "Rover" series (Chapter 4).

13

Secondary Play

Stance (Figure 173a)

Head—The head should be erect with your eyes on your key.

Shoulders—The shoulders are parallel to the line of scrimmage; do not turn inside or outside.

Back—The back is straight with the buttocks løw to allow the weight to be on the balls of your feet.

Arms—The arms are free and hanging to the sides. The hands are never on the hips or knees.

SECONDARY STANCE

Figure 173 a

Legs—The knees are flexed so you can react as quickly as possible in any direction.

Feet—The feet are about the width of the shoulders. The outside foot is staggered to form a brace for a quick start. The toes are pointed straight ahead and the weight is evenly distributed on the balls of the feet. The stance for all backs, based on a man-for-man technique, is the same.

Drills

At Florida, we use only the drills that simulate game situations. We feel that it is a waste of time to use drills just to keep our players busy. We have eight secondary drills that we use each practice session. Repetition is of prime importance, since we try to form good habits and instant responses executed automatically.

1. *Back Pedal.* The success of our secondary depends on how well the defensive backs execute this maneuver. They must head up the receiver until he declares his pattern. In order to head up a receiver, the defensive back must be able to back

BACKWARD RUN

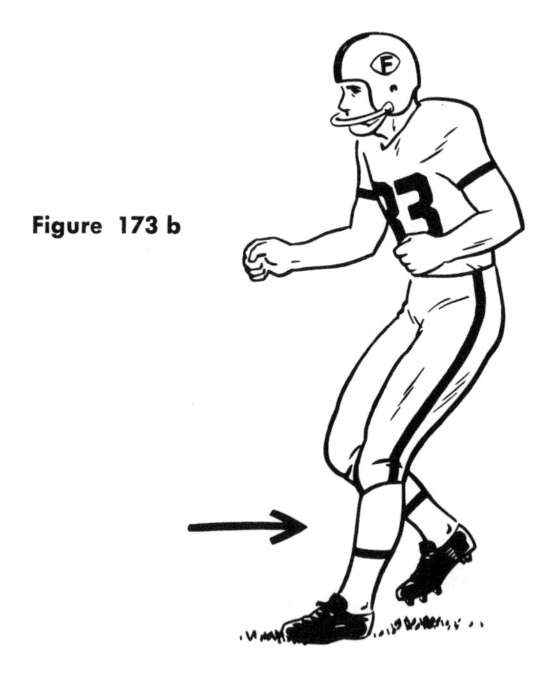

Figure 173 b

pedal well enough to keep the receiver a distance of three yards from him until he makes his break (Figure 173b).

From the basic stance, with the coach in front, the back is given the signal to back up.

Head—The same position as in the stance.

Shoulders—The same position as in the stance.

Arms—The same position as in the stance.

Knees—The knees remain flexed while back pedaling. Emphasis is on keeping the weight over the knees and on the balls of the feet.

Feet—The feet remain at shoulders width. Pick the feet up only as much as is necessary to allow the cleats to pass over the grass.

The coach signals back-pedal. When he indicates right, the defensive back keeps his hips parallel to the line of scrimmage and gains as much depth as he can until the coach signals left. He should never turn toward the sideline because the receiver can turn opposite him. Also, by turning it takes more time to adjust in the opposite direction.

2. *Down the Line.* This drill serves two main purposes that are important in secondary play. It teaches quickness in direction change, and at the same time strengthens the ankles of our players. Do this drill in teams of four. The four backs are on a line; the coach is where they can see him give the direction change. The orders for the players to move right or left should be as quick as possible. Emphasize their change as soon as the coach gives the slightest indication. Do not pick the feet up any higher than necessary to get the cleats above the grass. The hips should remain parallel to the line at all times. Never cross the feet, but go to the next step, plant, and push in the direction of change. Do not allow the feet to get close together. Maintain a good base.
3. *Tip Drill* (Figure 174). This probably is one of the oldest and most useful secondary drills. It teaches the secondary to react to the unexpected and field the ball that has been deflected. If we expect our players to make interceptions, they should have time to practice making the interception.

   Line the players up, with the front man about six yards in front of the next man in line. The coach is in a position to throw the ball so the front man can tip the ball. The player

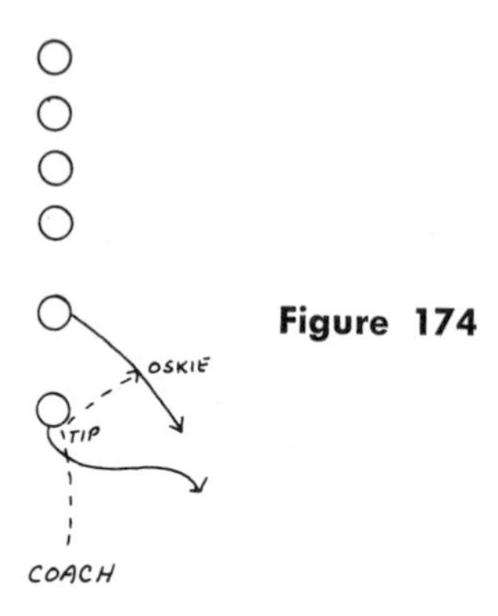

Figure 174

behind makes the interception at its highest peak and yells out "Oskie," our code word for the interception. The front man turns and blocks after he has tipped and made as many interceptions as time will permit. This drill can be used with two players running laterally. The tip and interception is made in the same fashion.

4. *Break on the Ball* (Figure 175). Let me repeat as coaches we expect our players to make the "Oskie," but we don't throw enough balls to them to get them the practice necessary to develop the good hands. This drill is designed to teach our players to break on the ball, and catch it on the move. The players are lined up about twenty-five yards from the coach. They run straight ahead on the signal as fast as possible, under control. To begin, the coach throws the ball at the players coming forward. After they have fielded a number of passes straight ahead, he simulates the quarterback's moves by turning

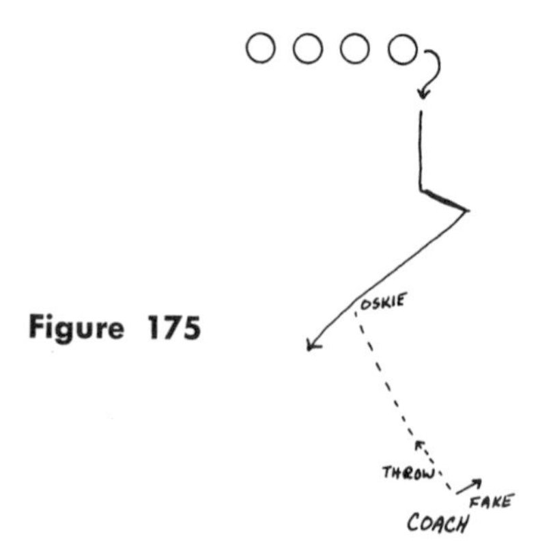

Figure 175

right or left. As soon as a player reads the slightest move by the coach, he breaks in that direction. The coach throws the ball at various angles to teach the player to react and catch the ball. The code word "OSKIE" should be used when the interception is made.

5. *One-on-One* (Figure 176). This drill is very difficult for the players, but it is very useful. We use this drill to teach our players to cover man-for-man. The one-on-one situation is the most critical position a defensive back can be in. At Florida, we explain these factors to our players. First, we try to get them to understand the overall defense. If we are man-for-man we have maximum rush to help them. Secondly, the pattern

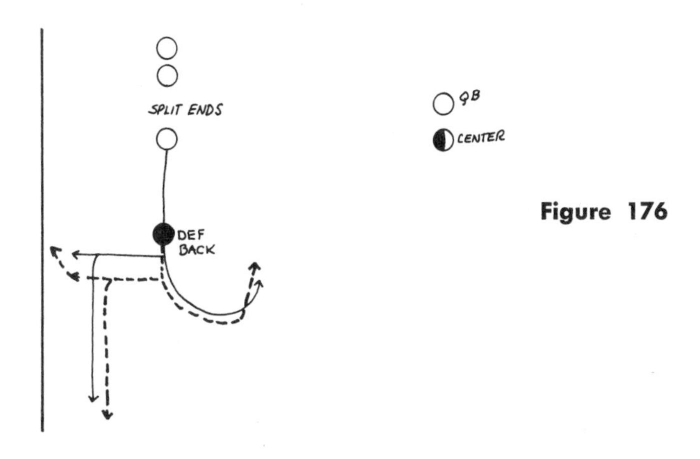

Figure 176

probably will not be toward them because of field position, or possibly a pass is not even called. Thirdly, there is the element of offensive error. The pass may be off-target or the pattern is poorly run. Fourthly, and most important, we tell our players that we are giving them the best fundamentals possible to cover the receivers.

To run this drill, get two or three split ends and a quarterback. Align the defensive back on the receiver. Use hand signals to call the cuts by the end. One finger is the curl, two is the sideline, three is sideline and up, and four is the post. Use a whistle so the quarterback won't hold the ball too long. Emphasize covering as closely as possible. Explain that in the game the rush and tempo will help the defender.

6. *Tackling*. A good tackling secondary is conducive to having a great defense. The tackle is the backbone of defensive football. Despite a reception by the offense, or a running play, the secondary is responsible to make tackles. At Florida, we work every day on form tackling, and hit live just enough to remain sharp (Figure 176a).

THE TACKLE

Figure 176 a

From the Basic Stance: Head—The head is cocked with the eyes on the offensive player's jersey number. The tackler's forehead should land on the ball carrier's numbers, and the top of his headgear should strike the ball carrier under the chin.

Shoulders—The shoulders are always level.

Back—The back should be as straight as possible to afford maximum power.

Arms—The hands and arms should be in a position to grasp and control the ball carrier.

Knees—The knees are always flexed for striking power and

ready to react with whatever movement is necessary to contain the ball carrier.

Feet—The weight should be on the balls of the feet. The feet should be about the width of the shoulders. When contact is made, the feet should move with short controlled steps to enable you to knock the ball carrier back. Also, if the feet are not moving you will slide off the target.

7. *Direction Drill*. This drill serves three important fundamentals for us. It teaches our players recognition of the various offensive formations, how to align our defense prior to the snap, and the proper position or rotation after the snap of the football. These basics are very important to us because our Monster figures in our coverages. He must be alert to proper alignment and rotation for our perimeter to be successful. We align the four defensive backs up on defense. We have a set of offensive ends and backs. The coach serves as the quarterback. You should form a huddle each time so the defense can work on recognizing the various formations.

   The coach should call the plays that will give the secondary practice in covering in all directions. Remember, the direction of the quarterback determines the rotation of "Blue" coverage. We use motions and shifting in this drill to make sure our backs are accustomed to making all adjustments. The coach should use a whistle. Blow the whistle and require the backs to stop where they are so you can check their position and rotation. Use play passes so they can see how the quarterback's initial step can mislead them. Emphasize that "Blue" rotation is determined by where the quarterback ends up.

8. *Perimeter*. This drill is the final phase of our group period. In this period our ends, linebackers, and defensive backs come together to form the "Perimeter." In this period we work on the running game as well as pass defense. This phase of our practice is where we put to use our basic fundamentals, and work on play recognition and execution. The "Perimeter" works against our "B" team and freshmen during the fall. In the spring we also work against the varsity. This is possible because of two platoon football.

   In our "Perimeter" two coaches work this phase. We emphasize recognition, getting set as soon as possible, and executing our defensive calls in detail. Above all, we, the players must practice aggressively. We practice to form habits. Insisting upon details, form the good habits necessary to good morale and sound defensive football. We spend 45 minutes per day on the "Perimeter." During the season, we work against what our next week's opponent does best. Scouting and films determine the things we have to stop. These things are emphasized during this drill.

Part IV

Organization

14

The Winning Edge

This chapter gives some of the extras that can spell victory instead of defeat—doing some of the same things other coaches do, but doing them better.

You can coach all the fundamentals required to field a respectable football team, but still lack the necessary morale and pride that breeds success. I hope the discussion of two of these extras on defense will inspire you to find others, and recognize the importance of inspiring as well as instructing.

Training the Defensive Quarterback

This does not seem like an important area of coaching. It is certainly easy to overlook, and so miss its importance in winning football games. It cannot be accomplished quickly, but can only be taught gradually, through repetition and experience. It is just as important to call the right defense in the right tactical situation as it is for your offensive quarterback to call the right offensive play. The defensive signal caller must be aware of this, and take pride in his responsibility. To make it easier, both your team and coaching staff must realize the importance of this. Work hard to develop the best possible defensive quarterbacking.

Selection of Personnel

This in itself is an important decision to make. The signal caller can play one of three or four positions, depending upon your basic defensive alignment, but he should certainly be somewhere close to the center of the defense. He should be where he can see the offensive alignments and variations, so he can check and adjust defenses. He should be able to make both sides of the line hear his calls. Usually, one of the linebackers is the logical man to call defenses. Start training your defensive quarterbacks from the time they are freshmen in calling your defenses with your theory and defensive thinking. The following is the information we give them at their first defensive meeting. This sums up most of our defensive theory, built around our defensive quarterback.

DEFENSIVE QUARTERBACK'S OVERALL ORGANIZATION

Purpose of Meetings:

1. To teach you to be a better signal caller.
2. To teach you the strength and weakness of every defense and defensive stunt.
3. To be in proper defense at right time.

Ways we intend to accomplish above:

1. Lecture
2. Discussion
3. Practical application
4. Studying movies

HINTS ON BECOMING A GREAT DEFENSIVE SIGNAL CALLER

1. Be a leader (Must take charge).
2. Know assignments (of everyone).
3. Check yard markers for down and distance and yard line on every play.
4. Anticipate different sets (be prepared to check defense).
5. Know the capabilities of individual teammates.
6. Know the strength and weakness of opponents.
7. Remind the team of opponents' special plays (draw, screen, reverse and bread-and-butter plays).
8. Always have a reason for calling defense.
9. Take pride in all calls and be in command at all times.

Defensive Theory: Never give a team the long run or the long pass—punt the ball and make them come a long distance, knowing they will make a mistake and stop themselves. We can stop their drives without their mistakes, if we are in right defense.

We should be in a defense, or stunt, where we will penetrate at one point on the line of scrimmage (where we anticipate their running). If they run at this point, we should tackle for a loss. If at another point, they should make three yards.

Try to build up pride and confidence in their ability to call defenses. Try to impress upon them that in every play on every defensive call, they must have a reason for calling their defensive signals, even though it may sometimes be wrong. I think you should continue each year to use whoever you select to call defenses at the same position. Boys who play this position must be selected with this in mind. Why the same position? Just as on offense, you stay with the same position because you can't take away this responsibility without hurting the morale of the personnel in this position. It shows a lack of confidence by the coaches in personnel. This works in reverse as well. It gives the boys who are selected to play the signal calling position each year the confidence of the coaches.

Teaching the Defensive Signal Callers

Separate the teaching and coaching areas. Confine the teaching to meetings and off-the-field work, and restrict the coaching to the practice in field work. In teaching you have to start with some very elementary actions, which the defensive quarterback must be conscious of at all times. One of the first laws of logic is if you are going to end right, you must start right. Start with a false premise, and you will end up with a false conclusion.

Down and Distance. This is the first thing a quarterback wants to know. With this in mind, he is immediately aware the situation is either:

NORMAL—which by our rules allows the defense approximately three yards per try on the remaining downs. Example: First and ten on the 50-yard line; third and nine on own 9-yard line; third and three on their 35-yard line.

LONG—with remaining downs, the approximate yardage to a first down or touchdown is greater than three yards per try. Example: third and twelve.

SHORT—with one remaining down and less than three yards per try for a first down or a touchdown. Example: third and two on our 40-yard line. There is one exception: second and one is automatically long.

Field Position—Are they where they can use fourth down? Are they in a field where they may not pass? One team we play has never passed in eight years in a certain zone on the field. Certainly this is important for our defensive quarterback to know, and a defense we might consider unsound in any other position would be the right call against this particular team.

Score—This one factor alone changes all the other rules for planning. We have certain rules which are ironclad, but we tell our offensive and defensive quarterbacks, "Break any rule to win." If we are behind 6-0, we will still play normal until we get ball position. If we are behind 14-0, then we are conscious that we must gamble and press more to get ball control and offensive position.

Time Remaining—This factor is very obvious even to the people in the stands, but how often do teams make a misplay either offensively or defensively in the last minutes of the half or the ball game! The only way to get results in these situations is to rehearse and practice this interval. How many times in a game have you seen halfbacks and safety men leading supporting running plays, with two minutes to go, as if it was the first play of the game! They certainly weren't aware of the score or time remaining. Eight percent of tied ball games are won or lost in the last two minutes of play. You should have the offensive and defensive two-minute drill every week. Review at this time all varied situations that may result.

Weather—Certainly, no one questions the importance of this factor, but how much time and effort do we spend preparing for undesirable weather conditions? Teach the factors involved: the wind and its effect on the passing and kicking game, or rain and a muddy field. These factors can make football seem like another game; on days like this it seems that the defense will either win or lose for you. It presents a different kind of defensive game, and you should have cards and charts to drill the boys on what you will do in such situations. You have as much opportunity to work under these conditions as you wish.

Specific Situation Calls

Third Down Calls—This is the most important call in football both offensively and defensively. Break this down into every possible situation and stress it both off and on the field. On the field stress the first down more in coaching the team, but with your defensive quarterbacks stress the third down call.

Kicking Situation Calls—Another field of defensive calls are the kicking situations. When to call for a return? When to call for a block kick signal? When to call for a single safety? When to call for a single safety with a running defense? When to mix up signal for return and block kick? Have the field areas divided and try to catalogue these choices of calls into different positions on the field. This also will vary with all the other factors we have already talked about: score, time remaining, weather conditions, etc.

Check Defenses—Everything we have done so far has been with one thing in mind: to win ten football games. We have tried to get a background that will enable us to meet every defensive situation and feel adequately prepared; to have our boys enter the game confident that there isn't any offensive formation that we cannot meet with a sound defense. I don't think we have ever been caught with a formation to which we were not prepared to adjust to since 1950, when Kentucky met us with an unusual spread offense.

In using our multiple defensive theory, we must decide what defenses we will stress against our next opponent. Sometimes we may have to make this adjustment during the game. In a big game recently, we saw an unexpected offensive maneuver, and we got hurt badly because we were not in the proper adjustment. Before we could get word in to our center, he had already anticipated our adjustment and started calling the proper defense. It was one we had not worked on since early September. With this call we stopped them cold, and this gave us the confidence and poise we needed to go on and win the game.

Game Plan Off the Field—However, most of our preparation is naturally done before the game. First, we study the scout report for the favorite running and passing plays. We pick out the plays they have been winning with—their bread-and-butter plays. We always try to sell our boys on the idea that we are not going to let them beat us with the plays we KNOW they are going to run. We go through all of their offensive formations, and wind up with their favorite plays and passes from each set. We put these plays on cardboards 12 X 18 inches. Then we study their different types of blocking at the hole, and decide what we think will be our best defensive calls and list them in order: first, second, and third choices, which are put on the back of the offensive formation cards for our centers to use later.

We do this on Sunday, and go through all of the opponent's offensive formations, including their kicking formations. We look for any field position tip or any personnel tip, and decide what we will try to do in regard to this information. There have been times when we felt that it was not advisable to play certain tips because you can sometimes have your team so conscious of playing tips they forget to play football, and if the tip doesn't develop, or the opportunity to take advantage of it doesn't present itself, it will affect the morale of the team.

Monday, we meet with the defensive quarterbacks and give them our plans. At the same time, we try to get some ideas from *them,* in a bull session type meeting. They have seen movies of their opponents, and have already given some thought to our defensive plan. We try as much as possible to make our plan of attack *their* plan of attack. We show them the formation, and favorite plays and passes, and ask them what they would call. It turns out that 75% to 90% of their thinking is the same as ours. This gives them the feeling that they have had a part in planning our strategy, and I believe they go about the job of preparation a lot quicker, and with more enthusiasm, when they feel that we have incorporated their thinking and ideas into game plans.

The centers now must work hard to be able to make the defensive call and get in as many correct defensive adjustments as possible. They take the cards and drill each other by giving down and distance, flashing offensive set, and making the defensive quarterback call the defense. Then they give the reason for calling every defense. As I have said before, we always try to have a reason for calling every defense, even though sometimes it may be wrong. We give them the goal line attack on Wednesday, going through a similar procedure.

Coaching the Defensive Quarterback

On the field, coaching is really putting into action what you have been teaching. During spring practice, 75% of our work is rough work. Here every drill, in which the center is working, the defensive quarterback calls defenses under a down and distance situation. Realize that the only way for them to gain confidence is by putting them in these defensive situations as many times as possible. Some boys will progress more rapidly, but all improve in proportion to the amount of work they have had in calling these defensive signals. Here are some drills that you can use to teach the quarterback and the defensive line to make these adjustments to different sets.

Shifting Drill—Use this drill for calling one defense and shifting to another defense on your signal. Have only the line of scrimmage and linebackers against a dummy line of scrimmage with the quarterback. The quarterback will call the snap count, and the center will snap the ball, with the offensive line of scrimmage taking one step. The defense will shift from one defense to another defense, and go to their responsibilities and hold. This gives the coach an opportunity to check their charge and position. Try to do this in ten minutes or less.

In this drill the centers get the experience of calling your shift signals and the opportunity to call your first signal as close to the snap of the ball as possible. With the non-rhythm snap count that most teams use, you will not always call the shift signal; this gives your line of scrimmage the experience of playing the first defense call instead of the second defense which you were to shift to.

Check Drill—This is a drill for coaching your centers to check certain defenses against every possible type of offensive alignment. You have taught them the first, second, and third choice of defenses you would like to have against these different sets, and when they recognize these sets, they must check the defense. The offense is dummy. They will come out and line up in these offensive sets and snap the ball. In this drill no offensive plays are run. Also incorporate in this drill man-in-motion, and your adjustments to motion. Always give down and distance.

Passing Drill—In this drill all the situations are long, from third and four to third and twenty-five. Again use only the line of scrimmage and the linebackers, but in this drill, throw pass patterns in the flat and spot areas, and make your ends, corner men and linebackers go to their responsibilities. This gives you a chance to check pass rushing by linemen, and pass defense position by linebackers, ends, and corner-men—if they are defending. Operate this drill between dummies at full speed.

In trying to coach dummy defensive football, it is a real challenge to keep your defensive line of scrimmage low and to keep them from getting sloppy habits, which will carry over in full speed work. Try at all times to stress the importance of learning, and of making as few mistakes as possible. In coaching dummy football you have an opportunity to emphasize the players' various responsibilities and to make them smarter football players. Early fall practice follows very much the same pattern as that given during spring practice. This specialized work, especially with your defensive quarterback, will win games for you.

Save-the-Game Defense

You can lose football games even with a Save-the-Game defense, but if you lose one game in a lifetime without a Save-the-Game defense, it is one too many. We are all aware of the importance of this defense, but it is still hard to find the time to put it in and work on it. It is really surprising how few coaches have a Save-the-Game plan.

It should be an adjustment from one of your basic defenses which should not require a lot of extra coaching or techniques for any personnel

Save-the-Game 5-4-2 (Figure 177)

Here is a simple adjustment from the Monster 5-4-2 defense. It requires only one substitution: A second safety for the Monster. This gives you the second safety you need against the long pass or long run.

Ends—Line up three yards outside of defensive tackle. They are responsible for containing on any roll action coming their way. On a straight drop back pass, they sprint to wide flat position ten yards deep. They should try to be in the line of the pass on a side line cut by any offensive receiver.

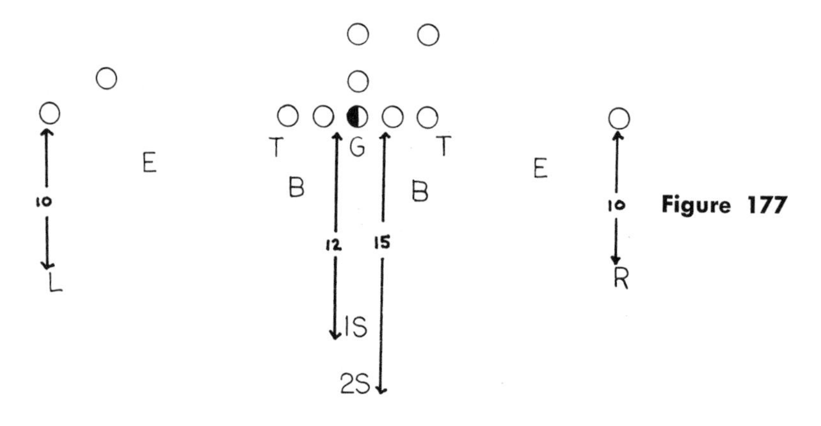

Figure 177

Tackles—Line up on outside shoulder of the offensive tackle. On a straight drop back pass, he is the container. On a roll out, the tackles rush the passer through his inside lane. They are the chase men on plays away.

Middle Guard—Line up one-half yard off the ball watching for the draw and rushing the passer hard through the center. Give him the option on the snap to shoot the gap between the center and guard sometimes, to be in a better position to rush.

Linebackers—Line up two yards deep on the inside shoulder of the offensive tackle. On passes they have the outside hook zones.

Halfbacks—Line up ten yards deep. On straight drop back passes, they shuffle to the outside and play their one-third zone area. On roll-out passes to their side, they shuffle forward to within six to eight yards of the line, picking up anyone in the flat zone.

First Safety—Lines up 12 yards off the ball. Plays the middle zone on all type passes with no revolve with flow. No one gets behind him and he plays the ball and overlaps the halfbacks after the ball is in the air.

Second Safety—Lines up 15 yards off the ball. On straight drop back passes, he slowly shuffles to the loaded side gaining depth. On roll-out passes, he supports the halfback to the roll action, gaining depth as he moves quickly to this position.

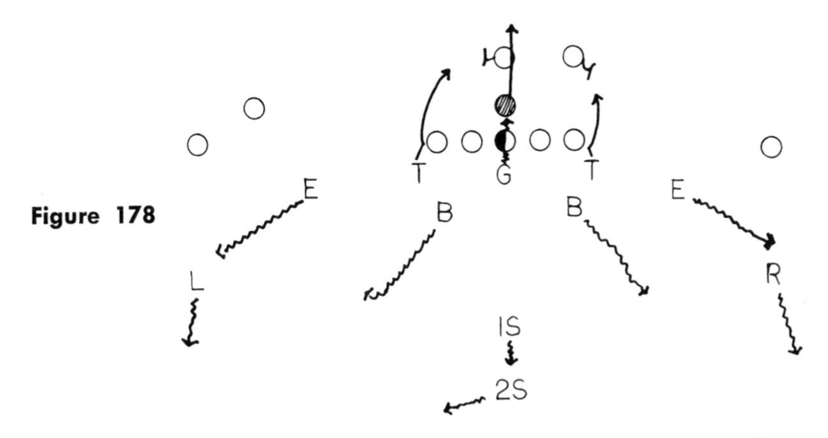

Figure 178

***Pocket pass—Save-the-Game Defense* (Figure 178)**

***Roll Pass—Save-the-Game Defense* (Figure 179)**

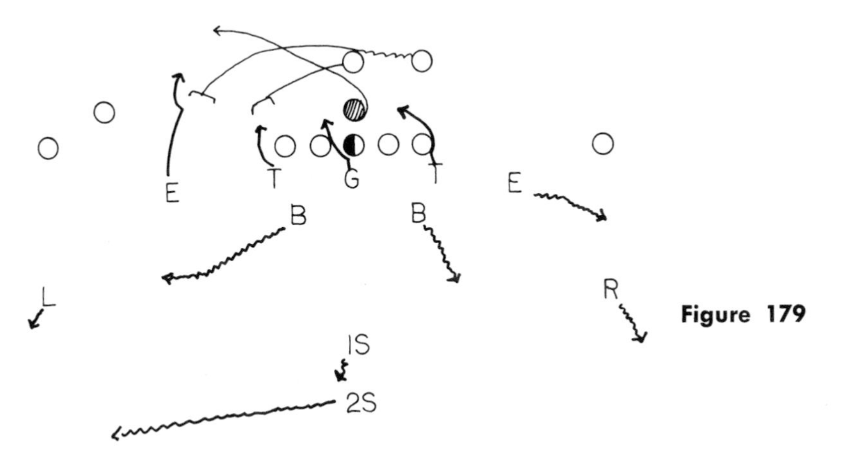

Figure 179

These defenses are simple and sound. They have less movement of the secondary to play their zone, since no one has to revolve. You are protected on all deep and throwback type passes.

Red-Dog Save-the-Game Defense (Figure 180)

No defense will stand alone. The basic defense is a cautious type of defense with only three or four men rushing the passer. For a variation of this, you can easily come back with the Red Dog stunt as a change of pace.

On this defense both the *Ends* come hard on the snap of the ball and are responsible for the outside with the jump on the on the snap.

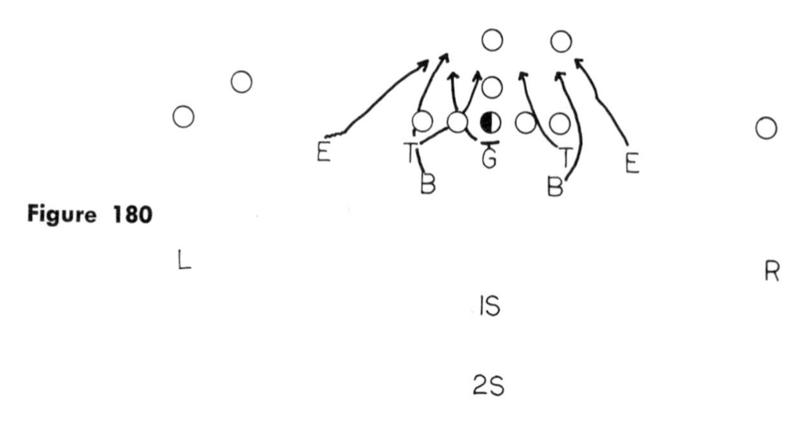

Figure 180

Tackles come hard on the snap over the offensive guards and become hard rushers up the middle.

The *Middle Guard* plays slow till he is sure there is nothing up the middle, then he has the option to rush either side of the offensive center. On the snap the *Linebackers* sprint to a position outside the offensive tackles and rush hard in the lane between the defensive end and tackle.

Any basic defense can be adjusted to a Save-the-game defense, but this is a must in any complete defensive plan.

Shifting Defenses

I have always been an advocate of shifting defenses. It is one of the few advantages football rules give the defense.

Shifting defenses can mean many things. It can mean calling a defensive shift from one basic defense to another defense. It can also mean moving on your call or the offensive snap count. It can mean checking some defenses, or variations of defenses, after the offensive team has lined up and shown another offensive set. Finally, there is the possibility of automatic shift at the line.

Why Shift?

1. It should be an objective to conceal and vary your defenses so the offense never gets the advantage where they can hit your weakness.

2. It is important for the team morale of your defense. For example, if a team lines up in a 6-3-2 defense, the quarterback calls an automatic at the line. It may be a live or dead call. Then the play makes a substantial gain and the defense will feel that they were hit at a weakness and the offense has an advantage. Sell your boys on the idea that the offense has no rhyme or reason for an automatic. You should vary enough to carry out this objective.

3. To control line splits. You give the offense a terrific advantage when you give them a set defense and let them take their offensive splits to isolate the man at the point of attack. There is a weakness in any defense. Line up so you do not give them the advantage of getting offensive blocking position. Line up in one defense and shift to another, and the defense has assumed an advantage. For example, a team will split an Eagle Defense to isolate the linebacker. We can line up in the Eagle Defense and shift to the Oklahoma 5-4-2 which will give the defense the advantage (Figure 181).

SHIFT FROM EAGLE TO 54

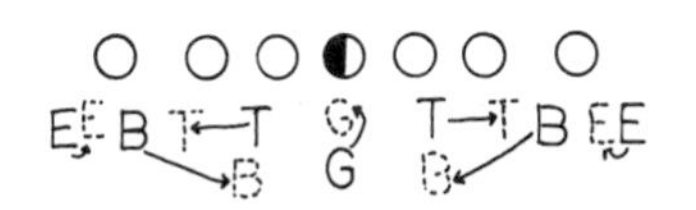

Figure 181

4. To get the best possible defense against every offensive set. In preparing for a game try to stop a team's bread-and-butter plays—what they have been winning with. If they beat you, they are going to have to use something different, and this seldom happens. A team in certain offensive sets tips off their offense—so in shifting and checking your defenses you are able to get in what is the best defensive alignment.

5. To make the offense "think." If, by some movement on defense, you can make the offensive quarterback think and linemen have to change assignments, you have gained an important advantage. There

are not many football players who can do very much thinking and still play inspired ball. After the Star Spangled Banner they are playing more to a pattern, and reacting by reflex. Making them think neutralizes some of their blocking potential. An offensive man going up to the line wondering who is going to block instead of how is not as effective an offensive lineman.

You can do this very simply. All of us have some basic defenses. You can call a shift from a gap defensive stunt to the 5-4-2 defense (as shown in Figure 182). On a call from your defensive quarterback, move

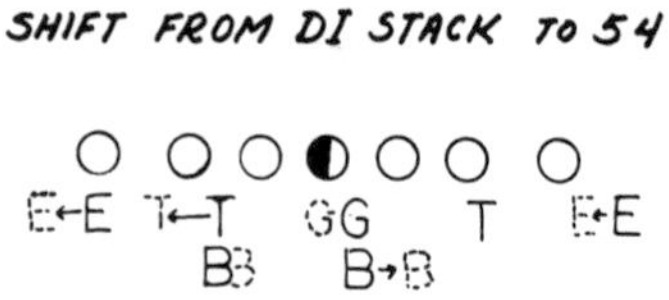

SHIFT FROM DI STACK TO 54

Figure 182

O O O ◐ O O O
E←E T←T GG T E←E
BB B→B

as a team. This call should be loud and flat, and no word used in any offensive snap count which would interfere with the offense snap count. The shift should be sharp with quick movement. If you should be hit in the middle of a shift, everyone has responsibility of the defense you are shifting to.

Some of the most effective shifts are from an odd defense to an even defense—Oklahoma 5-4-2 to 6-3-2. A lot of teams adjust splits based on odd or even—3 deep or box defense. So try to show one and shift to another. Also go from a gap defense to heads-up defense. Also shift from a three-deep zone defense to a defense with corners.

15

Defensive Tests and Measurements

Grading

There are many types of grading systems used by colleges and high schools today. They all serve one purpose—to check on each player's contribution to the team effort. They also make the coach watch every player on every play. This information can be mishandled. A reverse result will occur if such information is allowed to appear in the press, or even if it is made available indiscriminately to the squad. Grade results should be analyzed by the coaching staff only. Individuals on the team can be given their grades privately by the coach concerned, and should receive only *their* grades. Mistakes should always be corrected in the film room at the time of the film showing. All good plays should be acknowledged by charts, etc. But actual grades and grade averages should not be posted.

Figure 183

DEFENSIVE GRADING FORM - GAME SIWASH

NAME	ONSIDE	OFFSIDE	PASS	KICK	TACKLES	OVER ALL GRADE	COMMENTS
COLSON	0011110 63%	111011 83%	101100 50%	1111 100%	1½ 1½ 11 4/2	24 PLAYS = 75%	MISTAKE ON SLANT POOR PASS RUSH
GAGNER	1111011110011 80%		11101 83%	1110 75%	1111 ½ 11 6/1	24 PLAYS = 80%	FINE GAME
LANGLEY	111001 66%	11010100 50%	11111 100%	1100 50%	11½ 2/1	24 PLAYS = 66%	BAD PURSUIT ANGLE
JOHNSON	10 50%	11 100%	1 100%	0 0%	1 1/0	6 PLAYS = 66%	MISTAKE ON PUNT RETURN
WARNER	11 100%					2 PLAYS = 100%	INJURY EARLY
CUTCLIFFE	11	00	0	1	½ 0/1	6 PLAYS = 50%	DIDN'T CHASE
McCOLLOUGH							DIDN'T PLAY
BRAY		11	1	1	1½ 1/1	4 PLAYS = 100%	MUCH IMPROVED
SMITH							DIDN'T PLAY

Coaches' grading forms should be made up before the season starts. Each coach should work with the same forms (Figure 187 shows a sample form).

To keep from getting too complicated, the grading coach marks either a one or a zero in the appropriate place. This means the player either did his job or he didn't. You can eliminate, to a degree, a natural desire by the grading coach to grade some players easier than others.

This system makes final per cent grades easier to figure. For example, if a player was involved in 37 plays and got 26 ones, his grade is figured by dividing the plays into the number of ones. In this case the grade figures 70%. Keep separate grades on the different type of plays the player must make as well as an overall grade. Sometimes a player can go almost a half a season and have relatively few plays come directly at him. This could be deceiving if only the overall grade were kept. All pertinent information is written down on the form so compilation can be made for incentive charts.

Incentive Charts

The defensive team should have a meeting room of their own. This room should always have a projector set up so players can drop in between classes and watch films on their own. The incentive charts should be hung in this room.

Figure 184

OVERALL RUN

TEAM									TEAM TOTAL
SMU	3+6	8+37	3+8	5+4	3+8	7+17		4+11	33+91 2.7
M. ST.	8+146	2+1	2+0	3+5	3+8	1+1	1+0	4+31	24+192 8.0
LSU	4+7	3+5	1+4	4+22	4+34	3+46	7+34	3+13	29+164 5.6
MISS.	1+0	5+24	3+4	2+6	4+2	4+11	2+4	1+2	22+53 2.4
USC	3+5	2+21	5+14	4+5	1+0	3+6		3+8	21+59 2.8
ALA.	7+27	9+13	3+18	4+10	4+8	2+8	7+47	7+48	43+200 4.6
AUB.	3+8	7+32	2+6	4+12	2+5	5+13	6+21	3-7	32+90 2.7
GA.	5-1	15+61	2+7	3+24	4+12	5+10	11+47	2+9	47+165 3.5
FSU	4-2	8+42	3+4	4+13	3+8	7+23	13+47	2+8	44+143 3.2
MIAMI	8+34	2+4	3+9	2+1	3+30	1-1	2+8	9+50	30+135 4.5
SEASON TOTALS	56+230 4.1	61+241 3.9	37+74 2.0	45+102 2.2	31+115 3.7	38+134 3.5	49+208 4.2	48+173 3.6	365+1292 3.5

1. Defensive Results Charts

(a) Overall defensive run record chart shows total defensive records at each hole (Figure 184). In each pair of numbers, the first is the number of attempts and the second is the number of yards gained. Totals are given in average yards gained per try.

(b) Overall defensive pass record chart shows pass defense by area (Figure 185).

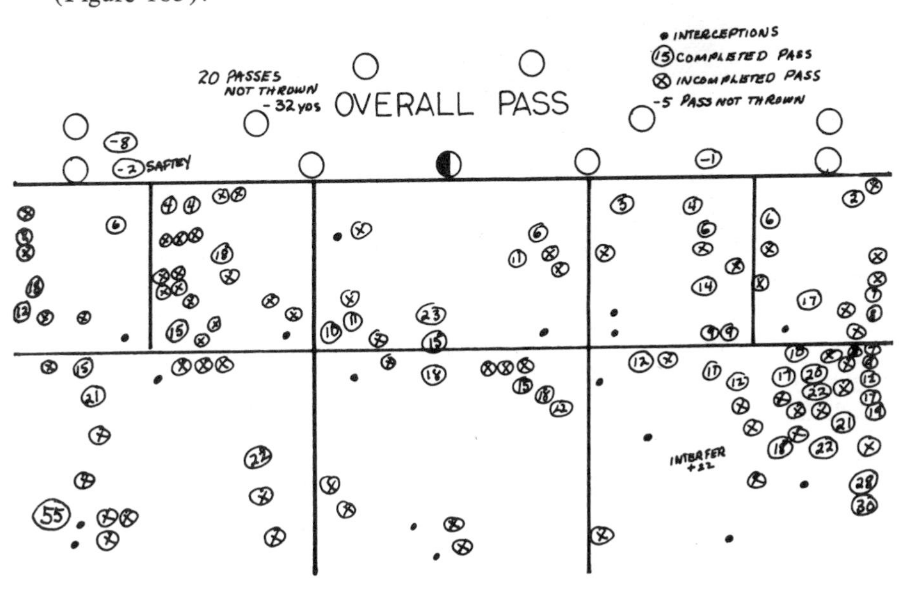

Figure 185

Figure 186

54 REGULAR

PASSES ATTEMPTED 101
PASSES NOT THROWN 20 - 32
PASSING YARDS 293
INTERCEPTIONS 11

PASS 121 + 293
RUN 115 + 417
TOTAL 236 + 710
AVE. THIS DEF. 3.0

TEAM									TEAM TOTAL
SMU	1+2	2+4	1+2	1+1		2+4			7+14 2.0
M. ST.	4+17			2+5	2+8			3+36	11+46 5.6
LSU				2+15			2+13		4+28 7.0
MISS.		2+10	2+2	2+6	4+2	2+8		1+2	13+30 2.3
USC			2+8	1+2					3+10 3.3
ALA.	1+4	4+21	1+9	1+4	1+4	1+4	2+10	2+23	13+79 6.0
AUB.	2+1	1+4	1+4	2+7	1+0	2+8	1+5	3-7	13+22 1.7
GA.	2-3	8+34	2+7	3+24	2+12	4+6	9+40	2+9	32+129 4.0
FSU		1+14		2+13	1+1	3+10	4+16		11+54 5.0
MIAMI	1+0		1+4	1+1	1+1			4-1	8+5 .6
SEASON TOTALS	11+21 1.9	18+87 4.8	10+36 3.6	17+78 4.5	12+28 2.3	14+40 2.8	18+84 4.4	15+62 4.1	115+417 3.6

(c) Individual defense record chart shows results of plays directed at this particular defense. Have one of these posted for every defense you use. Figure 186 shows one of these defenses.

At the end of the season a defensive report should be made, with statistics showing records of overall defense, the defensive record of each defense, and an analysis with recommendations for how to correct failures.

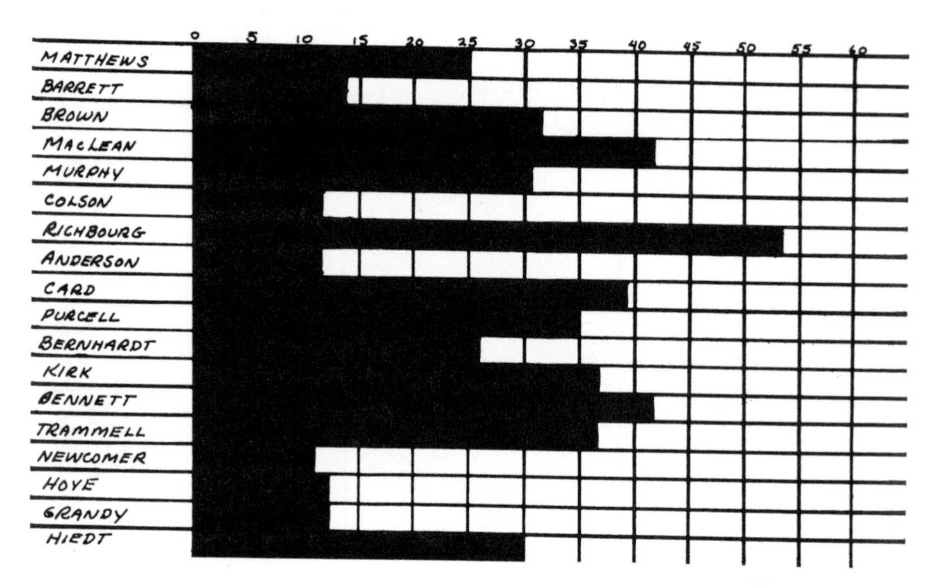

Figure 188 **Figure 187**

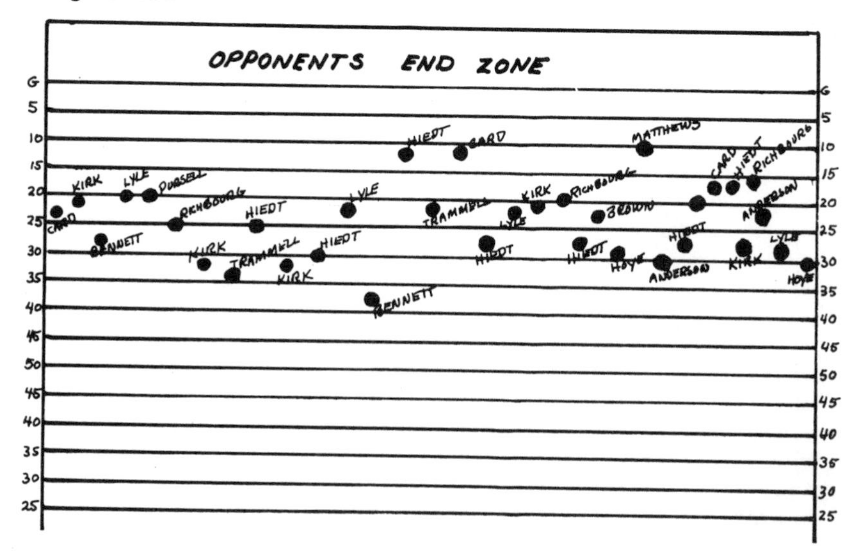

(d) *Tackles and Assists Chart* (Figure 187). The diagram should be self-explanatory.

(e) *Kickoff Coverage Chart* (Figure 188). Each kickoff covered is plotted and the main (or key) tackler is given credit.

(f) *Punt Return Chart* (Figure 189). Lack of space prevents showing all the punt returns, but this diagram shows how to keep records of them.

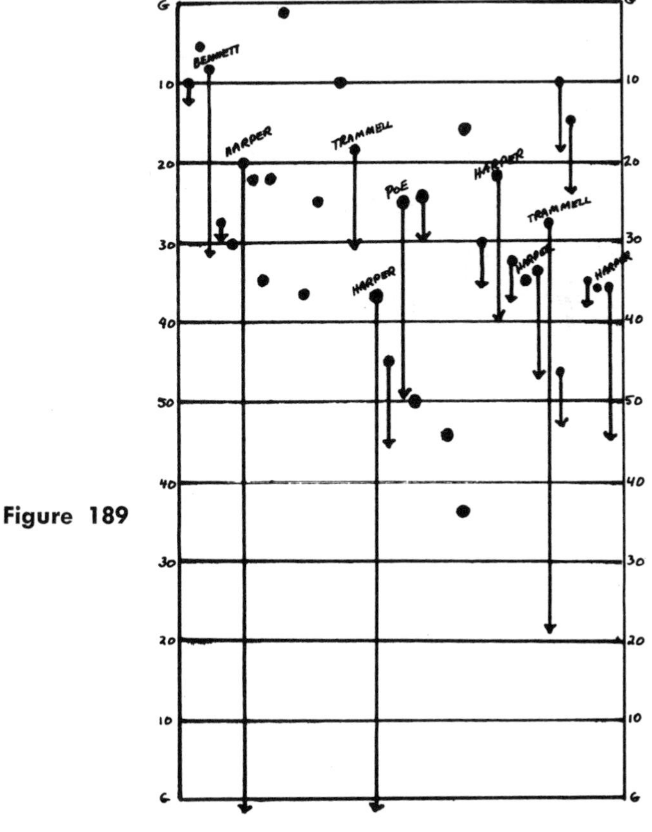

Figure 189

(g) *Big Play Chart* (Figure 190). This chart shows by colored stars the "big plays'" made each week. Give a red star for a big loss. (A big loss is actually any tackle made for minus yardage.) Green stars indicate pass interceptions and fumble recoveries. A yellow star indicates a fumble or interception caused (hard rush or hard tackle). The blue stars mean tackles on kick off coverage or punt coverage. Black stars are for key blocks on punt returns or interception returns. Any colors will do, so long as these plays are clearly labeled.

NAME	INTERCEPTION OR FUMBLE RECOVERY	CAUSE A FUM. OR INTERCEPTION	BIG LOSS	TACKLE ON KICKOFF - PUNT	KEY BLOCK PUNT - OSKIE
MATTHEWS	☆		☆☆☆	☆☆☆	☆☆
BARRETT		☆	☆	☆	
BROWN	☆☆	☆☆	☆	☆	☆☆☆☆☆
MACLEAN	☆	☆	☆☆☆☆		☆☆
MURPHY	☆	☆	☆☆	☆	☆
COLSON	☆		☆	☆	
RICHBOURG	☆☆☆	☆☆☆	☆☆☆☆☆	☆☆☆☆☆	☆☆☆
ANDERSON		☆	☆☆	☆☆☆	☆
CARD	☆☆☆☆☆☆	☆	☆☆	☆☆☆☆	☆☆
PURCELL	☆☆☆	☆	☆☆☆	☆☆☆	☆
BERNHARDT	☆☆☆	☆	☆	☆☆	☆
KIRK	☆☆☆☆☆☆		☆☆☆	☆☆☆☆	☆☆
BENNETT	☆☆☆☆☆☆			☆☆☆	☆☆☆☆☆
TRAMMELL	☆☆☆☆☆☆☆	☆☆☆☆		☆☆☆☆☆	☆☆☆☆
NEWCOMER	☆☆☆				
HOYE	☆☆			☆☆	☆
GRANDY	☆	☆		☆☆☆☆	☆☆
HIEDT	☆☆☆☆☆	☆☆☆	☆☆☆☆	☆☆☆☆☆☆	

Figure 190

(h) *Player or Players of the Week.* Each week the staff votes for the defensive player who contributed most to the effectiveness of the defense. His picture is framed for the next week with a resumé of his accomplishments. This may be posted anywhere: the training room, dining room, dressing room, or the defensive room.

(i) *Defensive Honor Roll.* At the end of the season, the outstanding senior defensive players are picked and their pictures are put up in the letterman's club lounge (or anywhere that alumni or returnees annually visit). This area is designated as the school's Defensive Honor Roll.

Written Tests

Each week the defensive team and signal callers are given a written test. At home games this test is given at the Friday night meeting. On road trips the test is given on the bus or plane. This test is usually on the scout report and assignments. These grades are kept and averaged to go into the master personnel sheet. The three defensive coaches are asked to make separate tests so the questions are all applicable to each position. Here is a sample test for interior linemen.

NAME ____________________ POSITION _______ DATE _____

1 Name, in order, the plays we must stop this week.

a.

b.

c.

d.

e.

2. Give names and numbers of this week's opponent's best backs.

3. At what place on the field and what down and distance may we expect their favorite plays?

Plays	Position	Down and Distance

4. What are our opponent's side line tendencies?

5. What changes have been made in the following basic defenses that effect you?

54 Regular

54 Slant fire

61 Rover

6. When will our opponent pass?

7. Write down techniques and aiming points of 54 slant.

8. What do we look for when #24 comes in the game?

9. What return is on if our opponents quick-kick or kick on the third down?

10. Name our opponent's favorite plays, in order, on the goal line.

MASTER PERSONNEL CHART

ENDS	HT	WT	CL	SPEED 40	T+A 64	PLAYS '64	GRADE '64	TEST AVE	SPRING '64	SEASON '63	SPRING '63	SEASON '62	COMMENTS
MATTHEWS	62	214	JR	5.0	36	422	84%	91	80%	79%	74%	FROSH	ALL CONF '64
BROWN	63	230	JR	5.0	31	408	82%	92	82%	80%	80%	RED SHIRT	MOVED TO OFFENSE
HOYE	62	205	So	4.9	18	132	85%	89	73%	FROSH	HS	HS	CAN SWING
BARRETT	511	200	So	5.2	11	98	80%	95	68%	FROSH	HS	HS	PLACE KICKER
THOMAS	62	210	JR	4.9	OFF.	OFF.	OFF.	✓	OFF	78%	75%	FROSH	MOVED TO DEFENSE
TACKLES													
MACLEAN	63	237	SR	5.3	52	477	85%	96	84%	80%	72%	70%	SIGNED WITH PROS
MURPHY	62	260	SR	5.2	39	402	80%	82	89%	80%	81%	80%	SIGNED WITH PROS
COLSON	62	230	So.	5.1	20	118	78%	87	71%	FROSH	HS	HS	BETTER ON LEFT SIDE
JOHNSON	510	240	JR	5.4	8	80	69%	82	65%	JC	JC	JC	TRANSFER
McCOLLOUGH	61	210	JR	5.4	2	17	61%	91	60%	JC	JC	JC	TRANSFER CAN PLAY LINEBACKER
LINEBACKERS													
CARD	56	168	So.	4.9	68	301	88%	86	85%	RED SHIRT	RED SHIRT	FROSH	HURT KNEE IN GA. GAME
PURCELL	61	199	SR	5.0	49	321	86%	90	81%	72%	70%	FROSH	KNEE OPER. SPRING 65
HIEDT	60	200	JR	5.1	46	222	87%	93	78%	69%	58%	FROSH	ENDED SEASON STRONG
BERNHARDT	511	205	SR	5.2	51	238	86%	99	85%	85%	83%	81%	GRAD.

Figure 191

Master Personnel Records

Each week the season grading charts are up-dated. After the season, and after spring practice, a master personnel sheet should be compiled. The information is too extensive for a typed sheet so charts must be used. Figure 191 is a sample showing just the defensive ends, tackles, and linebackers. Naturally all positions are compiled.

16

Defensive Organization

Staff Organization

Where possible, the coaching staff should have three offensive coaches and three defensive coaches. These are the varsity assistants. In addition, of course, there are freshman and B team coaches. Defensive organization should follow through all the teams within your squad. For example there should be an assistant designated as head of the defense. He bears the overall responsibility for the success or failure of the defense. The three varsity defensive coaches should split the positions in the following way: The Interior Line Coach coaches the middle three linemen, a Linebacker and End Coach who coaches the two inside linebackers and the two defensive ends, and a Secondary Coach who handles the four deep.

By breaking down assignments in this way you have a coach working with the players whose responsibilities are similar. Also this organization has other logic behind it, such as film grading and breakdown drills. Also on the defensive staff is the defensive B team coach. His job is to prepare the defensive scout team to be able to put on the opponents' defensive maneuvers. Lastly, there should be a defensive backfield and line coach on the freshman team to start the young players out in your defensive plan. These freshman coaches can be graduate assistants.

This makes a total of six coaches who specialize in defensive coaching. The Defensive Head-coach is responsible for putting out a defensive play book and instructing his staff on all defensive plans and procedures.

Most scouting assignments are handled by the B team coaches, and whenever there is another scout he must work through these men. Naturally, the offensive B team coach works on the defensive field against the defensive team, so in a sense, he is more a part of the defensive staff than the defensive B team coach.

With the widespread use of film-swapping, the varsity Defensive coaches are able to work on their game plan before the scout returns.

Sunday is a big day for the coaching staff. By 2:00 P.M. all defensive coaches are to have turned in complete grades, number of plays, tackles and assists, and bonus plays taken from our game film. The Defensive Head-coach compiles them and hands in this information to the Head Coach. From 2:00 to 6:00 P.M. all coaches study the next week's opponents films and get the scout report. A beginning game plan evolves.

At 6:00 P.M., all coaches dine with the players on the training table. At 6:30 P.M., everyone meets in the projection room. The past Saturday's game is run for the team. The Head Coach makes corrections and hands out praise at this time. At 8:30 P.M. the squad is dismissed, except for the signal callers. They are briefed on the next week's opponent. The defensive staff continues to review the opponent's films and works on the game plan. This work continues on until midnight. Tuesday noon is the deadline for a written defensive game plan. The following is a sample of the type of game plan that is handed out to all coaches and signal callers.

SIWASH GAME PLAN (DATE)

I. *Comments* - Tough run team. Less than average passing team. One good receiver. Use I, shift, slot, motion both ways, option. Lots of power.

II. *General Plan* - Major in eight-front defenses. Heavy rush. Press a lot. Use stacks on run downs—Stop Graboski #33. Double cover Hansen #81 on long yards. Monster and Squirm come up fast and turn in sweeps; TX and Razor vs. split end.

III. *Repertory*

Read	***Press***
54 Regular	**Eagle Fire**
Eagle Regular	**Slant Fire**
54 Slant	**Stack Fire**
lt. 80 rush, pick & part return. Fourth down—80 rt. & Stack	**Split Stack Fire**
	Rover
	Rover Bullets
	65 Goal Line

Punts

Third Down - Def. Called, Rotate Left, Single Safety, Left

IV. *Special Adjustments*

A. Monster Rules

1. Declare to tight ends #82 T.
2. Close on slants & stacks
3. Bullets (off on motion).
4. Same rotation as last week.

B. Secondary

1. Blue on all regulars vs. tight ends.
   Orange vs. split ends.
2. Eagle to Monster on long yards, hold up tight end.
3. Call only one Back coverage in 3 and 4 zone (eagle fire).
4. Watch #81 Hansen (Split end).

C. Ends and Linebackers

1. Ends double on reads, inside position on wide split end, outside on nasty split.
2. Ends jiggle the option.
3. Linebackers play closer than usual, watch for lead plays.

D. Special Keys

1. On regulars, middle guard use quick around to split end side.
2. Linebacker to split and side, key tailback in the I. If he comes your way, fire. If he goes away, cover for middle guard.
3. Secondary - Watch #24 when not a flanker. He is always a lead blocker.
4. Goal line offense—Slot sweep first—FB jump second - QB sneak last.

Squad Organization

A defensive team should be two deep at each position with possibly a few spares of a utility nature. Most coaches claim they can't find 44 players (22 offense, 22 defense) capable of playing in their particular league. Therefore, they try different methods of swinging some kids both ways. This is a waste of practice time and narrows the two-way boy. An average athlete, if he is worked with, will respond and do as good a job as a great athlete trying to play both ways. Further, you improve squad morale if 44 boys all feel they are an important part of the team.

Selection of personnel should be one of the coaching staff's main topics of discussion. After spring practice every player should be measured in every possible way. Accurate height and weight should be taken. Measure their speed in the 40-yard dash. Get statistics from the weight room on strength measurement. Compile all past grades and set up a form sheet with comments. As a basic approach, the offensive coaches should have first choice of backs and receivers, while the defensive coaches get first choice of linemen and linebackers. After the first 22, both ways, have been set, the rest of the varsity goes to the B team. In case of injuries, B teamers move up to the first 22. One season we won our last game of the season playing our seventh linebacker the whole game.

Practice Organization

From staff and squad organization we will go right into practice organization. You must have at least two football fields, one offense, one defense. The Frosh can work around the edges, and should be needed

Figure 192

DEFENSIVE PRACTICE
15 SEPT 1965

PLANS			TIME	REQUIREMENTS		
ELLENSON	BROWN	KINARD		ELLENSON	BROWN	KINARD
CALLYS	CALLYS	CALLYS	3:55 4:00	NONE	NONE	NONE
SPECIALTY: FLIPPER + SHIVER KO COVER	SPECIALTY: PASSING GROUP KO COVER	SPECIALTY: PUNT CATCHING KO COVER	4:00 4:20	NONE B TEAM REC.	NONE B TEAM REC	NONE B TEAM REC
INDIVIDUAL: 1 ON 1 2 ON 1 RUSH PASSER	INDIVIDUAL: BAG DRILL 1 ON 1 WARD OFF HAMBURGER	INDIVIDUAL: BLACK COVER BLUE COVER FLOW	4:20 4:40	5 LINEMEN 1 CENTER 1 QB	1 BACKFIELD 1 CENTER 2 ENDS 2 GUARDS	1 BACKFIELD 2 ENDS 1 CENTER
SEMI GROUP: 5 ON 5 ALT. LB w/BROWN	SEMI GROUP: WIDE OFFENSE ALT LB WITH ELLENSON	SEMI GROUP: WIDE OFFENSE WITH BROWN	4:40 4:55	SAME AS ABOVE	← 1 FULL TEAM EXTRA QB + CENTER →	
ICE BREAK	ICE BREAK	ICE BREAK	4:55 5:00	ICE	ICE	ICE
PERIMETER: DEF VS RUN FULL LINE ALT LB + M.	PERIMETER: WITH KINARD ALT LB + ENDS ↔ NORTHWESTERN PASS ROUTES	PERIMETER WITH BROWN ALT. MONSTER NORTH WESTERN PASS ROUTES	5:00 5:40	ONE FULL TEAM	ONE FULL TEAM ↔	
TEAM DEFENSE	TEAM DEFENSE	TEAM DEFENSE	5:40 6:00	2 FULL TEAMS ALTERNATING		
SLED + SPRINTS	SLED + SPRINTS	SLED + SPRINTS	6:00 6:10	NONE	NONE	NONE

for varsity work only in certain areas. When injuries move B teamers up to the varsity, the B team gets a little slim to provide personnel for both the offense and the defense. Freshmen must fill these gaps. Another function Frosh can handle is running pass routes against the defensive perimeter.

Time is the one factor that must be carefully planned. Afternoon classes and evening tutoring will allow a maximum of two hours a day for everything. Injury treatment must be taken care of during class breaks. As we mentioned in the chapter about the kicking game, every practice should start with a specialty period. Every practice should end with some form of conditioning. A good idea is to combine Quick-quick and wind sprints, along with heavy sled work. The heavy seven man sled is the best isometric there is for developing conditioning.

Figure 192 is a sample practice organization sheet. This sheet is made up in the morning and posted before practice. Every coach carries one on the field. There is also a personnel sheet attached showing complete available depth.

This is a work day schedule. Mondays and Fridays during the season are much lighter, but the same form is used in putting out practice plans.

Game Organization

The players are allowed to sleep on game morning until 9:30. They are given orange juice and coffee and then board the bus back to the campus. They are taken directly to the pre-game meal. This meal is usually steak and eggs, toast and tea. From the pre-game meal they all go to the dressing room for taping. They are to be dressed and in the ready room by 1:00 P.M. They are not allowed to see anyone (except for emergencies) on game day until after the game.

In the ready room, coaches go over reminders and comment on their written tests from the day before. Warm up procedures start at 1:25 P.M. In the South a 20 minute warm-up is plenty. Any kind of warm-up plan that calls for each man to get to do his job during the game is okay. By 1:45 the players should go back to the ready room for ten minutes. Seven minutes before kickoff, a minute of silence is allowed, for each boy to pray in his own way. Then the team takes the field. Here the Lord's Prayer is said by everyone. Right after the kickoff, bench organization is in effect. The Offensive team occupies the South benches and the Defensive team the North benches. There is a place in the middle for chairs in which specialists—such as the kickers—belong. The defensive signal caller reports to the defensive phone when he is not in the game. Defense has a runner sitting in the specialists' area.

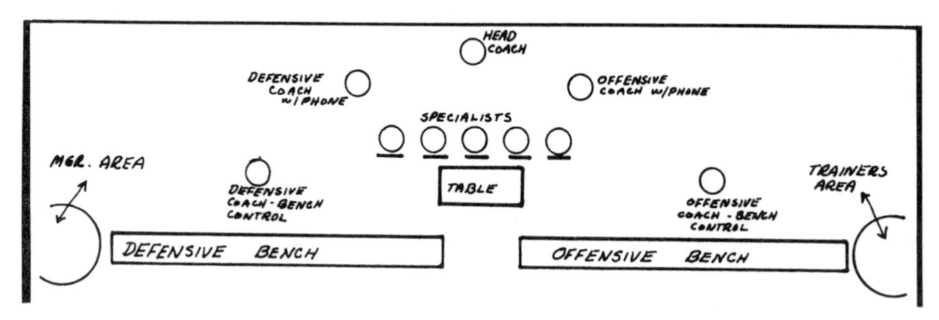

Figure 193

He is the number one sub, to carry information from the phone. There is one defensive coach in the press box, one on the phone on the field. The other defensive coach keeps control of the bench and substitutions. All entering subs clear through the Head Coach and report to the proper official. Figure 193 shows a bench organization chart.

17

Responses of Players and the Team

This chapter will deal with attitude and mental preparation, what the Army calls *Esprit De Corps*. Whatever you call it, it is the most important thing you, as a football coach, can do to get your team ready to play great football. This particular phase of coaching is the one that is the least discussed. There has been very little written about this subject and almost no one has ever set up a particular guide to go by in this vital part of the game.

The reason there is no set pattern is because of the broadness of the subject. There are no two human beings that will respond in exactly the same manner. There are no two football coaches whose philosophies are exactly the same, and finally, the set of circumstances that surround each football game are different. Many coaches have approached this problem in different ways, and been successful using opposite methods. This is why it is so difficult to categorize emotional responses.

How often have you heard a coach wonder, before an important game, if his team was "ready?" Since this is such an important factor, I am going to give you some basic rules drawn from my personal experience and beliefs. This is not intended to be an unshakable guide, but my experience has proven these things to be successful.

The Individual Player

The whole morale pattern is a gradual process that begins with your handling of the individual player. From the time a youngster comes under your guidance—until he leaves, he must be treated with equality and fairness. Nothing will kill an individual's morale quicker than to feel he is not getting a fair chance. It is equally bad to give one player the feeling that he is more important than the rest. The others will feel this, and resentment can't help but creep in. Being completely fair is a tough job. Movies are a great help. Any boy who feels he should be playing more should be taken to the projection room and shown why he is where he is. This takes time and effort, but it will pay off. While on the subject of movies, it should be brought up again how important thorough film grading is to the morale factor of a team.

In handling the individual player, each coach must create an atmosphere of discipline and good humor. There is an old cliche, "firm, fair and friendly," which is pretty much true. Football players have a hard job to do and it isn't all fun, but the work can be made interesting. This is where coaching personality comes into play. Some coaches have a natural knack for giving praise (or criticism) at just the right time. They have a "feel" for the boys they are coaching. I'm not talking about a comedian, or wise guy, but the ability of a leader to apply the needle or the "juice" just when it is needed. In order to do this you must know when such leadership is required. Let's take a particular time for an example. The third morning of two-a-day sessions is probably the toughest practice there is. Soreness has set in, rest has been reduced, and these plus early rising all bring out ill temper. Look around during calisthenics and you'll see plenty of grouchy faces. Some coaches get tired, too. The natural tendency is to growl at the squad and tell them to get going right now or you'll give them extra sprints, or some other disciplinary exercise. Some coaches can scare their squads into a working frame of mind, but the results are better if one kidding remark hits home and produces a lift for the whole squad. Such things as "Call the trainer, Peters just had a heat flash" or "Johnson, you look like you smell something bad, but you just can't quite locate it." Of course, Peters or Johnson must be the player that will bring out the smiles in everyone. Every squad has one or two characters that are good foils for humor. Sometimes there is a *player* on the squad who can do these things—he should be encouraged. I could go on and give you other examples, but the point is clear. "Lead, do not drive, your player through the difficult times."

There are a few other things that also come under the handling of players individually. Always keep your office door open to members of your team. This to me is one of the great challenges to a coach, as well as one of the great rewards. They are going to fight for you, and you must let them know you are willing to fight for them. You are going to be called upon to counsel, guide, and help with everything from girl and family troubles to brushes with the law. There are times when the coach has to take one of his players to the woodshed. When a boy is wrong, he expects to be punished. To let him go is to do him a dis-service. Every possible chance should be given to regulation breakers, and every effort should be made to correct the wayward lad. Most of the troublesome cases can be corrected and most boys can be straightened out. Occasionally you will run across one that repeatedly lets you and the team down, and sooner or later he must be dropped for the good of all concerned, but *you* have been defeated.

Discipline should be started early, and each freshman should understand what is expected of him and how he is to act. Once this pattern is set, the older boys will be the example. Here is a set of behavior patterns that all freshmen should learn immediately.

1. Be on time!
2. Keep a neat, clean cut appearance.
3. Use the expression "Sir" to all faculty and staff. It sounds better than any other form of address.
4. Be honest—it's the only policy.
5. Do not associate, or talk to, anyone connected in any way with gambling.
6. Stay out of any establishment that serves alcoholic beverages and away from any parties during the season where there is drinking.
7. There will be no smoking allowed during the season and during spring practice. The rest of the time do not smoke publicly.
8. Budget your time. Regular hours are essential for your school work, athletics, and rest.
9. Do not steal from yourself by cutting classes.
10. Stand tall and look proud—you are a football player.

A final truism should be mentioned regarding the handling of the individual, and that is *interest*. If you are genuinely, sincerely interested in your boys, they will know it and believe in you. If you are the least bit phony, they'll spot it and react accordingly.

Getting the Team "Ready"

I would like to devote the rest of this chapter to the important function of getting a squad mentally ready to play better than they know how. Many coaches do not believe in mental preparation. Their philosophy is simply, get them ready through game plans and conditioning. Once they are prepared they'll play well enough by sheer motor response and discipline. They more or less rule out the old Rockne approach. Many of these coaches are successful, but it is my opinion that they have not tapped a great source of inspired effort. I do not believe that modern boys are blase and sophisticated, are not impressed by pep talks, and cannot be inspired to great heights. They will get chill bumps as readily as their fathers did. Thank God there are still youngsters among us who are emotionally involved. I like to see a player who gets a lump in his throat when the flag goes by or when he hears a particularly stirring band number.

Down through the ages men have jumped up with a club or pitch fork and charged some enemy because they were fired up into a fighting frenzy. Often the underdog army has swung the tide of battle because of just such actions. One small group can trigger such a change in events. People like Joan of Arc, the patriots at Bunker Hill, Sergeant York and many others have led their forces through pure inspiration. The perfectly trained army does not win all its battles. There must be a dominating will to win.

Football is a war with rules. To win there must be the same mental attitude as in any battle. There must be a strong mental involvement. Each player must become so emotionally committed that, in a way, he loses his identity. Here we come to the one crucial word in getting 30 or 40 young men really eager to engage in this war with rules. That word is "oneness." There must be a single purpose, a single goal. Each participant must lose himself in the forging of a single spirit. This is not easily accomplished. Most of us are too self-conscious to give in to a group feeling. We look around quickly and say to ourselves "Someone is looking at me and thinking I'm a darned fool." However, once this self-consciousness is lost, the individual can melt into the singular purpose, however savage it may be.

It requires real leadership and real selling to convince a whole squad to become "one," to forget the petty animosities that always divide any group. It cannot be done fifteen minutes before kickoff time. To get this feeling of being able to charge into Hell with a bucket of water, you must start the week before. The whole attitude must build slowly until it reaches a crescendo by game time. Remember, nothing is corny as long as you, the coach, are completely sincere.

Start off each game with a slogan of some kind. There may be more than one slogan, but we pick one and have it printed on a sticker similar to bumper strips. These are stuck up around the campus and anywhere our squad may be. They are small enough to be plastered to headgear. If the game is a key one, we may even have the slogan sewn on our game jersies, or dropped from a small airplane on bits of paper. This will impress the team with the magnitude of the impending contest. Use any gimmick you think might impress some of the squad. I don't think you have lost anything if it doesn't impress the entire squad.

Most kids will accept a real challenge and very often we challenge them with posters and slogans. One of the best ways to set a mental attitude for everyone is a squad meeting the night before the big game. When we are at home, we have a squad meeting in our projection room on Friday evening. The coaches are not always invited. The players themselves decide on what kind of meeting they want. Sometimes a certain coach will have a special reason, and he will give the team a talk. Sometimes we will write the squad a letter. Other times a certain type of story is called for. Then again, the squad will close the doors and not allow any coaches to participate in this "honing" of their mental attitude. After this meeting, we always have a war movie, or any good shoot 'em up film with plenty of action in it. I've seen our squad with such a sharp mental edge for battle that every blow that was struck, in a routine movie fight, was cheered vociferously. As soon as the movie ends, we have busses take us to a small motel 20 miles out of town. This is the beginning of "quiet time." No one speaks unless it is necessary. There is something very dramatic about silence. They are given a snack and retire. The silence continues on the ride back the next morning. You can't help but think of all the things that have been done to set the mental edge. Nervous? yes. We want them nervous and edgy, but determined to pay the cost of victory.

An incident several years back illustrates this. We had just lost a heartbreaking game to a fine Duke team. It was one of those games where the result was almost inevitable. We had a 21-0 lead at half-time and then proceeded to do everything in our power to lose it—

which we did, 28-21. The next week our practices were lousy. We were playing a strong Texas A&M team, and our morale was low. Our kids just weren't snapping back from the Duke loss. By Thursday evening, I was pretty low myself because everything I had done to get the players back into a fighting mood had failed. All our coaches were aware of the state of morale and one of them, Gene Ellenson, who handles our defense, came to me with the idea of writing a letter to the squad telling a true story about combat experience. I was impressed by his idea and gave him the go-ahead. He worked late Thursday night and the next morning he put it on my desk. It was a masterpiece. Tears came quickly to my eyes. Gene had hit the nail on the head. This letter was given to every player at the Friday night meeting. Here is a copy of that letter.

Dear (*Player's Name*)

It's late at night. The offices are all quiet and everyone has finally gone home. Once again my thoughts turn to you all.

I feel I have something to say to you because what you need now more than anything else is a little guidance and maybe a little starch in your backbone. You are still youngsters and unknowingly, you have not steeled yourselves for the demanding task of 60 full minutes of exertion required to beat a determined opponent. This sort of exertion takes two kinds of hardness. Physical, which is why you are pushed hard in practice—and mental, which comes only from having to meet adversity and whipping it. Now all of us have adversity—different kinds maybe but adversity. Just how we meet these problems determines how solid a bottom we are building our life on; and just how many of you stand together to face our team adversity will determine how solid a bottom our team is built on for the rest of the season.

No one cruises along without problems. It isn't easy to earn your way through college on a football scholarship. It isn't easy to do what is expected of you both academically and athletically. It isn't easy to keep on fighting when others are quitting around you or when your opponent seems to be getting stronger while you seem to be getting weaker. It isn't easy to continue good work when what you're doing isn't appreciated by others. It isn't easy to go on strong when bedeviled by aches and pains and muscle sprains. It isn't easy to rise up when you are down. The pure facts of life are that nothing is easy. You only get what you earn, and there isn't such a thing as "something for nothing." When you truly realize this—then and only then will you begin to whip your adversities.

If you'll bear with a little story, I'll try to prove my point. On midnight, January 14, 1945, six pitiful American soldiers were hanging onto a small piece of high ground in a forest somewhere near Bastogne, Belgium. This high ground had been the objective of an attack launched by 1,000 men that morning. Only these six made it. The others had been turned back, wounded, lost or killed in action. These grimy six men were all that were left of a magnificent charge of 1,000 men. They hadn't had any sleep other than catnaps for over 72 hours. The weather was cold enough to freeze the water in their canteens. They had no entrenching tools, no radio, no food—only ammunition and adversity. Twice, a good-sized counterattack had been launched and beaten back, largely because of the dark and some pretty skillful grenade heaving. The rest of the time there was incessant mortar bombardment of the general area, and the trees caused the dreaded tree bursts which scatter shrapnel like buckshot: The attackers were beginning to spot the location of the six defenders

Then things began to happen. First a sergeant had a chunk of shrapnel tear into his hip pocket. Then a corporal went into shock and started sobbing. After more than six hours of incessant mortar barrage, two close counterattacks, and no food perhaps since the day before yesterday, this was really demoralizing.

Then, another counterattack; this one made it to the small position. Hand-to-hand fighting is a routine, terse military expression. I have not the eloquence of diction or imagination to describe what this is really like. A man standing up to fight with a shattered hip bone, saliva frothing at his mouth, gouging, lashing with a bayonet, even strangling with his bare hands. Alone, the five fought (the corporal was out of his mind) until the attackers quit. Only the sergeant with the broken hip and two others were left after the last attack, not counting the crazy one. The snow ran red with blood and at least a dozen bodies lay dying around this little knoll. Then the mortars began again. All this time the route to the rear lay open but this little group never took it.

At early dawn a full company of airborne troopers relieved them. It wasn't quite light yet. One of the group, a lieutenant, picked up the sergeant with the broken hip and carried him like a baby; the other led the incoherent corporal like a dog on a leash. The last two of the gallant six men lay dead in the snow. It took two hours for this strange little group to get back to where they had started from 24 hours earlier. They were like returning ghosts.

The lieutenant and the one still healthy sergeant, after 10 hours of sleep and a hot meal, were sent on a mission 12 miles behind the German lines and made the link-up that closed the Bulge. Today, two of the six lie in Belgium graves, one is a career army man, one is a permanent resident of the army hospital for the insane in Texas, one is a stiff-legged garage mechanic in Delaware, and one is an assistant football coach at the University of Florida.

This story is no documentary or self-indulgence. It was told to you only to show you that whatever you find hard now, others before you have had as bad or worse and still hung on to do the job. Many of you are made of exactly the same stuff as the six men in the story, yet you haven't pooled your collective guts to present a united fight for a full 60 minutes. Your egos are a little shook—so what? Nothing good can come from moping about it. Cheer up and stand up. Fight an honest fight, square off in front of your particular adversity and whip it. You'll be a better man for it, and the next adversity won't be so tough. Breaking training now is complete failure to meet your problems. Quitting the first time is the hardest—it gets easier the second time and so forth.

As in most letters, I'd like to close by wishing you well and leave you with this one thought. "Self-pity is a roommate with cowardice." Stay away from feeling sorry for yourself. The wins and losses aren't nearly as important as what kind of man you become. I hope I've given you something to think about—and remember, somebody up there still loves you.

Sincerely,
Gene Ellenson

How did the letter affect the players? It's in the record book: Florida 42—Texas A&M 7. Not only did that one letter pick us up for that one game, but we gained a momentum that carried us to the Gator Bowl and one of Florida's finest victories over Penn State, 17-7. Incidentally, this is the game where we had Confederate flag decals placed on our head gear. The year before Penn State had clobbered Georgia Tech in this same Gator Bowl, and we were out to vindicate the South. Emotional responses aren't everything—but they can make a lot of difference in the big ones. Think about this area of coaching; it is a real challenge.

18

The Coach and His Relations with Press, Public, and School

The very interest which has built up collegiate football into such prominence also ranks it with politics and weather as a major topic of conversation and news.

It is primarily because of this that a coach must do a good job in the field of publicity and public relations with press, alumni, fans and friends. The goal in this field is promoting understanding of your program, and the creation of the correct and proper image.

While a coach can master proper coaching techniques and have the material and facilities to produce winning teams it is vital that he do a good job in the field of publicity and public relations in order to succeed in the long run. He must be able to communicate with those who are interested in and involved with his program.

The first step in creating proper understanding and image begins with members of the news media—press, radio and television. No coach is a true success unless the public believes him to be so, and most of the thinking, pro and con, of the public is generated by what is read, heard and seen.

The Coach And The Newsmen

To begin with it should be a cardinal rule among coaches that honesty be the key maxim in all relationships with newsmen.

This is not to say that you, or your publicity man, should run out and volunteer all bits of news whether or not they adversely affect your program. However, neither should a coach attempt to deceive newsmen or attempt to use their writings for personal gain by giving false impressions.

In the long run it is not to your advantage to be pessimistic, for example, downgrading the team during the week in order to look better if you win on Saturday. By doing things in this manner you are building your relations with newsmen on an unsure foundation which will crumble through lack of understanding and respect in times of crisis.

You should, by your own actions and words, convince the press of an intention to be honest and, by the same token, should expect as much of newsmen. Criticism in news media should be taken in the proper spirit with your only desire being that critics print facts and attempt to get the entire story from all sides.

College coaches would be wise to make room in the budget for an adequate sports publicity staff, which will be capable of keeping newsmen informed. Such a staff can keep your program in front of the public by supplying news media with stories, information, pictures and statistics on your football program. High school coaches would also benefit by having an interested follower of the team handle these duties.

These are the day-to-day functions which must be carried on in order to promote a football program and keep the newsmen informed. Now let's go into more detail on the points which can make or break a relationship between coach and newsmen.

The Interview

Without personal contact between coach and press there can be no communication of ideas and no understanding of decisions and goals. Coaches should make themselves available to newsmen for interviews whenever possible.

College coaches can all find some period during the normal daily practice routine to answer questions from newsmen. This period can be set aside before, during, or after practice.

Likewise, following all games, a coach should set aside time to talk to the press privately. It is an advantage to find a room away from the general confusion which follows a football game and spend time talking to the press with no fans or other people present.

It is also helpful to set aside time later that evening to talk to newsmen. By this time a coach has had time to think matters and events over and might have explanations and thoughts which will give further insight into the just-concluded game.

Again, the key thought to remember in all such interviews is to shoot straight with newsmen. Whether they are good or bad answers, let them come straight from the shoulder.

Running the Press Box

There is a marked tendency among college coaches to disregard the public relations value of the press box and the effect you might have on newsmen by the way you operate it.

It is important that college and high school coaches alike remember that the press box, to a newsman, is a place to work while covering a football game. It isn't a social or entertainment session for a newsman, but rather his office away from the office for the day.

While it might possibly be of benefit to any program to allow certain fans or alumni in the press box area to view a football game, you should make every effort to keep these people separated from working press. Restrict the working press area to officials such as public address and statistics crews and the press. This holds true for high school or college games.

The working press area of a press box should have a crew which supplies game programs, rosters, statistics at halftime and end of game and a play-by-play where possible. If possible, it is also a good idea to serve refreshments such as sandwiches, cokes and coffee to members of the working press and radio.

A Typical Week

In order to provide some insight into how much publicity and public relations work is done at the University of Florida let's take a look at a typical week during the football season:

Monday—Coaches check early in morning, or late Sunday evening, for latest report from head trainer on condition of boys injured in Saturday game. Newspaper men begin calling at 7 A.M. and status of injured players is main news at this time. These calls are not in the least bit discouraged.

Head Coach and all assistants, in addition to Sports Publicity Director, are available to reporters until approximately 9 A.M. when a staff meeting is held.

At 11 A.M. Head Coach does video-tape interview in his office which is sent to several state television stations for use during the week.

This program deals primarily with the condition of the Florida team and reports on the next opponent.

Monday afternoon practice is usually light and Head Coach is available to press during a good portion of the drills. Remainder of the week a pre-set time for a daily press conference is used, this coming at approximately 5 P.M. each day.

Tuesday—In addition to the normal routine of calls from, and interviews with, members of the press, Head Coach and two of his assistants tape a radio program which is used all over the State of Florida.

Head Coach and assistants also do a great amount of speaking at luncheons and other functions early in the week.

This routine continues until Friday on the week of a home game. Friday night all reporters in town to cover Saturday game are taken out to eat and talk by Sports Publicity Director. Coaches are along when they are not tied up scouting high school games.

Saturday—Head Coach and Assistants spend most of the morning talking to high school football prospects and their parents. Newsmen also find this a good time to hold brief interviews prior to the game. Coaches are made available to these newsmen.

Approximately ten minutes after the game, the entire Florida staff retires to a private room and meets the press. Soft drinks are provided and nobody is admitted to this session except newsmen and coaches.

That night a party is held at one of three places (1) Head Coach's house, (2) Sports Publicity Director's house, (3) A local hotel in a private, large room.

All Florida coaches and their wives are at these functions and at some time during the evening, although writers are free to interview anybody there at any time, Head Coach sits down with them and discusses the game and plans for the following week.

These interviews are conducted in a very informal fashion so that all parties are relaxed and can clearly attempt to determine what happened and why in the recently concluded game.

Sunday—Head Coach does a live television show which is shown in most sections of the state. He is also available to press by phone in the morning and later that afternoon after game films of Saturday's contest have been seen.

Sports Publicity Director compiles and writes a four-page newsletter called "Gator Tales" which is printed by Monday morning and mailed to all members of the booster club and active alumni. This pamphlet includes a letter from the Head Coach, a scout report on the upcoming opponent, up-to-date statistics and other news of interest.

Football As Part of the Academic Framework

Coaches should remember at all times that football, high school or collegiate, is an integral part of the overall scholastic program and must be operated within an academic framework.

The days of the football player not knowing his "ABCs" are gone and at most institutions the football player lives under the same scholastic rules as the remainder of the student body. Certainly this is right and as it should be.

Perhaps it would be a good idea to go a step further where relationships between football and faculty and other students are concerned.

We tell boys at the University of Florida that as a football player they have an opportunity and an obligation. The opportunity, of course is in making a name for themselves and gaining an education. The spotlight of public attention is on these boys and by their progress they can gain recognition which few obtain.

However, we stress being in the public eye charges football players with more responsibility than the average student. When the average student fails to make the grade academically, or in other areas, it is of vital concern only to that person and his immediate friends and relatives. When a football player encounters the same failure it is considered news worthy of public notice.

This attitude is what we attempt to sell our boys on from the start. Football players should fully understand the obligation they have to faculty, student body, and studies and act accordingly. If anything, a football player should work harder in school than the average student.

Coaches should also go out of their way to cooperate with school officials and to help promote the school goals and projects. In helping your school you are also selling your program and at many schools, such as Florida, a major recruiting weapon is the academic climate under which a boy might advance himself.

Collegiate coaches should make every effort to aid the alumni association by speaking, showing films, and helping to encourage support of the university.

A Game for the Students

Spectator interest has made football one of the finest games in the United States. This interest comes from many sources but the primary source, indeed the major reason for the existence of football, is the student body.

Coaches should encourage student body participation in support of the football team. A coach should aid in any manner the efforts of pep squads, cheerleaders, the band, and student government groups concerned with football.

By making himself available for discussion with student groups a coach helps to create understanding about his football program among the students. This understanding should go both ways, with the coach hearing student thoughts with friendliness and sincerity.

Cooperation with the school newspaper, helping its representatives to do a good job and to understand the decisions and goals of the program, is an important task for any coach. Such representatives should be encouraged to ask questions and seek facts in regard to the football program.

Keep the Alumni Aware

Alumni groups and booster clubs contain the school's most loyal supporters. These groups can praise one day, be critical the next, all in what they consider to be the best interests of the football program.

Coaches, through personal appearances and in various other ways, can get in contact with these alumni in virtually every important area. This is an important way to maintain communications and understanding between coach and alumni.

Coaches should encourage alumni to take an active role in the development of a football program. Alumni and booster groups, operating within NCAA rules and fully informed as to what these rules entail, are excellent sources of aid in the recruitment of high school athletes.

No favoritism should be shown between the various alumni and booster groups. Coaches should make it a point to attend functions over a broad area and where possible speak to all groups which are active.

Working in conjunction with the university Alumni Secretary the coach should make it a point to be active in attending meetings of alumni groups during the off-season.

Special publications by the sports publicity department can also be helpful. Brochures, pamphlets and other special booklets which describe your program should be sent to active members of booster clubs and, if possible, it is a good idea to send out newsletters during the fall.

Such newsletters can also be produced in conjunction with the office of alumni affairs and should be sent to all active members of the alumni association.

High school coaches should make every attempt to speak to booster groups such as quarterback clubs and also to civic organizations and parents as a group.

Who Gets Tickets and Where

When the demand for tickets and good stadium location gets heavy you inherit with it many problems in the field of public relations.

There is only one fair method of ticket distribution when there is this demand for good tickets. Some sort of priority system must be established so that all concerned understand tickets are not just sold on the basis of "who-knows-who" or some other unfair method.

It's difficult to say just how such a priority system should be established because situations vary according to the school. The important thing to remember is that a system which best suits your school should be established, so that all understand there is a method by which good tickets can be obtained.

Most schools operate a priority system on the basis of ticket distribution to booster club member, active alumni, ex-lettermen and so on down the line until you come to the general public.

All such systems are in addition to ticket distribution plans for students and faculty.

Index

N

O

P

Q

R